DELIVERING HUMAN SERVICES

DELIVERING HUMAN SERVICES

ROY S. AZARNOFF, Ph.D.
*Institute for Communication
and Professional Studies
California State University
Northridge*

JEROME S. SELIGER, Ph.D.
*Department of Health Science
California State University
Northridge*

Prentice-Hall, Inc., Englewood Cliffs, New Jersey 07632

Library of Congress Cataloging in Publication Data

AZARNOFF, ROY S.
  Delivering human services.

  Includes index.
  1. Social work administration—United States—Mathematical models.   I. Seliger, Jerome.   II. Title.
HV91.A96   361.3'068   81-5855
ISBN 0-13-198317-2   AACR2

Printed in the United States of America

10   9   8   7   6   5   4   3   2   1

Editorial/production supervision: Jeanne Hoeting
Cover design: Diane Saxe
Manufacturing buyer: Edmund W. Leone

Prentice-Hall International, Inc., *London*
Prentice-Hall of Australia Pty. Limited, *Sydney*
Prentice-Hall of Canada, Ltd., *Toronto*
Prentice-Hall of India Private Limited, *New Delhi*
Prentice-Hall of Japan, Inc., *Tokyo*
Prentice-Hall of Southeast Asia Pte. Ltd., *Singapore*
Whitehall Books Limited, *Wellington, New Zealand*

To **Shawn**, an eleven-year-old wise beyond his years, who gave up a lot of baseball practice so that his dad could complete this "ballgame," special thanks and lots of love.

To **Pat**, who makes the impossible possible because she cares, and to Julie, Lamar, Karen, Moshe, Kate, and Sam, who make a very special cheering section.

Contents

Foreword

The role of government at all levels in the provision of human services is increasing. Support for our needy citizens, traditionally provided by families, churches and charitable institutions or not provided at all, is becoming more difficult to manage. Greater costs and the requirement for more technical skills are making government intervention common.

The policies and systems for providing human services are still evolving. There are no final answers. While the scope of services enlarges continually, the day-to-day work of assisting others must still be done in the local community by caring people working with those who need help. Their understanding of the processes and alternatives involved is important in achieving the effective, efficient delivery of services which we all desire.

This book will be an asset to providers of service and to those who work with them as volunteers or board members because it gives an extensive overview of the major service delivery components and practical suggestions for improvements.

Tom Bradley, Mayor
City of Los Angeles

Preface

Since the mid-1960s, enmormous amounts of public money have gone into the provision of human services. Thousands of new human service agencies have started, while many have ended. The lives of millions of people have been touched. Yet, with so many projects and programs behind us, human service practice continues to vary considerably from one setting to another. Certainly human service delivery is complex. Helping people and assisting them to help themselves is difficult. Ironically, human service providers, who give others assistance, tend not to seek help in organizing for service delivery. When a new agency opens its doors or a new program director is hired, too often past experiences are ignored. Unfortunately, starting from scratch may be quite costly.

Throughout the years and in different communities one issue has continually recurred. Newcomers and seasoned practitioners alike are dismayed that they do not have resources from which to learn practical techniques for handling problems. The establishment of an effective human service delivery system calls for a wider range of information and understanding than many practitioners have, no matter how positive their expressed intentions. We have written *Delivering Human Services* to meet this need.

Our intent is to provide concerned practitioners and volunteers with a resource they can use to improve the way in which they organize and provide human services. Over the years, we have been asked for help by directors, board members, and program staff from every type of human service agency. Their requests have included "how-to" information about such things as proposal writing, recruiting volunteers, service planning and evaluation, training and board-staff relations, needs assessment, and serving clients from minority groups.

This book is designed to help human service providers learn from the experience of others. The concepts, strategies, and techniques described are derived from the three decades we have worked in human services. Our experience ranges from short-term consultation assignments to administrative roles. We have worked in urban and rural areas as employees, employers, and board members; with traditional human service providers such as hospitals and local government, and with less traditional community-based organizations; and we have directed training and technical assistance for numerous human service agencies.

We wrote this book with the most frequently voiced needs in mind. We have included examples of strategy and service problems and methods for handling them. Examples are drawn from a variety of human services to highlight the broad application of practices generic to human services. What works in one agency can often work well in another. For example, the steps involved in researching and writing a proposal for a maternal and child health community intervention project differ little from researching and writing a proposal for a senior citizen transportation project.

We also have aimed to meet the needs of human service practitioners and volunteers who move from one agency to another. People in the human services are job mobile. This is probably a result of the uncertain and time-limited nature of much grant funding. When service providers move from one service to another — from a community mental health center to an information and referral project, for instance — they may fear they lack technical preparation for their new assignment. We demonstrate that most processes are applicable to a wide variety of human services, and that many provicers, therefore, can transfer successfully their experience and skills to new areas.

In the first chapter we posit a community services model for organizing and delivering human services from the identification of needs to the assessment of the services delivered. In each of the subsequent chapters, we systematically examine components of the model, such as assessing needs and setting objectives, implementing services and evaluating programs, or those related to increasing the quantity or quality of services, such as training and technical assistance, coordination, publicity, advocacy, and the use of volunteers.

Most chapters contain figures to illustrate the text and have materials such as charts and sample forms appended to them. Care is taken to explain technical terms within the text, but a glossary is provided for further clarification. The book is designed for ready use by human service practitioners, volunteers, board members, and students. We believe beginners as well as more advanced practitioners can benefit from the systematic overview, the prescriptions for action, the appended materials and the wide range of examples.

Experience has taught us that most human service providers and government bureaucrats are decent, competent people. They often work under conditions which limit what they can accomplish. Usually the needs they seek to ameliorate are greater than the resources they have available. Organizational and political considerations sometimes outweigh program and personal considerations. Record-keeping requirements can occasionally become more important than services. Yet they continue to keep their faith and caring and somehow manage to go on helping others.

We wish to thank our many friends and colleagues at California State University, Northridge, who continually encouraged us, especially Len Glass, Jim McDonald, Seymour Eiseman, Ben Kogan, Don Hufhines in the School of Communication and Professional Studies and in the Department of Health Science. Mary Sue Hebert, who typed and retyped drafts, deserves our gratitude. We both agree that without her help the book would never have been. Lynne Ericksson did the graphics. Her patience and ideas helped greatly.

We owe more than we can repay to the many service providers from agencies, the board members and volunteers with whom we have worked, and to the Los Angeles City Council on Aging. They were gracious enough to say we were helping them, while they were teaching us so much we now say that we know.

Roy S. Azarnoff
Jerome S. Seliger

DELIVERING HUMAN SERVICES

Service Delivery Models

1

The delivery of effective, efficient, responsive human services involves numerous decisions about who will receive them, the nature and quality of the services, how the services will be organized, and who will pay for them. For human services to be delivered successfully, agencies must have adequate information; social, financial, and political support; and competent, caring salaried and volunteer personnel. Providing human services is complex and the results are often difficult to determine. Yet the quantity and variety of such programs is increasing regularly in the United States, with the demand for services often exceeding available resources.

Human services have always played an important role in our society. For the most part, their provision rested with the family and alternatively with the church until the upheaval caused by the Great Depression of the 1930s. The federal government then began funding human services with the passage of the Social Security Act and other related legislation. The role of government at all levels in human services has been increasing dramatically ever since. Today, federal spending on human services, including health, education, social services, and recreation, exceeds its spending in all other sectors, including defense. When local and state government expenditures are considered, and if insurance dollars and other private spending are added, their spending for human services easily outdistances even the federal government in this area.

Human services as a term has been defined in many different ways. However, the general controversy over definition need not prevent us from seeing that certain common factors appear consistently. The definition offered in the Allied Services Act of 1974 is useful: Human services are those which enable the consumers of the services to achieve, support, or maintain the highest level of economic self-sufficiency and independence. This legislation includes two of the three most commonly

1

used services, life-sustaining services (e.g., health care) and life-support services (e.g., transportation), but does not specifically include life-enhancement services (e.g., education). In our opinion, to sustain and support life without provision for growth or quality of life is something less than "human." Figure 1-1 represents these three types of services and suggests that there will always be needs unmet by any services provided.

There appears to be some agreement that human services are meant to include services provided by agencies and service institutions and not those provided by families. Sense can be made of an approach which seeks to establish the *functions* of human services. The four categories of function identified here are obviously just a different way of looking at the types of services indicated in Figure 1-1. In the first category are those programs whose function is providing *access* to other services. Programs to provide referral information, outreach, transportation, and escort services are examples. A second category, *protective*, includes programs such as child welfare, the guardianship of mentally incompetent adults, drug abuse prevention, and crime abatement. In the third category are those programs aimed at *personal growth*, or enhancement of the quality of life, such as recreation, education, and arts programs. The fourth category consists of programs providing basic services necessary for *survival*, including health care and housing.

Human services are delivered by public agencies and service institutions, such as the recreation department of a city, a state-operated mental health clinic, or a

Figure 1-1

SERVICES ORIENTATION

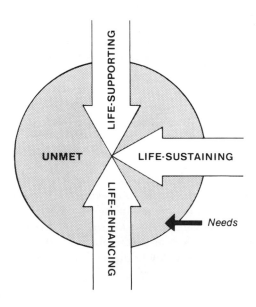

Veterans Administration hospital. Private nonprofit agencies provide a vast array of services, such as youth employment, economic development, adult education, child care, and consumer counseling. In addition to the public and private agencies, millions of people receive human services from profit-making organizations, such as a rehabilitation hospital or a home health firm. Together, these agencies and service institutions form a vast network for the providing of human services.

There are numerous approaches to organizing services for people whose needs are met through this network. Regardless of approach, however, the basic elements of service delivery are the same for all agencies and service institutions. In this chapter we will briefly examine these elements from two perspectives, that of the clients and of the agencies.

The client services model, depicted in Figure 1-2, has the three elements of services with a client focus: (1) an intake process, (2) a receipt of services, and (3) an exit process.

Once the need for a particular service is determined, the intake process requires that those who meet the criteria be identified and taken into the system and that those who do not meet the criteria be screened out. In some service projects, the screening out is given far higher priority than the identification and intake process. People who meet the criteria, however, move on to the next element, the receipt of services.

The kind, quality, and number of services that consumers receive are determined by a number of factors, not the least of which is the agency's explicit objectives. Clients in a drug treatment project may reasonably expect help to overcome their abuse of drugs. This is not always the case, however, as agency goals can be

Figure 1-2

CLIENT SERVICES MODEL

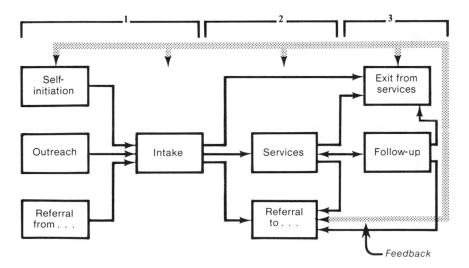

displaced or altered to fit other, implicit agency goals. Thus an agency may alter the type of services it delivers in order to obtain more funds, to meet unanticipated needs of its clients, or just to survive. A health care project may discover that more social services and less health care services are required to genuinely meet the needs of its consumers. A project serving the counseling needs of runaway youths on an outpatient basis may find it more suitable for its clients and easier for its staff members if it runs a shelter instead.

Disregarding funding or organizational considerations, consumers of a service have a right to expect that it be *available, accessible, acceptable,* and *appropriate.*

AVAILABLE—the quantity of service promised to help ameliorate a need can be obtained.

ACCESSIBLE—no physical or other barriers exist which will prevent an available service from being obtained.

ACCEPTABLE—the manner in which an available, accessible service is provided is consonant with the social and psychological orientation of the clients.

APPROPRIATE—the service is potentially effective in ameliorating a need.

At some point the client and/or the agency personnel may decide the relationship should be severed or perhaps moved to a new phase. The final breaking of the direct support relationship between client and agency can be understood either from the point of view of the client, who no longer has need for help, or from the view of the agency, which has the constant job of balancing needs against resources, the many against the few, effectiveness against efficiency.

As an example, let us consider a project of a community mental health center designed to assist battered wives (women who are habitually beaten by their husbands). Such a project could receive its clients in one of three ways: (1) Women might be contacted through outreach efforts of community workers from the center who obtain the names of potential clients either by attending meetings and speaking about the project or by going through the community knocking on doors and explaining the project. (2) Women in need of the services might seek out the project on their own after reading about it in the newspaper or hearing about it on the radio or television. Or (3) women might be referred from a physician, a friend, the police, or another agency.

The resulting intake procedure can result in three outcomes: (1) provision of the services, (2) referral to another agency, such as a hospital or welfare department, or (3) in no services being offered. Again, if services are offered, three outcomes are possible: The women, after being served, can be (1) discharged from the project, (2) assigned to follow-up status, which means periodic checks to determine if services are needed, or (3) referred to another agency. For those for whom follow-up is deemed necessary, three outcomes are once again possible. These women may later be: (1) discharged from the project, (2) provided additional or new services, or (3) referred to another agency.

Note that any effective service delivery system will plan for and maintain a feedback component so that information about how the processes are working can be furnished to personnel involved in all stages of the project. This enables modifications to be made which will help achieve the project's goals. Feedback is a vital part of any system of service delivery. It can be better understood from the example of an automobile driver who is blinded by fog. As the fog lifts, the driver is able to see the road ahead and to compensate for changes in the direction of the road by turning the steering wheel. Thus the car can be kept on the road as long as the driver has the needed information about the direction of the road. Without feedback, the system breaks down and unfortunate mistakes can easily be made.

The community services model is agency oriented and differs from the model with a client focus in its changed perspective. It has five basic elements, as depicted in Figure 1-3.

The decision to fund a program or project, especially at the federal or state level, is most often made to meet widely identified needs not necessarily specific to any one locale. For this reason the schematic representation of the community services model shows the funding decision as outside the basic system because the decision to provide particular services locally is not always made on the basis of a local assessment of priority needs, but sometimes simply on the availability of funds to provide those services. Fortunately, the funds usually do provide for services that some people can use, even though the program may not offer the services that the community would choose if unrestricted funds were available.

Agencies generally respond to perceived needs in the same sequence as that shown in the model. For example, suppose a hypothetical agency named Help Incapacitated Retired Elderly, Inc. (HIRE) discovers that 25 percent more persons are eligible for its services during the current budget year than it had anticipated. (No. 1, assessment of needs.) Upon closer examination, the agency finds that almost all of these persons could work productively in its sheltered workshop if space were available. (No. 2, setting of objectives.) It decides, therefore, to create more workshop opportunities, but without extending its costs beyond income. For this objective, alternative ways of handling the situation present themselves. (No. 3, development of strategies.) The agency can develop a new site and place less severely disabled current and new clients there or it can place some clients with another agency, or it can discontinue services to some of its current clients in order to provide space for new ones. The last two alternatives do not fit the agency's objective of creating more work opportunities, however, so they are not chosen. This review of the advantages and disadvantages of these possibilities puts the board members in a position to choose an alternative, which is then implemented. (No. 4, provision of services.) If the board has chosen well, the new site should provide the needed space for its sheltered workshop with no loss of revenue. In any case, after implementing its decision, subsequent events will enable the agency to evaluate the results of its actions. (No. 5, evaluation of results.) If it has decided improperly and the space does not become available or funds are overexpended, feedback will enable it to choose a new plan or strategy for action, or even to set new objectives.

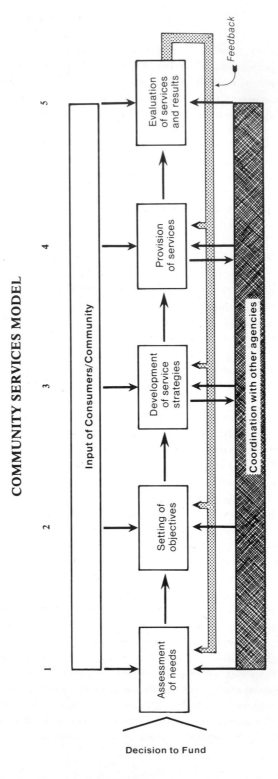

COMMUNITY SERVICES MODEL

| 1 | 2 | 3 | 4 | 5 |

Input of Consumers/Community

Assessment of needs

Setting of objectives

Development of service strategies

Provision of services

Evaluation of services and results

Feedback

Coordination with other agencies

Decision to Fund

Figure 1-3

Each of the five elements is a logical progression from the previous element, although in the actual delivery of services many programs do not follow the sequence in such an orderly fashion. Some projects never develop objectives or attempt to measure their accomplishments in any meaningful way. Others provide services without any definable plan or strategy, although it could be argued that no strategy is a strategy. Some projects deliver services without ever determining whether a reasonable need for the particular services, in the amount they are willing or able to provide, exists. Generally, however, most agencies and organizations do go through each of the elements in the development of programs to deliver services, even though they may not do so in a planned and sequential fashion.

Figure 1-3 also indicates the external forces which influence the system. First, the input of the community, especially from potential or actual consumers of the services, is an integral part of the entire system. Second, the input of other agencies and organizations is part of the system at each stage. Third, data about the elements and their effects, in the form of feedback, are an important part of the model, as the information can help to modify the decisions and practices throughout.

For our purposes, this community services model is the conceptual framework which best illustrates how human service programs are developed and implemented. To envision how the elements function, imagine that in one community the clergy who head the churches, synagogues, and temples get together and form a nonprofit corporation called United Ministry for Service (UMS). Each congregation donates money annually to help pay a director and several staff people, whose job it is to provide emergency food and shelter for persons in dire need who have no other source of assistance. The staff members, in addition, offer referral services to other agencies that can provide aid of a more substantial nature over a longer period of time. The board members of UMS realize after a few months that far more help is required than their few employees can give, so they instruct the director to seek additional resources. The director discovers that UMS is eligible for Title XX, Social Security Act funds from the Social Services Department to provide emergency services. The director also learns that the federal, state, and departmental regulations which UMS must follow in order to receive the funds will require substantial changes in the amount and types of aid the agency has been giving. The model's elements generally apply to this point. The decision to provide emergency services funds was made outside the community, while the assessment of needs developed from actual agency experience in the community.

Looking ahead, the board members select several lay persons to represent them on an advisory committee established to oversee this project. The director, at the same time, creates a technical advisory panel whose members work for agencies to which the project refers clients. With the help of this technical advisory panel, the director conceptualizes the strategies for services, determining who will be eligible for how much of what services and for how long. The decision as to whether the staff members will work with clients where they find them or bring them back to the office is also made and a set of measurable objectives developed. These decisions are shared with the advisory committee, altered in accordance with its suggestions, and then submitted to the UMS board of directors. Though the community services model elements apply here, note that the sequence does not follow that of the model.

Continuing our hypothetical example, assume that with the board members' approval, an application for funds is submitted and a grant awarded to UMS. UMS then begins providing services to those in the community who meet its newly established eligibility criteria. As time passes and more services are delivered, data begin to accumulate which indicate to what extent the agency is meeting the objectives it had established. Board and advisory committee and technical panel members, people in the community, and consumers all begin to express their opinions about the quality of services, the approaches being used and their effectiveness, and the efficiency with which the agency is operating. The feedback obtained is then incorporated as new strategies are developed and operational changes are made.

This example, although considerably simplified, illustrates the elements of the community services model. No single focus or model can describe any human service delivery system perfectly under all circumstances, but this model does provide a useful tool. It explains program elements and their interrelationships so that learning is facilitated about alternative ways of developing and implementing human services.

"Programs" and "projects" are two terms we frequently use throughout the book which need defining. Some people loosely use the terms as synonymous with "agency." They refer to the Back Street Drug Abuse Agency, the Back Street Drug Abuse Program, and the Back Street Drug Abuse Prevention Project and intend the same meaning for each. These are not the same, however. *Back Street* is an agency which has a *drug abuse program*, one project of which is the *Back Street Drug Abuse Prevention Project*.

"Program" is generally used to indicate a category of services, such as programs for the elderly or educational programs. Programs are long-term affairs with wide application. "Project," on the other hand, denotes a specific short-term effort with a narrow focus. An agency can have several programs, each with several projects, as shown in Figure 1-4.

As more and more organizations take on the task of service delivery, the need for a systematic framework from which reasonable decisions about competing alternatives can be made becomes apparent. No single approach to delivering services works under all conditions, but by increasing their understanding of the elements common to all approaches everyone involved can learn to make more informed, more rational decisions about human services.

AGENCY, PROGRAM AND PROJECTS

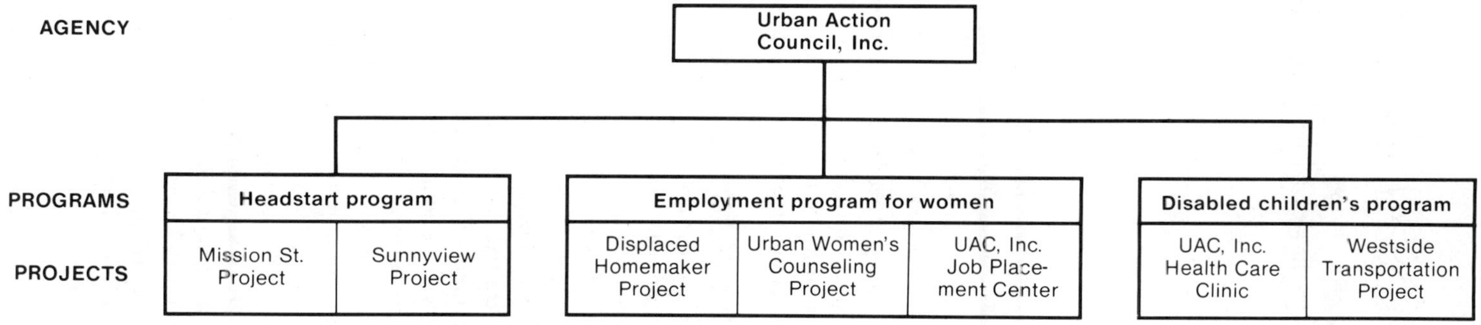

Figure 1-4

AGENCY

Urban Action Council, Inc.

PROGRAMS

Headstart program	Employment program for women	Disabled children's program

PROJECTS

Mission St. Project	Sunnyview Project	Displaced Homemaker Project	Urban Women's Counseling Project	UAC, Inc. Job Placement Center	UAC, Inc. Health Care Clinic	Westside Transportation Project

9

Assessing Needs and Setting Objectives

2

Since the amelioration of need is the basic reason for providing human services, importance must be given to understanding needs and how they are determined, and their crucial relationship to the strategies and methods for implementing services. But what does "need" mean and in what ways can it be determined?

Need, as defined in most public legislation, is a vague standard or concept in which the community expresses concern about an individual or group problem. For example, the fact that some individuals or a group of people in the community live in houses with no indoor plumbing is seen as a need. Since between 30 and 50 percent of inner-city minority youths are unemployed, we say there is a need for job opportunities for these young people. However, in many nations indoor plumbing is a luxury, not a necessity, and persons living in housing without it are not deemed to be "in need." In the United States a four percent rate of unemployment is considered to be full employment. Should this figure be reached, does it mean that some persons still unemployed no longer require work and, therefore, do not have a need? How much of a concern must there be in order for a need to exist?

Need has two dimensions, quality and quantity. Need is stated qualitatively as a difficulty which the community recognizes. Many women have to work to support their families and need day care facilities for their young children. People who are alcoholics need care. Children who commit crimes of a minor nature need a program which will divert them from the criminal court/penal institution system. Notice that need is a judgment that a problem exists and that a remedy, usually in the form of a program, can be made available.

Need is also expressed quantitatively. How much? How many of which kind? In what places? To determine the degree of need for child care services, for instance, requires assessing the number of working mothers, the number of their children, the number of centers already providing services and their licensed capacity, and the number of children already being served. The population "in need" minus the number of persons already served equals the extent of need.

If need is a judgment, in what ways can the judgment be made? Usually definitions of need begin with a *normative* comparison of people to a predetermined standard. If the standard is not met, a need is said to exist. If the standard in the United States is to have inside plumbing, then houses without inside plumbing are identified as substandard. As societal conditions change, so do the *relative* needs of people. When compared to most people, a few people will always be in a worse condition — thus, in need. Persons below the desirable minimum income level, called the "poverty level," as defined by the federal government are needy. *Normative* and *relative* are two ways of describing need.

Expressed need is a third way of describing need and is defined by the number of people who indicate their need either verbally or by seeking services. Suppose that 600 children require care in a day care center, but only 400 places are available. The parents of 200 children perceive a need which is unmet. If the parents of 100 of the children made other arrangements for the care of their youngsters or gave up the attempt to place their children in day care centers while the parents of the other 100 registered for the waiting lists, the expressed need would diminish, but not disappear. When people know that others in similar circumstances receive assistance and they do not, their expectations change markedly. Expressed needs are influenced by expectations which people have about the availability of services. The more they expect, the greater will be their requests for services, and therefore their expressed needs.

Another way of looking at expressed needs is in terms of cultural expectations — what people value, what they feel is important. The level of human services in any community tends to reflect what the people there expect. Their expectations change as the community values change. When new people move in, when government action starts new programs, or when the news media reflect new ideas, their cultural values begin to change, thus creating changes in expectations.

Years of medical shows on television have tended to alter people's views of what is and what is not "good" health care. The impact on people in a low-income neighborhood may be quite considerable. Acculturation to TV's brand of medical practice can change the level of expectation in such a community away from relative satisfaction with public health clinic services toward a demand for the personalized health care portrayed on television. This media-induced value has altered expectations. The people involved are no longer as readily satisfied as before and their new criteria of need may require a drastic alteration of existing services and concepts of service.

Determining what needs exist and who has these needs can be easy or difficult, costly or inexpensive, time-consuming or quick, depending on what information is available, how complex the data are, and the degree of resources an agency can devote to this task.

Surveys which have been either completed or updated recently are one obvious source of information. Probably the best-known example is the United States census. The data collected have great value in many program areas. They include such information as the number of people in various age ranges, family income, heads of households, housing conditions, vacancy rates, and the number of persons belonging to particular racial groups. Census data are published by census tracts, which are small predetermined geographic areas. For larger areas, the data can be aggregated; i.e., census tracts counted together. However, for smaller areas, such as city blocks, the data may not be readily available. The census is done once every ten years and it takes more than a year to analyze and publish the data. As time passes, however, the data become less valid since few communities remain constant. Also, the census costs many millions of dollars to prepare and carry out. The census illustrates the advantages and disadvantages of surveys generally.

Surveys can of course be done on a much smaller scale, collecting information from individuals about almost anything and on a sample size of almost any percent of the total population to be surveyed. It is possible, for example, for a clinic to make decisions on the health care needs of children in its catchment (service) area by selecting either a representative or a randomized group of children to survey. If the survey is done well, what is learned about the children surveyed will apply generally to all the rest. To get meaningful, valid data the clinic must take into account factors relating to cost, sample size, availability of children who will participate, community attitudes about surveys, and the reliability of the survey instruments and method. Because they are difficult to do, valid surveys usually require expert assistance.

Care must be taken to ensure that surveys do not create needs by arousing expectations for service that did not previously exist. The very act of asking people about their needs may skew their response. People have a tendency to tell interviewers what they think the interviewers expect to hear. There are a number of factors at work in such a situation. The respondents may be intimidated by the interviews or the interviewers, or the respondents may feel grateful for the personal attention the interviewers afford them and may respond affirmatively to questions, while downplaying their true feelings. Another explanation for the tendency of interviewees to respond with what the interviewers want to hear is the way in which the questions are asked. The questions themselves may influence the response that emerges from a needs assessment. In other words, the suggestion by the interviewers that a need exists can bias the response to questions about need.

The following is illustrative of other possible biases. Suppose researchers are trying to identify the mental health needs of a community by gathering data from secondary sources, such as federal and state government reports and county health department records, and from primary sources, such as interviews with residents. To look only at secondary sources could be quite misleading in understanding mental health needs. Indicators such as numbers of persons institutionalized with a mental illness or rates of alcoholism or drug abuse certainly would point to aspects of the problem, but would not necessarily get at environmental factors such as unemployment or overcrowding that can affect mental health. If the assessors of needs are not aware of these and other relevant factors, any interview schedule, or questionnaire, that they administer to residents may miss whole categories of response.

Similarly, gathering data about the availability of mental health treatment facilities in a community only from the traditional agencies may ignore important, nontraditional local institutions and individuals.

Service providers are another source of information, in addition to surveys, which can be helpful in determining the needs of specific groups. A nutrition project for the elderly, funded with Older Americans Act funds, for example, may be serving an average of 300 meals a day, about 7,500 meals a year, and have a waiting list of 60 persons. This would suggest that a twenty percent increase in the number of meals is needed. However, many eligible persons who are in need may not know about the program or may not have put their names on the waiting list.* Depending exclusively on the information from service providers can be misleading and waiting lists can be the most misleading of all.

Public hearings can provide data on needs. Many state and local governments, as well as the federal government, require that agencies hold hearings for some programs which are designed to provide human services. Hearings can be an excellent forum for the articulation of needs. All too often, however, hearings are used for show and not substance, the decisions about service provision having been already determined.

Clients, potential consumers, and interested persons from the general public form an important source of data about needs. They are, after all, the ones who will use the services which try to ameliorate their needs, or, in many cases, will pay for the services through their taxes. Agencies conducting hearings should not depend only on experts but also should give these persons a chance to state their views. However, needs assessments based only on the perceptions of clients can be like a grocery list made by family members. It can have many satisfying items, but may not enable the homemaker to provide balanced, nutritional meals at reasonable cost.

Expert testimony is another valuable source of information about needs. Well-trained, knowledgeable experts can render professional judgments about needs that may be helpful. The experts may be quite familiar with existing research and survey data and be able to provide an analysis of needs for specific population groups or in specific substantive areas, such as family planning, juvenile delinquency, or employment training. Agencies should recognize, however, that some dangers

---

*Eligibility is presumed to be evidence of need. Under the Older Americans Act, persons 60 years old and older are eligible for program benefits. Some persons who qualify may have sufficient funds, knowledge, companionship and ability to eat regularly, yet seek out the meal service. Others, also eligible, who cannot cook or do not have funds for adequate food may not know about the program or may not participate. Or they may want to participate, but have been put on a waiting list behind many who can manage on their own. To make the latter group "more eligible" than the former is to create a "means" test, which tends to degrade the persons who are allowed to participate. Subjected to a means test, many needy persons will not participate because of the values they hold. Without sufficient funds to serve all eligible persons, the determination of need becomes extremely complex, value-laden, and controversial. Who is excluded can become more important than who is included. For a further discussion of this issue, see Chapter 5, Developing Human Service Strategies.

exist. Because of their heavy concentration in a given subject area, which is what made them experts, professionals may have a narrow focus that enables them to recognize only those needs that fall into limited parameters. They may also have professional biases which influence the scope of their understanding and range of information.

Relatively simple assessments of need are possible. Imaginative and persistent agencies can get relevant data and analyses of need without doing extensive surveys or employing costly consultants by taking the following steps:

setting specific criteria for geographic and/or program areas,

identifying sources of information,

working with the appropriate mix of persons to determine what conclusions can be drawn from the available data.

Too many agencies flounder and then withdraw from serious needs assessments because they have not sharply limited their investigation to important and manageable facts. Much data collected and analyses made fit the equation stated in the words of people who work with computers, "Garbage in equals garbage out." That is, the data were useless or faulty to begin with, so they can only lead to useless or faulty conclusions. The two overriding criteria for collecting data about needs can be stated in the form of two questions: Does the information relate directly to persons, conditions, and locations about which this agency can do something? Are the data fairly simple to collect? Put another way, the questions can be used as a guide to investigation: What directly applicable and easy-to-collect information is available that will indicate the nature and extent of needs for the programmatic and geographic areas in which this agency might provide services?

Care must be exercised to see that the efforts and cost to obtain data about specific populations are reasonable in relation to the anticipated results. In one project relating to services for the elderly, the only readily available data by census tracts were based on persons aged 65 and over. But eligibility began at age 60. So, instead of going through the effort and expense of a survey to determine the exact number of persons between age 60 and 65 for each census tract, the overall percentage of persons aged 60 to 65 in relation to the population 65 years old and over was calculated. The number of people represented by this percent was added to the 65-plus figures for each census tract to determine the approximate number of eligible persons. These approximate figures were good enough for the purposes of the project and the savings in time and money were substantial.

A technique that works well with groups where there is a high degree of cohesion is self-study. A juvenile justice agency that worked with gangs was able to augment the usual secondary source assessment (police arrest records, school attendance, etc.) by getting gang members to gather data about themselves. The agency staff members brought two leaders of each active gang together at a neutral site, to avoid potential "turf" hostility, and told them that the type and extent of summer youth jobs available in their neighborhoods would depend on the amount of proof of need that they and their friends could help the agency gather. Several participants from each gang were trained in the use of a survey instrument. When the survey was completed, the findings were compiled and the surveyors were asked to place the identified needs into priority order.

This approach had three purposes. First, it built on the cohesion within each of the gangs and got the gang members involved. Second, it prepared potential consumers to accept the services. Finally, the self-study identified needs that probably could not have been documented as well in any other manner.

The availability of relevant information and access to it will vary from one place or agency to another. However, some information is available almost everywhere. For example, probably every school in the United States collects the number of student absences. Any agency interested in aiding frequently truant teenagers can tap its local schools to obtain the information. To the extent that information exists, new data will not have to be generated. Therefore, to save effort and expense, find all possible data sources which already exist and adapt the available information to the populations under examination.

The federal government produces a great variety of data on a regular basis, in addition to publishing the census. Most published data on employment comes from the Bureau of Labor Statistics. The Internal Revenue Service publishes a biennial analysis of adjusted gross income for the 100 most populous metropolitan areas. The FBI publishes *Crime in the United States — Uniform Crime Reports*, which lists statistics on a variety of offenses by Standard Metropolitan Statistical Areas (SMSA). Data on juvenile court offenders are provided by the Department of Health and Human Services. This department also produces many periodicals and reports that give information on social security, public assistance, and social services. The Department of Education provides a variety of useful data in its annual *Digest of Educational Statistics* and has data retrieval centers throughout the nation called Educational Research Information Centers (ERIC). (See the Appendix for a list of ERIC addresses.) Each ERIC specializes in a specific topical area, such as the handicapped or early childhood education. Health statistics are numerous and come primarily from the National Center for Health Statistics of the U.S. Public Health Service. At the community level, health planning agencies tabulate and make these data available.

Every state has data on needs and services for many areas of human need, including health, housing, employment, and social services. If the data are not collected by geographic areas which match the service area of the particular agency, approximations can be made. Each state is required to prepare plans for a number of federal agencies. Examples include the Title XX Comprehensive Annual Services Program Plan (Social Security Act), Health Systems Agency Annual Implementation Plan (National Health Planning and Resources Development Act), and the Annual Plan for Aging (Older Americans Act). These plans contain quite useful demographic and service information.

Agencies can usually obtain data on a variety of topics from municipal or county governments that have planning units. Local entities operating with Housing and Community Development Act block grant funds will have data on housing needs and other important demographic information. In addition, police departments keep records of the number and types of crimes committed by persons of each age group. These data are available from local criminal justice planning organizations. Public and university libraries have reference works with valuable data on numerous subjects and the local United Way/United Fund organization ordinarily has much information on social services needs and resources available. For a small fee, health care data and research can be retrieved through computer search systems such as Medlars and Medline, available at university libraries. Sometimes all the data desired do not exist, but more often a little digging at local, county, and/or state levels produces much useful information.

Once information is obtained, it must then be analyzed. This requires classifying, evaluating, and interpreting the data gathered. Even with the availability of trained planning personnel, agencies find an appraisal panel a serviceable instrument for developing a needs assessment. The appraisal panel should include persons such as agency staff and board members, professional experts, current clients and potential consumer representatives, as well as, where feasible and desirable, the representatives of local political officials and other agencies. This latter group should be invited, if for no other reason than "what they are not up on they are likely to be down on." Care must be taken, regardless of the composition of the group, to keep the assessment objective. An appraisal is needed that makes best use of the judgment of all participants acting as individuals, without the biases of their organizational affiliations. This stricture also applies to the staff and board members of a sponsoring agency.

As suggested earlier, the need for a service basically equals total need minus the service which is already provided. Therefore, any assessment of needs must include an inventory of resources as well.

Resource inventories can be organized in several ways. Some begin as a resources listing with geographic areas, cataloguing all types of services available within given boundaries. Others begin with services for groups traditionally "in need," such as the mentally retarded, drug abusers, or low-income families. Still others list resources by the groups they serve, such as youth, blacks, disabled persons, or by service categories, such as housing programs, information and referral programs, transportation programs. As inventories become more focused on specific needs, combinations of categories will no doubt occur, as when services available for physically disabled persons are sub-grouped into transportation, employment training, and housing.

Inventories of resources are limited in several ways. First, the agencies giving the services generally provide the information. This may create problems of inaccurate data and interagency jealousy leading to the withholding or exaggerating of data. Second, the nature and amount of services, eligibility criteria, and location of service delivery sites change frequently, requiring continual updating of information. Finally, the development of discrete categories of service understandable to lay persons and useful to professional service providers and planners is not easy to accomplish. The decision about the category in which to place a particular service often is arbitrary. Suppose that a crisis intervention program for alcoholics and their families is put into the category of counseling programs rather than under substance abuse programs or that a medical transportation program is listed under transportation rather than medical care. Such seemingly harmless and trivial decisions have been known to cause much ill will and confusion among agencies.

Philosophic and political considerations also play a role in prioritizing, if not determining, needs. Many agencies and organizations have neither the staff capability nor the funds to review the entire needs of their community and probably could not obtain the money to meet all the identified needs, anyhow. Agencies ordinarily focus on one or a very few areas of human service that result from the agency's history, the availability of funding, or political and social pressures.

Philosophy and politics are important in deciding which factors will be labeled as "needs" as well as which will receive priority because there are not enough resources to deal with all areas of concern. For instance, without the funds to meet both needs, a decision might have to be made between saving marginally deteriorated houses from becoming dilapidated as against repairing dilapidated houses so they can be used for shelter. Should people who are underemployed receive supplemental incomes since they are trying to help themselves or should income only be provided to the unemployed who are unable to help themselves, when insufficient funds are available to assist both groups of people? Are the frail elderly, who are most dependent on government assistance for maintaining their existence, more in need than relatively independent elderly persons, who are at risk of becoming more dependent unless they receive governmental assistance? These are both philosophic and political questions, since values and funds are at stake.

Elected officials often determine which needs will be paramount for reasons not entirely related to the factors commonly thought of as "need." A public official might well wish to dramatize those programs (1) which are visible, such as hot meals programs for elderly and disabled persons, (2) which are likely to quiet complaints, such as adding crossing guards for schoolchildren at corners identified as dangerous by the PTA, (3) which reward constituents whose support is needed, or (4) which have been previously funded and cannot now be terminated without causing ill will.

Service agency staff members also play a role in determining priority of need by their actions in providing or withholding services. Sometimes an agency will ignore a new area of need because it is easier to do what has previously been done than to address new circumstances. A school may continue to teach students as it did when they were all English speaking and middle-income even though the majority of its current student body are Spanish-speaking youths from low-income families. Staff members may also have an investment in perpetuating certain services or ways of giving services because of their training, limits to their skills, or their reward system. For instance, state legislation might require all children's day care centers to meet the needs of physically, educationally, and emotionally disabled children by mandating that each center have a certain percentage of its clients with one or more of these disabilities. It is not difficult to imagine staff persons who would resist actively recruiting such children or trying to meet the day-care needs of these youngsters.

A basic issue in needs assessment is how to develop and carry out an assessment that taps real needs not met by other resources. In the final analysis this problem is one of validity. Bias is a human trait virtually impossible to eliminate and it may not even be desirable to try to do so. Therefore, identifying the biases of the determiners of need and the influence these biases have on the persons in need is vital. To cope with bias and make a needs assessment as valid as possible, it is important to ask who prepares the assessment criteria and who collects and evaluates the assessment data. It seems axiomatic that if people who live in a community to be assessed are involved in the design, implementation, and evaluation of a needs assessment, its validity will be greatly enhanced, as will the possibility for finding resources and ways to meet the identified needs. This is not to say that professionals in the human services cannot adequately prepare and carry out a needs assessment, but rather to suggest that potential consumers of the services should be involved as well.

Whether an assessment of needs comes first, as logic would indicate, or plans to establish a service come first because money is available, as reality sometimes dictates, any systematic approach to meeting the needs of people for services requires that objectives be set before plans are firm and activity steps are implemented.

Purpose, goal, objective, and activity are discrete terms used to describe agencies' intended actions at various levels of abstraction. They begin with an abstract end and move toward greater specificity and possibility for accomplishment as depicted in Figure 2-1. Note that each level is linked to the one below and above. The activity steps are the actions which are necessary to attain the objectives.

Statements of purpose are more abstract than goals and global in what they seek to accomplish. Goals are not precise either, but they relate to a more specific future condition which agencies desire to achieve. Usually goals are stated in general phrases, such as "to improve housing for the people of Chicago." Most specific are objectives, which identify concrete ends to be accomplished at specific levels and within specific periods of time. Objectives link directly with goal statements so that attainment of the objectives results in the attainment of the related goals. As a result of not linking objectives and goals, goals can be displaced and an agency can lose its way. It can get involved in actions little related to the desired future conditions stated in its goals. Confusion may exist between the meanings of the terms "objective" and "activity." Objectives are desired results, outcomes, ends. Activities are actions, or means, which will lead to the accomplishment of the objectives.

Figure 2-1

HIERARCHY OF ENDS AND MEANS

A purpose is a generalized statement of ultimate condition to be attained at some undetermined future time. Suppose that in response to an identified need and the availability of funds an agency decides to create a substance abuse treatment center. To determine the agency's purpose, we must answer the question, "What end should be achieved?" The answer is not a definitive description of a program but, rather, reflects the agency's hopes and desires and suggests the direction its projects will take. The statement of purpose might be: "The purpose of this agency is to help create a community in which all people maintain themselves in healthy social, economic, and personal functioning."

Goals are a reflection of the purposes which agencies have established and represent the ideals toward which the agencies aspire. For an agency which is establishing a treatment center for substance abusers, a goal could be: "To assist drug users to maintain themselves healthfully, independently, and lawfully in the community." This statement is more specific than the purpose statement, but less specific than the objectives the agency will derive from the goal.

A goal is a broad statement of a desired condition that resolves an identified need sometime in the future, without specifying the time or extent of accomplishment. Purposes and goals are needed to give direction and keep programs focused on the longer-term impact expected.

Objectives are required also, for they specify (1) what will be accomplished, (2) when it will be accomplished, and (3) to what degree. Goals are a promise, objectives are a prediction. Remember the link between objectives and evaluation. If we do not know in the short range where we are going and when we should get there (objectives), we cannot know if we have arrived at the right place and on time (evaluation).

Objectives fall into two categories: those which state product outcomes and those which state process outcomes. An example from an agency seeking to create a substance abuse treatment center illustrates the difference. Its main objectives might include the following:

1. At least 50 percent of the project participants will obtain employment within a three-month period after entering the project, and an additional 25 percent within a six-month period. (*product objective*)
2. At least 80 percent of the persons admitted to the program will attend not less than 13 weekly counseling sessions within one year. (*process objective*)

In the first objective the outcome, or end, is obtaining employment, the degree is 50 and 25 percent, and the time is three months and six months. The outcome is the *product*, or result of having participated in the project. In the second objective the outcome is attendance at weekly counseling sessions, which is part of the *process* of participating in the project. The degree is 13 sessions, and the time is one year.

Care should be taken not to confuse activities with objectives. "To establish a substance abuse treatment center that will serve 100 abusers" is not an objective, but an activity. Likewise, "to provide 40 hours of pre-employment training" is an activity and not an objective.

Suppose an assessment of needs in a particular rural community indicates that a large group of migrant farm workers find it difficult to get employment after the picking season is over because they are unable to read, write, and do simple arithmetic. A statement of purpose for an agency wishing to serve them might be: "To enable every person in the community to be capable of participating fully in the life of the community, including participating in opportunities for employment." The goal of the agency with this purpose might be: "To assist migrant farm workers in obtaining off-season employment by helping them to learn reading, writing, and arithmetic skills."

Objectives the agency could undertake might include statements such as:

1. Within six months, teach 50 adult farm workers sufficient reading and writing skills to enable them to correctly complete the employment application form of a local business or industry. (*product objective*)
2. By the end of one year, recruit and enroll 20 adult farm workers in specialized reading, writing and arithmetic classes at the community college. (*process objective*)

Activity steps for accomplishing these objectives would relate to the recruiting of participants, the hiring of teachers, the development of class materials, etc.

The four levels of the ends–means hierarchy in Figure 2-1 are summarized in the following example: An agency engaged in mental health services might have as its long-range purpose: "To create a society which fosters mental well-being for every individual." This purpose, if it could be brought to pass, would certainly not be achieved in the very near future. Therefore, one goal could be: "To create a treatment system that will enable each mentally ill person to benefit from an appropriate mix of community outpatient treatment centers, institutional care facilities, and research." An objective might be: "To diagnose and refer for treatment, within ten months, at least 300 previously untreated persons believed to have varying degrees of socially or psychologically dysfunctional behavior."

Activity steps are actions designed to implement projects so that they will result in the objectives being accomplished to the degree and in the time period specified. Suppose, to take a new example, a child abuse prevention program has as one of its objectives the reduction of incidents of abuse by 50 percent among its target population. Numerous action steps might be required to achieve this objective, but we will list only a few.

1. Meet at least bimonthly with relevant agencies in the target neighborhood to discuss the effectiveness of the agreed-upon procedures for coordinating activities on behalf of project participants.
2. Meet at least twice weekly with all parents accepted into the project either at the project site or in their homes.
3. For each youngster whose parents are in the project, prepare a monthly school attendance record and send them to the Social Service Department by the fifth day of the following month.

GOAL/OBJECTIVE/ACTIVITY STEPS

(Prepare one of these forms for each program objective)

Statement of Goal: _____

Statement of Objective: _____

Activity Steps

	Activity	Completion Date[s]	Person[s] Responsible
#1			
#2			
#3			
#4			
#5			
#6			
#7			
#8			

AGENCY SELF-ASSESSMENT CHECKLIST: ASSESSING NEEDS AND SETTING OBJECTIVES

INDICATORS	STATUS			PERSON RESPONSIBLE
	Yes	No	Partial	
1. The agency has a procedure to assess the needs of target groups on a regularly scheduled basis, including obtaining input from clients and potential clients.	____	____	____	_____
2. The agency has a procedure to routinely collect data from secondary sources about the target population.	____	____	____	_____
3. The board of directors regularly reviews projects in the light of identified needs.	____	____	____	_____
4. All agency persons responsible for data collection are trained to use the collection instruments accurately.	____	____	____	_____
5. The agency has an established resource inventory that is easily accessible to program staff.	____	____	____	_____
6. Procedures used in data collection assure confidentiality for each respondent.	____	____	____	_____
7. The agency has a procedure for routinely checking the degree to which program activities relate specifically to program objectives.	____	____	____	_____
8. Data collection procedures are consonant with grant or contract requirements.	____	____	____	_____
9. Objectives of all agency projects reflect needs identified by the established needs assessment process.	____	____	____	_____

Finding Funds

3

Since funding resources are finite, but human needs are without limits, human service agencies must devote considerable time and effort to the pursuit of money. That agencies compete with each other for the scarce dollars is little wonder. The massive effort by these agencies to obtain funds for services has many aspects of a game, a game with rules, referees, and competitors. This chapter examines some of the rules of the game and identifies resources, strategies, and techniques which are generally a part of successful efforts to keep services funded.

The search for funds, and the behavior that results from it, has similar aspects at all levels of the social service structure. Members of the Congress, for example, attempt to ensure that the areas they represent will receive an equitable share of funds from legislative enactments. The same concept motivates elected officials at state and local levels just as it motivates personnel from agencies dependent on outside sources for financial survival.

Agencies can influence several of the factors that aid their success in raising money. Knowing, and using to advantage, the rules of the game is important, but in the long run a good record of service to people in need, good program ideas, and competent leadership are probably more important. A successful grant management track record is also important in getting funds, since this makes funding sources more comfortable. They believe agencies that managed grants well before can do so again. Like incumbents in elected offices, funded agencies have a public record. They also have constituencies that can complain if the agencies' services are ended.

Public planning for services tends to reflect short-range policy objectives. The plans are subject to a variety of influences besides the demonstrated need. Trends, fads, personal influence, costs, and tradition all play a part in determining which agencies will receive money to provide services. When Kennedy was President, programs for the mentally retarded received considerably more funds than previously. President Johnson emphasized programs to aid the poor, with millions of dollars going for this purpose. The Nixon and Ford administrations added millions of dollars to law enforcement programs. In the Carter administration, the accent was on mental health and manpower programs. The Reagan administration has sought to reduce federal assistance for human services generally, earmarking more for national defense. Like presidential administrations, governors, members of Congress, state and local legislators, and mayors are fickle about services. One year money is pumped into drug abuse programs (sometimes for control of illegal drug traffic, sometimes for treatment programs, and sometimes for prevention programs), and the next year these programs are downgraded and a big push is given to projects serving runaway youths. One year large sums of money go to cancer research and the training of allied health professionals, and the next year to stockpiling missiles.

The state of the economy also affects the amount of program dollars which will be made available. In an expanding economy, income from taxes increases and so does spending. In less expansive years, the funds made available for social services decrease or perhaps hold steady. In election years, more money is spent for jobs, construction projects, and human services. When commitments in other countries require large amounts of dollars to be spent there or military needs predominate, funds for human service programs tend to be reduced. Factors such as these are generally unrelated to need as perceived by the needy, by those committed to providing services to them, or by the people who live in the sunbelt, the frost belt, rural areas, urban areas, or by the rich or the poor. As the economy changes, the amount of dollars that foundations have available for human services changes too. In other words, needs, no matter how well articulated and documented, are not by themselves reason enough for funding.

In this constantly changing environment, where all plans for human services are subject to fairly rapid and relatively unanticipated changes, where factors other than need may influence funding appropriated for programs, and where lobbying by special interest groups many times is rewarded, agencies must learn how the funding mechanisms function so that they can make them work to the advantage of the people they wish to serve.

Federal programs provide so much of the funding now being used to support the delivery of human services that an understanding of the federal system is necessary. Congress passes legislation creating national programs to meet needs which it sees as having high enough priority to warrant the expenditure of federal funds. Pieces of legislation are called Acts, such as the Elementary and Secondary Education Act, the Comprehensive Employment and Training Act, or the Older Americans Act. An Act is divided into units called Titles. Titles are divided into Parts, which are further divided into Sections.

An understanding of this classification scheme is necessary because many times funding authorizations are identified by their classification rather than their program name. For example, disabled persons and those who provide services to them are concerned about the progress of 504. Public Law (P. L.) 93-112 is known as the Rehabilitation Act of 1973. This Act is divided into several Titles, one of which, Title V, establishes the rights, and procedures for guaranteeing those rights, that disabled persons have for equal access to all services funded by the federal government. Section 504 of Title V specifies what recipients of federal funding must do to conform to Title V regulations.

Congress authorizes and appropriates funds for scores of programs, usually with mandates for the allocation and expenditure of the funds. Authorizations and appropriations are not the same. Congress may authorize funds to carry out a program for several years, but almost always appropriates funds for one year at a time. It may appropriate less funding than authorized, or even no funding at all, if it wishes. There are so many programs each year, in fact, that the *Catalog of Federal Domestic Assistance* takes over 850 pages to list them.

Funding going through the federal system may end up allocated or used somewhat differently from what Congress intended. After Congress passes an act authorizing a particular program, the federal agency responsible for administering that program develops regulations to interpret the intent of Congress and what procedures or guidelines will be followed in expending the money. These regulations and other pronouncements interpreting acts may lead to the money's being spent in ways different, to some degree, from the original conception of the legislation.

If the federal money is distributed to the states or local governments for their use or for redistribution to subcontractors, a formula for allocating these funds is used. Generally, the formula is based either on total population or on population characteristics, such as age or income. Sometimes other factors are used as well, such as the percent of unemployed persons or number of families receiving welfare benefits. State and local governmental agencies responsible for administering a particular program may make further modifications in the program through the guidelines and regulations which they issue. The intent of Congress or of state legislatures is not always clear, sometimes purposely so. Still other changes may occur because of the variety of approaches taken by the service delivery agencies. The variability created by these processes can sometimes lead to innovative, constructive programming or perhaps to inefficient, uncoordinated projects.

When the regulations for a particular program are promulgated, or officially announced, the administrative machinery is put in place by the unit of the federal department or agency which Congress has charged with overseeing the program. When the appropriation bill has been signed by the President, the program may begin. In some federal programs the funds are dispensed directly to service agencies from the federal agency. An example is the Drug Abuse Community Service Program administered by the Alcohol, Drug Abuse and Mental Health Administration. In other federal programs the money is given to the states, which may then redistribute it to sub-state agencies. These can be governmental, such as county departments or agencies, or quasi-governmental, such as regional councils of governments (COGs), or nonprofit agencies. The local units may then subcontract with human service agencies. An example is the Older Americans Act administered by the Administration on Aging (AoA). AoA funds go to state-level aging offices, which distribute the money to local-level area agencies on aging. These, in turn, give contracts to local human service agencies to provide services. In still other programs, the federal money may go directly to local units of government, such as counties or cities, or to other sponsors, bypassing the state governments. The local sponsors may then contract for the services with other agencies or may operate the programs themselves. An example is the Comprehensive Employment and Training Act.

Federal funds for programs are generally provided through contracts, subcontracts, or grants. Contracts are documents which spell out precisely what tasks and/or products, such as reports prepared, services provided, or survey data analyzed, will be completed and at how much cost. A contract is written by a funding source, not by a service agency.

Subcontracts are contracts or grants once removed. For example, if a federal agency distributes funds via a grant or contract to a state or local government agency, and that agency in turn provides a portion of the money to a human service agency, the legal agreement under which the service agency operates is termed a "subcontract." So, a city might receive federal funding from the Department of Housing and Urban Development under the Housing and Community Development Act and then subcontract with several local nonprofit agencies to provide particular services.

Grants from a federal agency are somewhat different. The agreement about what an applicant agency will do is spelled out in a proposal for funding which it prepares and submits to a federal agency. The funding source, upon approval of the application, sends a Notice of Grant Award (NGA), which indicates the starting and ending dates of the project—before and after which the funds cannot legally be spent—the amount of funds awarded in each category, such as for personnel, equipment and supplies, and any special conditions which the applicant agency must agree to when accepting the funds.

Grants are generally preferable to contracts for a service agency to have. Grants are almost never monitored as closely as contracts, and the liability for failure to perform is usually limited to defunding the project. Indeed, some grants are not monitored at all, except for financial audits which may occur infrequently. This means that within the regulations, considerable flexibility in the implementation of a grant is possible. In addition, getting supplemental funds and renewals is generally easier with grants. Renewal requests require summary statements of progress to date but, except in the more flagrant cases of lack of accomplishment, renewals are fairly automatic for the terms of the projects.

A funding strategy is necessary before starting the writing of a proposal, contrary to advice often given even by experienced program proposal developers. A funding strategy includes the following elements.

1. An agency decision to find funds to accomplish particular objectives.
2. A search for funding sources.

3. An analysis of the impact that obtaining the funds will have on the agency.
4. A plan for delivering, and meeting the costs of delivering, services.
5. A strategy for obtaining the money.

The decision to seek funds is ordinarily taken because an agency sees a need for service that is not being met in the community. Sometimes a particular need is brought to an agency's attention as, for example, when a group of parents whose young children have cerebral palsy get together and pressure a nursery school to begin a special class for their physically disabled youngsters. Or an agency may make a decision to seek funds in order to enlarge and enhance a project it is already operating. Suppose an agency providing health and social services to women recognizes that it cannot be fully helpful unless it also establishes a job placement service for its clients. The agency may go after funds not only to make the added services available but also to increase the number of its funding sources so it will be less vulnerable should it lose its regular source of financial support. An agency may also go after funding because it recognizes that some client group other than its own is receiving a lot of support and it wishes to add funds in order to maintain its viability as a service provider. As an example, there are numerous agencies that once served only youth, but which have switched to programs for the elderly as well since a considerable amount of funds became available in the 1970s for services to the aging population.

A search for federal funding begins with the determination as to which federal department or agency has the statutory authority to spend money to meet the needs of the client group that the service agency wishes to serve. This information can be obtained from consultants, from other agencies currently providing services to this client group, and from publications of the federal government. People knowledgeable in the program area in which an agency wishes to provide services may often be an excellent resource. For instance, a rural sociologist working at a nearby college might be able to supply information about federal agencies which provide support for self-help housing projects. A transportation planner working for the local transit authority might have details on legislation providing funds for nonprofit agencies wishing to obtain buses to serve disabled persons. Staff members at a mental health center may know about funding available to create drug abuse treatment centers, while local community action agency staff persons can explain the procedure for obtaining VISTA volunteers.

Much written information from the federal government is available to help agencies find sources of funding. It publishes guides useful in any search for program funding. First and foremost is the *Catalog of Federal Domestic Assistance* which provides information on program funding amounts, deadlines, and requirements for applicants. Also valuable is the *Commerce Business Daily*, which contains the official listing of Requests for Proposals (RFP). An RFP is the mechanism used by many funding sources, including the federal government, to make known the availability of funds and the conditions on which the money can be obtained.

The following documents are useful when seeking federal funds.

Catalog of Federal Domestic Assistance contains a detailed description of the over 1,000 federal grant programs, including the purposes, beneficiaries, agencies, and organizations eligible to receive funds, application deadlines, persons or offices to call for additional information, total dollars authorized, range and average dollars of each program. Usually published in May of each year by the Office of Management and Budget (OMB), the *Catalog* is updated each November. Order from the Superintendent of Documents. See "List of Important Addresses" in the Appendix.

Federal Register contains the proposed and final regulations and rules relating to federally funded programs. The *Register* is published Monday through Friday throughout the year. For applications to a federal government agency, the issue with the regulations for the particular program can be helpful. Order from the Superintendent of Documents.

Commerce Business Daily contains a listing of federal procurement invitations, contract awards, subcontract leads, and sales of surplus property. Published Monday through Friday by the Department of Commerce, the *Daily* is the official listing of federal Requests for Proposals.

Legislation, which authorized the program for which the agency is seeking funds, can be obtained from federal elected officials or from the House and Senate Document Rooms. For the Washington addresses of Congresspersons and Senators see "List of Important Addresses" in the Appendix. Most have offices in their home districts which can be contacted for the needed materials.

Application packages containing required forms for submitting proposals and instructions for filling them out are available from the federal department administering the program for which an agency is seeking funds. Grant applications for the National Institute of Mental Health (NIMH), for example, are submitted on forms NIH 398 (National Institutes of Health). Application packages can be obtained from the department or agency in Washington or from a federal regional office. See the Appendix for a listing of Federal Information Centers and their addresses.

City council members or state legislators, or their staff people, can be useful sources of information about grants and contracts available. Another information source is the office staff of an area's Congressperson or Senator. They can gain access to funding sources more easily than most lay persons. Often they are sensitive to the local political climate and may be eager to please constituents by helping to find funds for services. In short, visits to the offices of elected officials can be helpful in identifying funding sources and these officials may be willing to write support letters for funding applications.

At the federal level, the project officers, staff persons in a department or agency whose unit has responsibility for funding the contracts or grants for which an agency is applying, are usually knowledgeable about their own areas. They are often willing to share information and to provide helpful dos and don'ts. Letters will eventually get to them, but phone calls are faster and more likely to result in reaching the right person. A call to the contact person listed for the appropriate program in the *Catalog of Federal Domestic Assistance* is a good way to get started. If the contact person for particular funds turns out not to be the project officer, he or she can usually make a referral to the correct person.

In most metropolitan areas there are local planning bodies which coordinate federal and/or state funding and are responsible for planning, such as health systems agencies (HSA) or criminal justice planning boards. One important role of these organizations is to work with service agencies which use federal funds. If a service agency wants to use federal dollars for health care, for instance, the local HSA is an obvious source for information and referral. These are some of the questions that could be asked:

When is the next deadline for application?

What are the funding agency's priorities for the year?

How many proposals were received during the last round of applications and how many were funded?

How much money is available?

If our agency submits a proposal for X dollars, is that a reasonable sum?

Does our agency qualify?

Are there any printed materials which would be of help in preparing an application?

Can you furnish an RFP and application package?

What are the relevant legislation and regulations?

Can you provide the applicable *Code of Federal Regulations* numbers and the date they appeared in the *Federal Register*?

An analysis of the impact of funding on an agency or organization is vital because project money may be a mixed blessing. Some agencies have found that the acquisition of staff to provide a service has resulted in a substantial decrease in volunteers, leaving the clients no better off than before. Others have found that the supporting effort for a newly funded project may dissipate the current staff's activities so much that morale and productivity decrease. The added paychecks and supply vouchers may be more than the bookkeeper can handle and cause serious delays. The added responsibility, especially at the time of starting up, may cause the director of the agency to become overstressed and less effective. Every formerly weak area may suddenly become a critical problem area. Careful consideration of such effects of any new funding on the ongoing operation must be considered before a decision to apply for funds is made.

Three areas seem to be most troublesome. Personnel problems can result if trained and skilled program staff persons are not available once the funds are obtained. Transferring program and/or support staff from current projects to the new one can easily cause role difficulties if not handled well. Also, differences in pay between current and new staff can cause concern. Governance issues have a way of sometimes becoming difficult when a new project is funded. For agencies operating on federal money for the first time, many new rules may have to be followed which members of advisory councils or boards of directors may not be aware of or may not like. Sometimes a new advisory group must be formed or the composition of the board of directors changed. When this happens, the role and relationship of the advisory group to the board of directors may not be clear and may take time to work out. Finally, the credibility of an agency is at stake. It must prove that it can provide the services for which is was funded in ways acceptable to both the clients and the funding source. If it cannot, then other of its programs may be jeopardized.

The development of a plan and budget for delivering services, called a "proposal," will be considered later. However, consideration should be given at this point to the relationship between the major tasks and the costs involved in a project. The development of an effective program idea into a specific operating project results from the interplay of resources (personnel and dollars) and benefits to clients. A project does not exist without clients, and services cannot be provided without resources. Therefore, contrary to the advice sometimes given, it is not wise to plan a project and then work out the costs. Since the amount of funds available is usually known, the development of a plan for services without regard to this figure is unrealistic.

Develop a strategy for obtaining the money requested in any application for funds. Agencies or organizations that have good records for getting funds are almost always those that do more than just submit proposals. There are factors which affect funding that can be dealt with directly by any agency. One of the most important is its reputation as a provider of services and its history of service and fiscal responsibility. Nobody wants to back an agency which cannot deliver on its commitments or which is suspected of using service dollars for other purposes.

Another way agencies can help themselves is by carefully tailoring their applications for funds to fit the priorities and requirements of the funding sources. This ordinarily means maintaining regular contact with one or more staff persons from potential funding sources to keep a steady flow of information coming in. This may also mean submitting the same project idea to several sources, changing the terminology to fit their differing requirements. While it is not right to *accept* funds from different sources for the same services, it is perfectly acceptable to *seek* funds for the same services from different sources. Also acceptable is the practice of seeking funds from different sources for the same project, as long as the money is not for the same services. A youth counseling project in junior high school, for example, might be seen as part of programs in mental health, education, criminal justice, and youth development.

Sometimes an agency knows that it will be funded before it ever commits an idea to paper. It knows that by the time an RFP comes out, if there is to be one, the decision about who to fund will already be settled in its favor. This process is called "wiring" and a grant or contract to a predetermined agency is said to be "wired."

How does this happen? One reason may be that an agency has some unique feature, outstanding staff, or other capability known to the funding source, which makes it especially suitable. Or an agency may not be uniquely qualified, but does have a good record of accomplishment on projects previously underwritten by the funding source. Occasionally the reason may be an illegal arrangement involving kickbacks or other forms of collusion. Within the programs of funding sources that use a peer review approach to screening funding applications the "old school chum" influence is sometimes felt. That is, the people who are chosen to do the reviews because they are experts in the content areas select others whom they know or know about to receive funds. These others may be their colleagues, persons who received their professional training at the same college, or persons who hold the same political or ideological views.

The friendship factors have diminished substantially in recent years at the federal level as the processes for awarding grants and contracts have become more available to public scrutiny and more regulated. State and local levels of government still vary considerably in the degree to which the merit of an application is the deciding factor. Publicity about the process is one of the best methods for ensuring honesty.

An agency or organization, as part of its strategy for obtaining funds, may wish to get the help of other agencies and individuals. Support letters from agencies and individuals with a high degree of credibility and a reason for being concerned about the funding of a project can be helpful. Asking a state office on aging to support a proposal for funds relating to improved nursing home care makes sense. Asking that agency to support a funding request for a youth athletic project probably does not. The main thing is that an agency asked to help be credible to the funding source.

Elected officials and/or some of their key staff persons can do wonders with an inquiry letter or phone call. Generally it is not a good idea for staff members, even the directors, of applicant agencies to directly solicit elected officials or government employees for help in obtaining funds. Such solicitations may be seen as self-serving. Any suspicion that clouds the funding atmosphere may adversely affect the good work the agencies have done. Requests for support for funding applications are better made by members of the board of directors who know the officials or who, as "public-spirited" citizens, can elucidate the good work of the agency. The support requested may be in the form of letters to be attached to the applications for funds or may be for more personal contact directly with the funding sources. However, heavy-handed inquiries by elected officials may cause the staff persons in charge of funding to feel unduly pressured, which can result in negative actions.

Also of help in many cases are program staff people of funding sources. If agencies already have money from funding sources, the project officers of the funding agencies can give effective support to renewal applications or new requests for funds. If an agency has never been funded by a particular funding source before, the staff in charge of the funds for which the agency is applying can aid materially if they have been kept informed about the proposed project, if they like the project idea, and if they have no conflict of interest in offering advice and help. They can argue on behalf of an applicant agency's proposed project both with the review committee and with the decision-makers. It pays for human service agency directors to visit with project officers, even if that means traveling to Washington, D.C., to seek them out at professional conferences and conventions and to call and correspond with them regularly. A recent study has shown a high correlation between this activity and success in obtaining funds. However, applicant agencies usually gain little advantage from trying to pressure review committee members or those finally responsible for the decisions on which applications to fund.

Support from professional associations related directly to the type of services being proposed can sometimes be helpful, especially if specific support activities are offered as well as the usual assurances about the importance of the project. Letters from clients attached to an application for funds tends generally to have little effect at the federal level. At the local level, however, visits, phone calls, numerous reasonable letters and politely worded petitions by clients or potential clients may be of use.

At least one other factor can be helpful to any agency seeking funding. If the funding application requires that a matching share (cash, goods, or services provided by the applicant) be provided, the applicant agency can offer a larger amount than required by the funding source. Since so many projects receive less money than is actually required to meet all needs, it follows that those responsible for funding projects would give weight in their decision to getting as many other resources put into the project as possible. The matching share, of course, is the primary mechanism for obtaining the other resources in most projects. Agencies have found it unwise to offer more match than they can realistically provide. The matching share becomes a formal requirement once a project is funded and failure to provide the amount committed can result in loss of credibility and/or funding.

Philanthropic funding sources are in some ways similar, and in other ways dissimilar, to governmental agencies which provide program funds. Private foundations rarely issue RFPs and are generally under no legal or political obligation to distribute their funds equitably in terms of demographic or geographic considerations. They are chartered, or sanctioned, by state governments and, within the terms of their charters which require charitable purposes, may provide funds to whomever they wish. They are not required to distribute their funds on a competitive basis. If they obtain Internal Revenue Service designation as a nonprofit, charitable organization, contributions to them become tax deductible. They must then give up the right to undertake specified lobbying activities. This tax deductible status is the reason most foundations exist. Private foundations' funds are generally from a single source, such as a family or corporation, while public charities, such as the American Cancer Society, have numerous sources of funding, including donations made by foundations and by individuals. Almost all foundations have interests in relatively narrow fields of service. The Kellogg Foundation, for instance, is particularly interested in education services while the Xerox Foundation is interested in community involvement projects. In some cases the interest is even more narrowly defined. A foundation may be interested in health, but perhaps only in providing funds for facilities construction and not services. In other words, pursuit of foundation sources must first involve a careful look at what the foundation will support.

As with attempts to obtain funds from governmental sources, agencies should develop strategies for obtaining funds from philanthropic sources. The previously proposed first step of deciding to seek funds applies to foundations as potential funding sources as well as to governmental agencies.

The search for foundation funding will lead to different sources of information. Just as the *Catalog of Federal Domestic Assistance* is the usual starting point for those seeking federal grants, so *The Foundation Directory* is the basic tool for beginning a search for private sector funds. The following documents are useful when seeking foundation funds.

> *The Foundation Directory* lists over 2,500 of the nation's largest foundations with assets over $1,000,000 each. The *Directory* indicates the type of grants and the range of dollars awarded for past grants from each foundation. The officers and members of the boards of directors are listed along with addresses for all the foundations. There are quarterly supplements updating the material. Each of the following documents can be ordered from Columbia University Press, 136 South Broadway, Irvington, N.Y. 10533.
>
> *The Foundation Grants Index* is an annual compilation of the *Index*, published bimonthly in the *Foundation News*. The *Index* contains a listing of recent grants of $5,000 or more made by more than 400 of the most active foundations in the United States. Each issue contains more than 1,600 grants listed by state, name of foundation, purpose, and amount.
>
> *The Foundation Center Source Book* is a two-volume publication with detailed information on foundations. It includes data on grants given during the year and includes application procedures. The Foundation Center compiles descriptive data and statistics on foundations and conducts searches of possible foundation funding for particular projects of agencies and organizations.
>
> *Foundation News*, published every two months by the Foundation Center, offers articles on the role of philanthropy and helpful information on grantsmanship. A subscription, which includes *The Foundation Grants Index* listing, can be obtained from the address indicated above.
>
> *Grantsmanship Center News* is published six times a year and contains articles on funding methods and philanthropic sources as well as up-to-date information on federal program funds. A subscription can be obtained from the Grantsmanship Center, 1031 South Grand Avenue, Los Angeles, California 90015.

These publications are invaluable for agencies seeking foundation funds. Instead of an agency applying to hundreds of foundations from which there is little or no chance of receiving grants, these publications make it possible to identify the foundations that have given money for projects in the program areas and geographic locations for which the applicant agency is seeking a grant. Since the *News* and *Index* list the dollars given for each grant funded, agencies can determine what constitutes a realistic request for funds.

The strategy for obtaining funds, the final step in an overall strategy, differs somewhat from that which proves helpful in obtaining project money from governmental sources. While it is important, even essential, to fit a project to a foundation's purpose and objectives, more latitude is possible than with most grants from government agencies. Smaller foundations often give in local areas, with the place of implementation of the project being as important as the nature of the project. These smaller foundations are frequently operated by individuals who are not specialists in the program areas supported by the foundations. Even the larger foundations, with professional managers, will often accept proposals for funding which are considerably off the beaten track, provided the applications show clearly what the needs are and how they will be met.

Credibility may be among the most important factors in decisions to fund. Therefore, an agency that can include a resume of a proposed project director which shows that person to be responsible, well-trained, and experienced will have an advantage. Also helpful are letters from established persons and agencies in the community which confirm the need and indicate their support for the project.

Since many foundations are operated by the family and friends of the individual(s) who established them, personal contact with members of the board of directors, often called trustees, can be helpful in obtaining a serious reading of a grant request. *The Foundation Directory* contains the names of officers and other trustees of the foundations listed. An approach by a member of an agency board of directors to a trustee of a foundation may be useful in getting a request for funds accepted. In larger foundations, where experts and staff members are hired to review applications for funding, this approach may still be desirable. With local foundations, the selection of a foundation trustee to serve on an agency's board of directors is not only ethical, but may bring other benefits beyond a possible increase in funding to the agency.

Before submitting a lengthy request for funds to a foundation, there are several steps which can be taken to save time and resources and increase the chances for obtaining funding. First, identify the foundations which give grants for the type of project and in the geographic location desired by the agency. Then send a one- or two-page inquiry letter, which briefly covers the need, objectives, proposed project activities, and credibility of the agency. In a follow-up by phone, ask the foundation staff if they publish guidelines for applying for their grants. If the foundation does not have written guidelines, seek information about what they like to have included in an application. Obtain as much information as possible about the foundation's current priorities for programs, their preference for length of projects, and the nature and extent of evaluation they ordinarily request from their grantees. This data, along with the range of dollars awarded, which is obtainable from *The Foundation Directory* and *Foundation News*, should enable an agency to put together a fundable application for a grant.

Charitable organizations can also be a source of funds and other resources. Fraternal organizations and churches provide funds for worthwhile projects in their communities, although the amounts are usually small. United Way/United Fund organizations, or their equivalent, raise money in their respective communities and allocate their funds to nonprofit human services agencies. These organizations generally allocate funds to member agencies only, but have procedures for admitting additional agencies to membership.

Some agencies cannot provide money but can provide other valuable resources in the form of free space, furniture and equipment, building renovation, transportation, volunteer services, printing, and supplies. These items provide a valuable matching share contribution for those grants which require it, and since the money provided for projects hardly ever seems sufficient to meet the need for services, these resources may spell the difference between success and failure.

AGENCY SELF-ASSESSMENT CHECKLIST: FINDING FUNDS

INDICATOR	STATUS OF INDICATOR			PERSON RESPONSIBLE
	Yes	No	Partial	
1. The agency has a process to catalogue all incoming requests for proposals and related grant materials.	____	____	____	_____
2. The agency has a grantsmanship library or a procedure to pool grant documents with other agencies.	____	____	____	_____
3. The agency has "boilerplate" statements about its community and its various service populations and they are updated annually.	____	____	____	_____
4. All applicable federal forms such as Civil Rights assurances, certificates of insurance, and indirect cost rate agreements are up-to-date and on file.	____	____	____	_____
5. The Board of Directors determines service priorities annually in accordance with which funds are sought.	____	____	____	_____
6. The agency routinely requests feedback about unfunded grant applications.	____	____	____	_____
7. The agency has a procedure for obtaining letters of support and coordination agreements.	____	____	____	_____
8. The agency has a procedure of obtaining community input into the fiscal and programmatic aspects of proposals as they are being prepared.	____	____	____	_____
9. The agency has procedures for integrating newly funded services into its fiscal and program operations.	____	____	____	_____
10. The agency maintains contact with government and foundation staff persons regarding possible funding opportunities.	____	____	____	_____

Developing Proposals

4

Proposals are basically plans for how services will be delivered or research conducted. A typical proposal will:

show that there is an important need,

have objectives which will significantly affect that need,

outline a plan for accomplishing the objectives,

establish the applicant agency as capable of carrying out the plan in an efficient, effective, sometimes innovative, manner,

specify the costs anticipated in carrying out the plan.

Every funding source requires a slightly different submission format, but each format has the same intent, which is to describe what will be done, why, how, at what cost, and by whom. Generally, formats contain some or all of the 14 proposal components indicated in Figure 4-1. Although a few foundations may require no more than a two-page letter outlining the proposed project, some foundations and nearly all government agencies insist on a more extensive detailing of activities and costs. They may ask, in addition, for select documents, such as articles of incorporation, letters of support from other agencies, and fiscal and civil rights assurances. The bottom line requirement for every funding source is to know what their dollars will be used for and who will be responsible.

The components of a proposal follow, some or all of which are requirements of the funding source.

Figure 4-1

PROPOSAL COMPONENTS

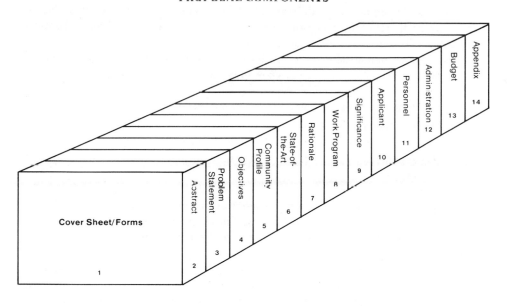

Cover Sheet/Forms — 1
Abstract — 2
Problem Statement — 3
Objectives — 4
Community Profile — 5
State-of-the-Art — 6
Rationale — 7
Work Program — 8
Significance — 9
Applicant — 10
Personnel — 11
Administration — 12
Budget — 13
Appendix — 14

COVER SHEET AND FORMS

Funding sources are quite particular about the way the cover sheet and other forms are prepared. Government sources usually supply the applicant with a package of forms that detail the order in which the proposal is to be submitted and how the forms are to be completed. It is not unlike preparing an income tax form. The best procedure is to read the instructions carefully and then fill in all the blank spaces. The funding source has its own rationale for asking for particular information. Therefore, if information is incomplete or missing altogether, the proposal may be rejected out-of-hand during the initial review. The rejection might even be made by a clerk who is concerned only with what the proposal document contains and not with what it says. Another reason for carefully completing forms is psychological. Whoever developed or requires the forms believes that the information requested is important. When a grant applicant appears to ignore the requirements, the response may be a rejection of the proposal.

Whether cover sheets are required or not, every proposal requires a title. Make the title concise and descriptive so that the reader can see at a glance what the project is all about. Keep the title under 53 letters and word spaces in length. If an acronym is used, list the acronym in the title, as in the example Health Experience Leadership Project (HELP). Sometimes, it is useful to identify the recipient as well as the activities proposed; for instance, Filipino Migrant Worker Dental Screening Project.

PROPOSAL ABSTRACT

An abstract is frequently required as part of the cover sheet or related forms. Even if not required, including an abstract is a good idea. Summarize the proposed project in 200 to 250 words, or about one-half page, so the reviewers will be able to quickly assess the document to determine its relevance to the interests of the funding source. The elements of an abstract usually are the following four items:

1. A paragraph of 2 or 3 lines that states the overall proposed project goal.
2. A paragraph of 3 or 4 lines that describes the need or problem.
3. A paragraph of 2 or 3 lines that summarizes the objectives.
4. A paragraph of 10 to 12 lines that outlines the proposed activities and expected outcomes.

Paraphrasing the abstract in the letter of transmittal which accompanies the proposal to the funding source adds unity. The abstract is also handy for preparing news releases or for use as a handout to give or send to groups that have an interest in the project.

An abstract gets attention. Without an abstract, reviewers are forced to go through the entire proposal to gain an understanding of the basic ideas. Unless the reviewers are particularly motivated to do so (a risky assumption), the absence of an abstract may be the factor that leads to rejection of the proposal.

PROBLEM STATEMENT OR DESCRIPTION OF NEEDS

This identifies a specific group of persons—the target group—and their specific needs *which the applicant agency proposes to do something about.* The entire proposal is a statement of intent to link the needs described in the problem statement with the objectives and the plan for services to be rendered. Make clear the connection between the problem statement and what follows in the proposal. For example, if a problem statement says that recovering alcoholics need employment and the work program contains nothing about providing job training, development and placement, or even job counseling, a funding source is likely to question the effectiveness of the project. Include only needs for which there are corresponding objectives and prospective services which can reasonably be expected to be effective in ameliorating those needs. Conversely, do not include unnecessary objectives unrelated to the description of needs. Nor should the work plan contain activities which are unrelated to meeting the specifically identified needs.

In Chapter 2 we outlined the data ordinarily used to describe needs and the means for gathering them. These data and the interpretation of them form the basis for the problem statement, or description of needs. The problem statement should describe the nature and degree or extent of each need along with the reasons for selecting the needs outlined.

Take, for example, a proposal to fund a group home for the placement of young women convicted of crimes, for whom placement in community facilities is deemed more suitable than incarceration. This proposal might detail needs drawn from different sources, including data and a narrative interpretation of the data. The data and narrative can be organized in the following way.

Scope of the problem: Cite national, state, and local recidivism rates (repeat offenses) for women. These data can be cross-tabulated against any number of variables, including ethnicity, age, years of incarceration, number of arrests, and type of arrest (felony, misdemeanor). The data can be depicted in matrix form, as illustrated in Figure 4-2, and then highlighted in a brief narrative.

Percentages or whole numbers can be used in the presentation of data tables. Use either one type of data or the other, however, and do not mix percentages with numbers. Data displays such as depicted in Figure 4-2 are quite useful in giving a sense of the interrelationships and complexity of the problem.

Data can be drawn from secondary sources, such as state reports, census documents, and survey findings done locally. Sensitivity to the proposal reviewers is shown by only citing cogent data which highlights the problem. Other data tangential to the problem should be placed in the proposal's Appendix section. When placing data there be certain to cite this fact in the problem statement. A statement such as "For further information, see Appendix A" will suffice.

Description of the relative effectiveness of treatment models: Incarceration versus community treatment models, for instance, can be compared in the narrative. The information can take the form of quotations from experts and from the research reported in scholarly literature. University libraries can be of great help in identifying literature citations. Local practitioners may be able to point out appropriate material. The purpose of this material is to show the degree to which incarceration is ineffective with this group of women. Do not include material unrelated to the statement of the problem, however interesting.

The clearest way to use such references is to divide the problem statement into sections. To continue with the incarceration example, the proposal might discuss the problem in categories such as: (1) trends or changes in treatment ("Jails gave way to workhouses in the 1930s, according to John Jones, noted Illinois criminologist, and this

Figure 4-2

**HYPOTHETICAL EASTDALE RECIDIVISM RATE
VARIABLES FOR WOMEN EX-OFFENDERS**
*(Data are drawn from Eastdale Regional Planning
Board Annual Report, 1981, pp. 113-17.)*

Race and ethnicity

	Caucasian %	Black %	Hispanic %	Asian Pacific %	Native American %
Age 18 – 25					
26 – 35					
36 – 45					
46+					
Eastdale					
National					
State					

resulted in . . . '') and (2) corollary changes in social values ("The 'Feminist Move-ment' is greatly affecting society's view of women and criminality. As the Second An-nual Report of *FMS* suggests . . . "). It is advisable to either footnote direct quotations or include the citations in the text. A sensible style used by professionals in many fields is that of Mary Claire van Leunen in *A Handbook for Scholars*, published by Knopf. Keep in mind that a problem statement is trying to tell a story. State the case adequately to establish the need, but do not overburden or distract the reviewers.

Description of the impact: State the significance of the problem to the nation, state, com-munity, and/or agency. In the same example, we might paint a picture of the problem as it appears "to the person on the street." Citing newspaper stories or providing a brief narrative description of what is happening to individual women would show the concern many people feel about the problem.

In this segment also indicate how interested agencies and groups in the community feel about the problem. Continuing with our example, the statement might say that "ten community organizations are actively concerned. . . . They have no resources similar to those proposed. . . . " Then it could refer the reviewers to the Appendix for letters of support and collaboration from these agencies.

The statement may illustrate the importance of the proposed project to the potential recipients of the services. It might refer to an attached letter from the Probation De-partment stating that many more young women require placement in community group-home facilities than presently exist. Those who do not get a placement must be incarcerated, with the attendant difficulties cited above, or else sent back to the envi-ronment where they previously got into trouble with the law. This shows that the need is real and immediate. Noting how others see the problem and then documenting their views with their signed letters corroborates the scope of the problem. This adds to the applicant agency's credibility.

Description of the resources in the community: In this section of the problem statement, sum-marize the appropriate projects, services, and types of agencies available to cope with the problem. The intent here is to suggest strongly to the reviewers that the service or activity that is proposed is not available, or is available in a quantity inadequate to meet the needs. In other words, make this segment of a problem statement highlight *gaps* in service.

A problem statement can depict available resources in a variety of ways. For most local needs give the name of the resource and indicate the quantity. For example:

1. Ann Smith Rehabilitation Center (capacity 4 persons).
2. Central City Halfway House (capacity 10 persons).
3. Catholic Big Sisters Home (capacity 12 persons).

Point to the gravity of the need by highlighting the list with a narrative such as: "As can be seen, Central City has three facilities presently available as alternatives to in-carceration for women. However, in the three facilities there are beds for only 26 women. This points to a critical need. For in Central City in each of the last five years more than 180 young women were sent to the state prison. About half of these women would have been eligible for our proposed program."

In summary, a problem statement component documents the nature, extent, and im-portance of the needs which the proposal intends to resolve. It narrows the needs down to a specific target group with specific difficulties and makes a logical connection between the evidence of needs presented and the program work plan which will follow later.

OBJECTIVES

The section of Chapter 2 that describes objectives, goals, and purposes should be reviewed now because the procedures for developing objectives described there are essentially the same as those required for writing objectives for a proposal.

Proposals require objectives rather than purpose or goal statements. Objectives are the specific outcomes expected from the proposed program and must define the ends of the planned activities in a measurable way. Objectives are not the means (activities), but the ends. "The funds from this proposal will be used to create a group home for delinquent young women" is not a satisfactory objective. Rather, concrete objectives are required that (1) state what the outcome will be, (2) in what quantity, and (3) within what period, such as, "During this 24-month project, a weekly average of fifteen young women referred from the Probation Department will receive at least one hour of individual counseling and four hours of group counseling." This is a process objective. An example of a product objective is, "The recidivism rate among participants during their stay in the project and for six months afterward will be less than 25 percent of that for a comparison group."

COMMUNITY PROFILE

This component is not always called for in federal grant proposals, but having a standard statement (called "boilerplate") ready is a big help. Make the profile brief and factual and give the readers a thumbnail sketch of the community. Depending on the purpose of the funds being sought, of course, a profile can include such information as the population by age (total age under 18, over 65, etc.), racial and ethnic groups, the number of persons in poverty, the percent of persons in poverty, the percent of substandard housing, and the setting (urban, suburban, rural). Include brief descriptions of unique features of the community, services offered, and the form of government (mayor-council, city manager). Data indicating general needs, as contrasted to the specific needs which are in the problem statement component, can be included here, too. These data must be brief and help to give reviewers, who may not know the community, a good picture.

The example which follows is *part* of a description of the County of Los Angeles and illustrates the kind of items that might be included.

Within the County government alone, there are thirteen separate departments involved in providing services to youth. This situation is further complicated by the immense population and geographic size of the County and large number of separate governmental entities involved, all of which either utilize or provide services related to the youth service system. Statistically this includes:

over four thousand square miles,

over seven million residents,

79 separate local government jurisdictions including the City of Los Angeles,

49 different law enforcement agencies,

95 separate school districts, including the large autonomous Los Angeles City Unified School District.

Based on the fiscal year 1975-76 data, when compared to the rest of the state, Los Angeles County contained 32 percent of the state's total population (6,920,700 for the County as compared to 21,520,000 for California); and 60 percent of the protective services caseload (68,068 in the County and 114,059 in California).

Preparing a short narrative description of the community that integrates demographic data with a physical description of the community is also useful. The following is illustrative:

The target community is a mixed residential and light industrial district. It is immediately adjacent to downtown and is characterized by garment industry and some commercial properties along the arterial streets. The community is virtually "walled" in by freeways.

The target community's estimated population of 95,000 lives in rooming houses, apartments upstairs of commercial buildings, and in single family residences. Approximately 30 percent of the single family homes are owner occupied. A relatively small number of persons live in multi-story apartment buildings. Housing is rundown; the commercial properties, interspaced with liquor stores and fast-food shops, are unkempt in appearance. Graffiti covers most exposed walls and fences. The population is mobile.

Based on school registration records, it is estimated that families move with a frequency more than three times as great as for the county as a whole. A cause for the mobility is the availability of low-income housing and jobs. The garment industry is labor intensive and seeks the unskilled. Employers readily hire "without asking questions." The undocumented worker thus has ready access to jobs and sees the neighborhood as desirable. Work in this industry is seasonal, however, and as jobs cease, people move on.

Income for a family of four in this community is well below that of the county as a whole. Further, unemployment for adolescents and male heads of household probably approaches 60 percent for the former and 30 percent for the latter. Garment industry jobs, though plentiful in season, tend to go to women rather than men.

The community's ethnic population is constantly shifting. The high transiency rate is certainly a cause if not a product. In the 1950s, the majority were Caucasian with a scattering of blacks, Asian-Americans, and Mexican-Americans. In the 1960s the community was predominantly black. In the 1970s, the shift toward Spanish-surnamed residents was quite marked. Today, 70 percent of the population are Mexicans or Mexican-Americans.

STATE-OF-THE-ART

A state-of-the-art component may not be needed for some types of requests, but most demonstration and model projects and all research projects require a piece on the state-of-the-art and a *current* bibliography. The purpose of this section in the proposal, sometimes called a "review of the literature" in research projects, is to demonstrate that a thorough investigation of the proposed work program has been conducted and that the proposers know what has been done previously in the program area, what research efforts have been made and the findings of that research, what has been written in books and professional journals about the topic, and what alternative models have been tried or could be tried. A funding source wants to be assured that it is not going to fund a demonstration project which has already been demonstrated elsewhere, that it is funding a model which stands a reasonable chance of succeeding based on the best evidence and thinking available, and that it is funding a project which will lead to materials and methods that can become the basis for similar programs in other places.

A state-of-the-art section is generally done in one of two ways: (1) a chronological sequence is described which brings up-to-date the history of the attempts to meet the particular need or answer the particular research question, or (2) a number of issues are examined, into which the previous program or research efforts can logically be divided. Suppose a proposal is asking for funds to establish a project which will pay family members to support older persons at home instead of institutionalizing them in nursing homes or other care facilities. A state-of-the-art segment, divided into three issues, might indicate data on (1) previous types of programs designed to prevent institutionalization of elderly people, (2) the financial costs of home care versus institutional care, and (3) the psychological effects of institutionalization. To justify the validity of the statements, citations are included in the text, with each source appearing in a bibliography.

Many research proposals are rejected because the relevant findings from the review of the literature, which establish the basis for the use of the particular model or theory, are not included. The findings must also support the selection of the specific research hypotheses which are to be tested in the program.

State-of-the-art statements are illustrated by the following two examples:

> The use of a patient advocate was pioneered in this state at Midvale Hospital. In that instance the patient advocate was able to reduce complaints reaching the hospital administrator by 40 percent in one year. This reduction demonstrated the efficiency of this new procedure. (Smith, 1978)
>
> The Public Health Service reported that the newest demonstration of consumer intervention in this area used consumer generated criteria for developing program standards. This activity showed a marked improvement over the traditional staff generated criteria. (*Bulletin*, 1980)

A good statement will not just review, but also will analyze the data and ideas. An effective review of the literature can help to establish the credibility of a proposed project and agency and may increase the chance for approval of the funds.

RATIONALE

This component is intended to explain why this approach, these methods, and this agency are the correct ones for meeting the needs or testing the hypotheses described in the proposal.

An agency with a history of meeting the health needs of a particular group of children from low-income families, for example, might suggest that it is applying for funds for a transportation component to its health clinic project so it can saturate its catchment area and provide services to children who otherwise would not be able to reach the clinic. The rationale is that this would be cheaper and more effective than other methods of providing the services, such as opening satellite clinics.

In another instance, an agency which has just completed a statewide survey of volunteer recreation projects in nursing homes might apply for funds to conduct a model project in local nursing homes in order to test whether what it had learned would work well. Or an agency without prior effort in a particular program might argue that its general management and service delivery capabilities made it a good candidate for funding and expansion into the new program area.

In summary, describe in the rationale component, clearly and briefly, why a particular approach to dealing with the problem has been chosen. Show how the approach selected will produce the best results. If a review of the literature has been done, references to that material can be helpful.

WORK PROGRAM

This component is the heart of a proposal. Sometimes the work program is called "scope of work," "action plan," "methods section," "approach," or "management plan." The component gives a detailed description of the activities which will be conducted over the course of the grant period in order to accomplish the objectives.

Contrary to the advice sometimes given in popularized versions of proposal preparation articles, it makes little sense to describe what the project is all about "in your own words." Many writers and readers of proposals talk about "keeping it simple," when they really mean "write clearly and logically." Clear is not the same as simple. Keep in mind that reviewers of proposals are often persons with an extensive background in the type of service proposed. As social services or law enforcement or health systems experts, they have a special language (jargon) they use when talking about their areas of expertise. Proposals not couched in terms familiar to them may seem amateurish. They often feel that someone not knowing the terminology probably could not comprehend the program. Whether for logical reasons or not, proposals sometimes receive negative recommendations for being too "simple." However, for requests to those foundations that do not use "professional" reviewers, the avoidance of jargon is desirable. The best approach is to write the proposal with the probable reviewers in mind.

The easiest way to make a clear work program is to list the major activities or components of the plan, describing each in turn by the tasks which comprise it. Be sure that each major activity or work component is related to the accomplishment of an objective, and that each helps to reduce a need.

To prepare a work program, always read a funding agency's instructions carefully before beginning. A work plan should be outlined first in a time/activity chart and then followed by a detailed narrative description of the major activities depicted in the chart. The following hypothetical example illustrates the method and format for writing the work program component of a proposal.

A church group in a poverty community decides that inflation has caused such a severe financial strain on their member families that a way of reducing the cost of living for these families must be found. Since the biggest cost is food, they decide to start a food cooperative. With a few thousand dollars from their parent church organization for equipment and initial supplies, they believe they can create a project which will substantially reduce food costs for the participating families.

Having identified the need, they decide on objectives; including the following:

1. Within six months of the start of services, recruit at least 100 low-income families who are purchasing at least twenty dollars' worth of food from the co-op each week. (Process objective)

2. At the end of one year show a savings on overall food costs of at least ten percent as compared with regular supermarket prices. (Product objective)

As the simplified time/activity chart shows in Figure 4-3, the four primary activities will take place concurrently. A sampling of the activities and tasks is detailed below:

Activity 1.   Open Co-op Site
Task A.   Building survey
During this period we will identify all the available stores and warehouses within two miles of the church that meet these criteria: (1) at least 1000 sq. ft. of floor space, (2) walk-in refrigerator of at least 50 sq. ft., (3) loading area accessible to trucks with 3-foot-high gate, and (4) ramp access for physically disabled persons.

This activity will be accomplished by employing two commercial Realtors (on a finder's fee basis only) to survey all suitable space within the target community. A lease will be signed on or before the third project month.

Task B.   Equipment survey
In the same time period we will identify, price, and order all equipment (shelving, scales, etc.) needed by the co-op. Staff will accomplish this activity using a buyer's criteria guide developed during the second project month.

Figure 4-3

SAMPLE TIME/ACTIVITY CHART

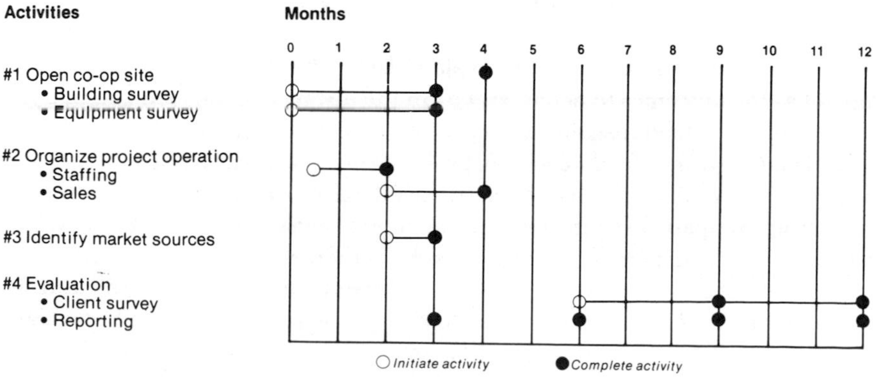

○ *Initiate activity*   ● *Complete activity*

Activity 2.   Organize Project Operation

Task A.   Staffing

This activity will take place during the first two project months. It involves four sub-activities: (1) publicize and recruit salaried staff and volunteers, (2) recruit a selection panel, (3) hold personnel selection sessions, and (4) hire salaried project personnel. The Personnel Selection Committee will use the job descriptions contained in Appendix A of this proposal document.

Task B.   Sales . . . .

An important part of a work program is the evaluation. Unfortunately, far too many program administrators are ignorant about or fearful of evaluation efforts. As a consequence they resist putting a serious evaluation component into their proposals. For some projects, such as demonstration or model projects, funding usually cannot be obtained without an adequate evaluation scheme. The reason is obvious. What good is a demonstration if there is no information about how well and under what conditions it will work? The evaluating of human service projects has become a more scientific and complex enterprise in recent years. Thus, the creation of effective evaluation methods and plans may require a considerable amount of technical knowledge. If no one in the applicant agency has the knowledge and experience to put together the evaluation section of the proposal, consider hiring an expert to write this part. Some knowledgeable college professors, professional evaluation specialists, or companies that do evaluations will write an evaluation section for a proposal provided they be hired on a contract basis to conduct the evaluation. This arrangement usually works well. The agency gets a professional evaluation for its proposal and a person or group to implement it who understand what the specific evaluation requirements are.

If a funding source does not require an extensive evaluation, a proposal writer should be able to put together a reasonable, if not sophisticated, evaluation plan. A good evaluation plan will answer at least these four questions:

What is to be measured?

What data will measure it?

How will the data be collected?

How will the data be analyzed?

One way to prepare an evaluation plan is to use the objective statements in the proposal as the outcomes to be measured. In the instance of the food co-op, a ten percent savings on food costs and a group of 100 low-income families buying at least twenty dollars' worth of food weekly are projected outcomes which can be measured. The data needed will be obtained from two available sources, the records of the co-op and from comparison shopping. This method of evaluation works quite well to the extent that the data measures quantitative activities.

To measure qualitative factors requires different approaches. For measuring the degree of impact on clients, or effectiveness, the co-op staff members might design a self-assessment form to be filled out by each participating family. This questionnaire could elicit such data as satisfaction with service and perceived improvement in economic status. An increased knowledge of good nutritional practices could be another qualitative measure. These data might be gained through interviews with a sample of the project participants. If the data collection methods are kept simple, a good deal of interesting, if not scientifically valid, information about the quality of a program can be obtained.

If proposal reviewers read any section carefully, it will most likely be the work program segment. Therefore, take care to ensure a logical progression from needs to specific objectives to activities (work program) designed to achieve the specific objectives. Show that the activities described can be accomplished with the staff and volunteers indicated and within the budget proposed, and that activities which require the consent or action of other agencies have been approved by responsible persons in those agencies.

A note of caution must be sounded here. Too often proposal writers and program developers are unrealistic about how much staff time or money it will take to do a particular job. They overstate the expected accomplishments or underestimate the time required, hoping this will make the proposed project seem more fundable. Practices such as this are dangerous for two reasons: First, many proposal reviewers are quite sophisticated about what it takes in time, money, and manpower to achieve a particular objective and will assume that the applicant agency is either dishonest or naive, and, in either case, should not be funded. Second, should the project be funded, the agency may be unable to meet its objectives at the levels or in the time frames stated. This not only disappoints the consumers and the community generally, but it also diminishes the credibility of the agency and makes getting new funds much more difficult.

SIGNIFICANCE OR BENEFITS

This component should be included prominently in the proposal even if the funding source does not require such a section. One aspect of significance is the importance of the project to the prospective clients whose needs are to be met. A project is significant when it will lead to knowledge about meeting needs which are not now known or will result in new or improved methods, materials, or models that have relevance for other projects. Also significant is the identification of new research hypotheses.

Funding sources may care about the described needs and the persons who have them, but they are more likely to fund a project if they think what is learned or demonstrated will have uses beyond the immediate place, time, and target group. Many federal, state, and foundation funding opportunities are for the purpose of providing direct services, but others are seen as "seed money"—that is, opportunities to get important results through carefully selected model or demonstration projects. For these, the significance statement can play a determining role in the funding decision.

APPLICANT ORGANIZATION

The purpose of this component is to establish the credibility of an agency in order to convince the funding source that it can operate the project successfully and handle money responsibly. Successful past and present projects should be included, as well as any special honors bestowed on the agency. An agency's organizational goals may also be included if they relate to those of the funding source.

Just as successful experience is a sign of credibility, so is stability over a period of time. How and why the agency was started may be of interest, if briefly stated. Therefore, include information as to when the agency was founded and incorporated. An unincorporated group providing service is not likely to receive money, since it has no legal status.

Also important to a funding source is an agency's credibility in its community. Letters of support for the good work done in the past from other agencies in the community may be included. Newspaper clippings also help. Less important, but sometimes helpful, are letters from Members of Congress, local and state officials, etc. Letters from local citizens are useful only for local foundations and charities.

In some cases inclusion of selected handwritten letters from consumers in the proposal appendix may be helpful. One project that provided mental health services to Mexican American junior high school students included letters from the parents of the students in its proposal to expand the services. Some of the letters were written in Spanish and some were in mixed Spanish and English. The parents used everything from bond stationery to scraps of notebook paper. The effect of the letters was to dramatize the human service needs of this target population. Readers could not help but sense the real people behind the support documents.

If an agency is newly established or has no experience to fall back on in the program area for which funds are being sought, the following devices can prove helpful. Prominent persons can be selected for the board of directors in order to lend their credibility to the project. A funding source will assume that they would not let their prestige be tainted by association with a fly-by-night project. Resumés of consultants who have credibility in the program area are helpful for the same reason. The resumé of a proposed project director may be helpful if this person has a good record of experience in the program area. Indeed, agencies often gain a foothold in new service areas on the strength of their proposed project directors. Include highlights from the background of these board members, consultants, and/or project directors, if necessary.

Some applications require an agency to make a statement about the facilities available. This can include such items as office space, computer facilities, research capability, and library or other materials available. The purpose is to demonstrate the capability of an applicant agency to carry out the purposes of the project.

PROJECT PERSONNEL

This component details the responsibilities of each of the major positions proposed. The following brief example is illustrative:

Community Outreach Specialist   100% time   12 months.

Duties: Working under the direction of the project director, conducts daily visits to local schools, prepares written documents for each school visit, organizes a project Advisory Committee composed of consumers and interested community persons and provides the Advisory Committee with staff assistance.

Note that in addition to a descriptive role title, the example also includes the percentage of time and duration of assignment. When known, state the name and degrees, if any, of the person proposed for the position.

Include a resumé for each person in a "professional" position, especially that of the project director. Of course, if the persons who will fill positions are not presently with the agency or have not been selected, no resumé can be attached. Resumés of consultants who have agreed to assist on the project should also be included. Never use a resume of anyone who has not given express permission to do so. Not only is it unethical but, if brought to light, can harm the project and the agency. The proposal may also include more expanded job descriptions which, along with resumes, are placed typically in an appendix.

ADMINISTRATION

This component usually consists of two parts. One shows how the project staff will be organized, the other indicates how the project relates to the agency as a whole, usually with tables of organization like the examples in Figures 4-4 and 4-5. If an agency will provide special arrangements or unusual support for a project, that information should be included in this section.

TABLE OF ORGANIZATION:
HEALTH & HOME CARE PROJECT PERSONNEL

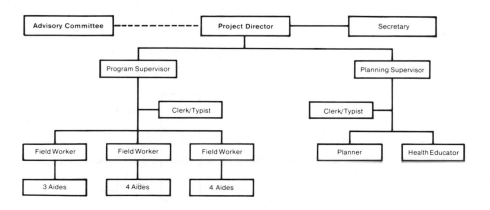

Figure 4-4

BUDGET

Budgets need not be mysterious or complicated. In their simplest form, budgets are a listing of anticipated income and expenditures. Unfortunately, budgets are rarely seen in their simplest form. A budget which is part of a proposal is composed

TABLE OF ORGANIZATION: AGENCY ADMINISTRATION

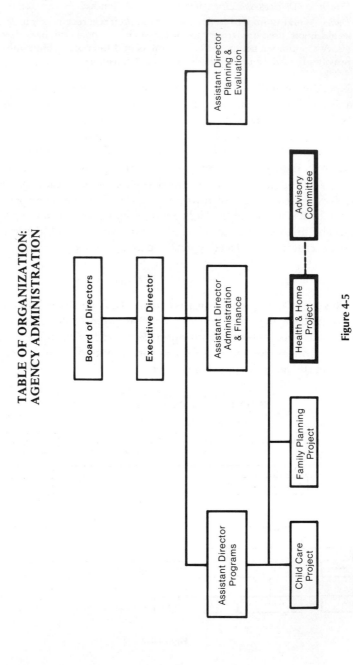

Figure 4-5

52

of expenditure categories. A category is a general area of expense, such as costs for personnel, travel, or supplies. Categories are further divided into individual expense items, called "line items," such as the salary of a project director, the cost for a typewriter, or the payment of rent.

A line item contains several bits of information necessary to the understanding of the costs. Following are three examples, one from a personnel category, one from a travel category, and one from the equipment category. An example of an entire typical small project budget is included at the end of this chapter.

THREE EXAMPLES OF BUDGET CATEGORIES

Personnel	Annual Salary Rate	Time on Project (%)	Cost
1 Project director	$22,000	100	$22,000
1 Social worker	20,000	20	4,000
3 Project aides	12,000	50	18,000
1 Secretary	11,000	100	11,000

Travel	Cost
Local mileage 1000 mi/mo. @ 22¢/mi X 12 mo.	$2,640
Out of town 1 R/T Minneapolis to Evanston: $175; 2 da. per diem @ $50/da.	275

Equipment	Cost
Typewriter 1 @ $900	$900
Tape recorders 6 @ $100	600

Note the designation of quantity and time commitments in the Personnel category. The listing of items in as descriptive detail as possible enables the reviewer to quickly grasp how resources will be allocated.

Different funding sources require line items to be placed in different categories. Telephone costs may be listed under a Communications category in one format, for example, but under an Other category in another format. Agencies will be wise to follow the dictates of their anticipated funding source, but are also wise to include all legitimate expense items, even though the funding source may not have specifically identified one or more of them. Following is a list of expenses which are ordinarily necessary for a human service project budget. These potential expenses are listed without regard to which categories they might belong.

Personnel positions are listed by position titles, with the principal investigator or director first. This position is customarily followed by the nonclerical positions in descending order of annual salary rate and then clerical positions in the same order.

Fringe benefits are usually listed as a percentage of the total wages (hourly rate) and salaries (monthly or yearly rate) of personnel receiving them. The amount usually varies between 10 and 35 percent, with 15 to 20 percent being the average for private nonprofit agencies. Benefits are any expenses paid by the agency on behalf of all eligible employees and may include such items as State Disability Insurance (SDI); Worker's Compensation Insurance; State Unemployment Insurance (SUI); Old Age, Survivors and Disability Insurance (OASDI), better known as Social Security, a benefit under the Federal Insurance Contributions Act (FICA); health insurance, and retirement pension contributions. Some fringe benefits are mandatory, but these vary from state to state. FICA, or OASDI, is a federal benefit that is not required for all nonprofit agencies and institutions.

Space includes rental or lease costs, or their equivalent if an agency owns the building in which the project is housed. Space is usually listed as the cost per month times the appropriate number of months if the actual space, and therefore the cost, is known. If office space has not been identified, an estimate can be made according to the following formula: 50 to 60 square feet times the number of staff members who will occupy the space times the average cost per square foot per month for rental space in the agency's geographic area times the appropriate number of months. Toilet, reception, program, and conference room space is additional.

Janitorial service, if provided by non-staff personnel and not included in space costs, is listed by the number of hours per week or month times the cost per hour times the appropriate number of weeks or months. Janitorial supplies, if provided by the agency, may be part of the category in which consumable supplies are listed.

Utilities, if not included in space costs, should be the estimated monthly cost times the appropriate number of months, plus any start-up fees or deposits.

Alteration and renovation of space, if not included in space rental costs, should be an estimated one-time expenditure. Significant alterations are usually itemized separately.

Books, subscriptions, dues to professional organizations, and registration fees to conferences are generally listed together as an estimated yearly cost.

Construction costs have many applicable regulations which should be examined thoroughly before a budget request is made. The funding source usually supplies the needed information.

Travel includes three categories: foreign travel, domestic travel, and local mileage. Foreign travel on federal grants requires specific prior written approval and is not often allowed. Domestic travel is usually listed in one of two ways: either the average cost per trip times the number of trips is listed when much travel is anticipated, or the specific locations and costs of each trip are listed when all travel requirements are known. The *per diem*, or daily cost for room and board, is figured at a maximum rate per day times the number of days. Air fare is listed at coach class rate. Local mileage is a reimbursement for the use of a personal car for job-related travel, usually figured at a cents-per-mile rate times the estimated average number of miles per month times the appropriate number of months.

Consumable supplies include estimated costs for nondurable items used in an office, such as paper, paper clips, typewriter ribbons, envelopes, soap, and towels. Office supplies are ordinarily listed as an estimated average cost per year times the number of staff persons. Program supplies, such as basketballs and arts and crafts materials for a recreational project or contraceptives for a family planning project or testing instruments for a counseling project, may be listed as a single line item. Desk-top supplies, such as scissors, calendar holders, staplers, tape dispensers, and phone indexes, are most often listed as a single line item at a fixed price, $25, for instance, times the number of staff persons in a project.

Printing, duplicating, and photocopying are ordinarily listed together at an average cost per month times the appropriate number of months, although large single items, such as the reproduction of a project final report, may sometimes be listed in addition.

Telephone includes estimated monthly average expense for local and long-distance calls times the appropriate number of months, plus installation fees, and any special communication equipment rental charges.

Postage includes stamps and any other mailing expenses at an estimated yearly cost.

Equipment (rented or purchased) should include the rental or purchase price for each durable item needed to conduct the project, such as typewriters, adding machines, file cabinets, desks, and chairs. In some grants only the items specifically listed in the budget can be purchased without written approval of the funding source at a later time, so it is important to include the entire inventory in a proposal. Prices indicated in the budget should be listed at the standard rate charged in the applicant's area for new equipment. The budget might be reduced by indicating that the equipment will be bought secondhand or, in the case of eligible organizations that are located near federal Government Services Administration warehouses, by picking up free secondhand equipment from surplus supplies. If agency-owned equipment is to be used, depreciation costs can be an allowable item of expense.

Equipment maintenance is ordinarily listed as a yearly cost and includes repairs to typewriters, adding machines, etc.

Insurance costs should be listed, including such types as liability, auto for agency-owned vehicles, plus fire and theft. Insurance which is included as part of fringe benefits should not be made part of this item. The cost for bonding those who handle money or sign checks is also a legitimate expense.

Consultant services include the number of scheduled consultant days of service times the average cost per day. Also included, generally, are the costs for consultants' travel and *per diem*, if any. No fringe benefits are paid to consultants.

Contract or purchased services, such as subcontracts for evaluation, financial audits, data processing services, or training are listed as separate items.

Direct and indirect costs are the two kinds of expenses recognized by governmental funding sources and most foundations. The costs cited above, for the most part, can be direct or indirect costs, *but can never be claimed as both*. A direct cost is one which can be identified specifically with a particular objective of a project. The allowability or unallowability of costs for the Department of Health and Human Services can be found in Subpart Q of Title 45 Code of Federal Regulations, Part 74, "Administration of Grants." This is referenced in the *Grants Administration Manual*, and is available from the U.S. Superintendent of Documents. It indicates, for example, that among items not allowable as a direct cost are the payment of bad debts; bonus payments to staff; contingency funds or reserves; entertainment expenses, including coffee-break supplies; honoraria, and foreign travel undertaken without prior written approval.

Not all costs can easily be directly ascribed to the activities of a given project when an agency has more than one project. Agencies have general administration expenses, such as payroll accounting or telephone switchboards, which benefit all their projects. They may have space and/or equipment the proposed project will use, and agency staff who will spend some indefinite amount of time to aid the project. There are three ways in which these "indirect" costs are usually recovered. One way is to include all expenses as direct line items. Second, governmental agencies allow an indirect cost rate to be added on as a percentage of certain direct costs. This method is explained later in this chapter. Third, foundations often allow these administrative overhead expenses to be included as a single line item. All of this will become clearer through examination of the sample budget at the end of this chapter. An indirect cost rate is negotiated with the principal federal agency from which a grantee agency receives funds and is applicable to all other federal agencies.*

Another look at the line items cited earlier will show that many items can be either direct or indirect costs, depending on the agreements that agencies have relating to indirect costs. Space will be a direct cost for some agencies, but indirect for others. Telephone equipment, insurance, utilities, janitorial services, books, subscriptions, some fringe benefits, support personnel, printing, duplicating, some supplies, and even postage are among items that may be charged as direct or indirect expenses. As indicated, however, they may never be both.

To calculate the amount of indirect cost due to an agency one of two methods can be used, depending on the agreement the agency has with the federal government. The first method is to calculate the indirect cost as a percentage of the total direct cost, minus the cost of equipment. This is done by subtracting equipment costs from the total direct cost and multiplying the result by the agreed-upon indirect cost rate (percentage). If the total direct cost of the project is $215,000, of which $3,000 is for equipment, $212,000 remains as the base. Multiply $212,000 by the agency's indirect cost rate (suppose it to be 23.2 percent) and the indirect cost will be $49,184. The agency will receive $264,184 ($49,184 plus $215,000) to operate the project. The second method is to calculate the indirect cost as a percentage of wages and salaries. Suppose that the indirect cost rate is 27.5 percent and the salaries and wages total $83,200, including fringe benefits. The agency will be entitled to $83,200 times 27.5 percent, or $22,880, plus the total direct cost of the project.

If indirect costs are not allowed as part of the project's expenses, then an Administrative Overhead item may be allowed. In this item will be the approximate agency cost for the proposed project's share of such expenses as bookkeeping and

---

*Formulas for determining indirect cost rates for colleges and universities, hospitals, and non-profit organizations applying to the Department of Health and Human Services for funds can be found in *Circular A-21*, Office of Management and Budget. The circular is available from the Superintendent of Documents. State, local and other levels of government applying for federal grant funds should use the formulas stated in the following document: *Uniform Administrative Requirements for Grants-in-Aid to State and Local Governments*, Office of Management and Budget, *Circular A-102*. For additional reference see the *Federal Register* for Monday, September 12, 1977, Volume 42, No. 176. Requests to establish indirect cost rates should go to the appropriate regional office of the U.S. Government. See the Federal Information Center addresses and phone numbers in the Appendix.

payroll, janitorial services and supplies, recruiting, telephone switchboard and central reception services, and supervision by the management staff, to name just a few of the possibilities.

If neither overhead nor indirect costs are allowed, then all expenses should be made part of some direct cost category. Perhaps, ten percent of the executive director's and of a bookkeeper's time and 20 percent of the space maintenance costs will appear as line items in the budget.

Budget categories and the line items included in them vary among funding sources. An example of one which has typical categories is that used by the Office of Human Development Services:

(a) Personnel (grantee agency staff, not consultants).

(b) Fringe benefits (percentage of wages and salaries).

(c) Travel (out-of-town travel for grantee agency staff only).

(d) Equipment (items that are non-expendable property).

(e) Supplies (items that are expendable).

(f) Contractual (itemized list of contracts, amounts, purposes, and recipients).

(g) Construction (costs of renovation or repairs).

(h) Other (all other costs, such as consultants and their travel, insurance, agency staff's local travel and space, not covered under indirect costs).

(i) Total direct charges (a + b + c + d + e + f + g + h).

(j) Indirect charges (the agreed-upon percentage of i minus d).

(k) Total (i + j).

Since many foundations have no specific way in which they want proposal budgets prepared, the following format may be useful as a guide.

(a) Personnel.

(b) Fringe benefits.

(c) Consultant services.

(d) Space, including utilities and maintenance if not included in the rent.

(e) Equipment (purchase and rental) and supplies.

(f) Travel, including local mileage.

(g) Communications, including telephone, postage, duplicating, printing, and photocopying.

(h) Administrative overhead, if needed and allowed.

(i) Other, including insurance, contract services, etc.

Do a budget justification for both governmental and foundation funding sources. Explain any items that may be questioned, such as pieces of equipment whose uses are not immediately apparent. List insurance types and coverage. Identify the destinations and purposes of out-of-town travel, when known. A budget justification is required for most federal funding applications and helps to establish the integrity of a budget for those funding sources that do not specifically require it.

   A matching share, or cost-sharing, is required for many federally funded projects and some foundation grants. A matching share is that percentage of the total cost of the project which is provided by a grantee agency. This share may be cash, called "hard match," or donated goods and services, called "soft match" or "in-kind."

   A common error made by applicant agencies is to figure the matching share as a percentage of the funds to be provided by the funding source rather than as a percentage of the total cost of the project. The total cost is a funding source's share plus an applicant agency's matching share. The formula for calculating the matching share is not complicated.

STEP 1. Dollars given by funding source ($215,000)	divided by	percent of total cost to be given by funding source (90%)	equals	total cost ($238,888)
STEP 2. Total cost ($238,888)	minus	dollars given by funding source ($215,000)	equals	matching share ($23,888)

   In the example above, an applicant agency is said to be making a 90%–10% match. The funding source's share is 90% of the total cost and the applicant agency's share is 10% of the total cost. For a project that is to be funded for $100,000 and that requires a 75%–25% match, the applicant agency's share would be $33,333. ($100,000 divided by 75 equals $133,333 and $133,333 minus $100,000 equals $33,333.) The three most common matching share percentages are 90%–10% (match is 11.111% of *funding source* share), 80%–20% (match is 25% of *funding source* share) and 75%–25% (match is 33⅓% of *funding source* share.) A simple alternative method for finding the matching share is to multiply the *funding source* share by the appropriate percentage. $215,000 multiplied by 11.111% gives the same matching share of $23,888.

   Agencies can provide cost-sharing contributions in three ways. They can give cash to a project and/or they can rebate indirect cost money due them. With a project to be funded at a direct cost of $100,000, an agency, based on a hypothetical negotiated indirect cost rate of 31.5%, would receive $31,500 additional for its indirect costs. Its 90%–10% cost-sharing contribution ($100,000 plus $31,500 divided by 90 equals $146,111 minus $131,500) equals $14,611. The agency could make its match of $14,611 by accepting only $16,889 out of the $31,500 for indirect costs. Agencies are also entitled to use the indirect costs due them on their non-cash matching share contributions as an additional cost-sharing contribution.

   Most frequently grantee agencies meet their matching share through in-kind contributions. In-kind consists of costs for goods and services defrayed by the agencies for which funding sources would ordinarily provide funds. The time of an agency's personnel not paid by project funds can be donated. So, too, can equipment or space rental equivalents. A large source of contributions by human service agencies is volunteer time. Donated renovations to space, printing, supplies, and mailing costs are also legitimate contributions.

There are two prohibitions on matching share contributions, however. No item paid for by direct funds can be considered match. Agency equipment, for example, which is purchased with funding source dollars cannot be used as match. In effect, the funding source would be paying for the equipment twice. Also, with the exception of certain federal revenue sharing funds and costs contributed by a Veterans Administration hospital, federal funds cannot be used to match federal grants.

As a general rule, funding sources will accept the local average rate or the actual cost for any item as the amount to be contributed. Suppose there is a photocopying machine in an agency and it costs 3.8¢ to reproduce each copy. The agency could claim as match the number of copies mady by the project times 3.8¢. Or suppose that several used desks and chairs are being donated by a local bank for a project. The cost of buying equivalent secondhand furniture would be the amount claimed for the matching share. If an agency owns furniture that a project is going to use, it should contribute as match the equivalent rental cost of the furniture and not the new or used purchase cost. All items bought with funds from the funding source, theoretically at least, belong to the funding source when the project ends. Therefore, agency furniture which is donated, not rented, to the project belongs to the funding source when the project is over.

The amount of match allowed for volunteer time sometimes causes confusion. Volunteers who have no professional education or training in the program area in which they are donating their efforts can always be listed at the minimum wage without problems. If they have professional skills and donate time in the area of their expertise, their time can be listed at the rate they ordinarily charge for similar services. So, for example, if a lawyer spends three hours at a senior citizens center helping to paint a wall, his or her services might be valued at the minimum wage per hour times three hours. However, if the lawyer spends three hours helping the senior center's Advisory Committee draft bylaws, his or her services would be worth considerably more as match, just as a professional painter's time painting the senior citizens center would be at the painter's usual fee per hour. Although it is infrequently done, volunteer time is supposed to be valuated at the rates set by the Davis-Bacon Act. These rates appear Fridays in the *Federal Register*. Most agencies, however, use the prevailing wage rates of their community for comparable work, and funding sources usually accept this approach.

Funding for subsequent years of a project beyond the first year is almost always part of an application when a project is proposed for more than twelve months. Usually an incremental approach to the budget is used. This means that the budget of the first year is repeated with any deletions or additions of line items and increases or decreases of costs added. Since personnel costs are the largest share of most budgets for human service programs, care must be taken in revising this category of costs for later years. A percentage increase in all salaries, and hence fringe benefits, is generally allowed in order to account for inflation and promotions. Up to a ten percent increase is usually considered reasonable.

In large projects, some delay in starting and turnover of staff is likely, with a consequent surplus accruing in unpaid salaries or wages. A two to three percent decrease to account for this vacancy factor is ordinarily acceptable in the first year. Since the project has no start-up delays in subsequent years, half the first year's vacancy factor rate might be used. For smaller projects, this factor is generally ignored. Savings from salaries and wages not spent are carried over into subsequent years, where this is allowed, or reprogrammed into other budget categories during the current year when carryover is not permitted.

Since increased costs are likely in goods as well as services, an increase in supplies and the local mileage rates might be anticipated as well. The category for equipment which is normally purchased at the start of the project may drop to zero. Subcontractors will be faced with salary increases, too, so consideration of the costs of any subcontracts in subsequent years should be discussed and anticipated increases reflected in the budget.

Rules of thumb are guides for testing budgets against experience, not iron maidens to fit whose forms budgets must be twisted out of reasonable shape. A few rules of thumb that have proven useful follow:

> *Personnel costs*, including fringe benefits, tend to be about 80 to 85 percent of a human services project budget. This does not include indirect costs.
>
> *The administrative costs* (as contrasted with program costs), normally scattered throughout the budget, when brought together average about 15 percent of a budget. This percentage may be considerably lower if many administrative functions are covered by indirect cost funds.
>
> *Evaluation costs*, whether done by project staff or contracted out, range from five to ten percent of model and demonstration project budgets; training costs average about five percent.
>
> *Salaries of project staff* in an applicant agency should be comparable to those from other agencies who are doing similar work and consistent within an agency among its projects.

> *Match for federal funds* cannot be made from federal funds. Do not offer equipment or personnel paid for by one grant as part of the cost-sharing contribution for another grant. Making match for federal funding with private and foundation funds, goods, and services is permissible.

Reminders on the proposal format are in order, especially since so many

proposals violate these common-sense "rules of the game." Remember, the proposal may be the only impression the funding source has of the agency.

1. Use plain white bond paper with *black* ribbon (to ensure sharp photocopying) unless otherwise directed in the application instructions.

2. Leave at least one-inch margins on sides, top, and bottom.

3. Double-space the typing, except for the abstract which is usually typed single-space.

4. Spell every word correctly and check grammatical correctness. Permit no typographical errors to show.

5. Avoid slang and "hells" and "damns" unless used for a specific purpose.

6. Do *not* use fancy, expensive covers and bindings.

7. Follow the format described in the application instructions as exactly as possible, even if this requires repetition of some text.

8. Always save the original typed copy (unless required to send it) and several photocopies. Use a dry copier, if possible, as the pages are easier to read and handle. The "original" copy is any photocopy signed in ink by a responsible person, not the originally typed copy. Send exactly as many copies as required, with the pages in order and bound or clipped.

9. Be sure the "original" copy is signed, in *black* ink only, by the person who is authorized by the agency and required by the funding source to sign such documents. This may be the chairperson of the board of directors, the executive director of the agency, or sometimes the fiscal officer of the agency.

10. A deadline date is almost always the time the proposal must be in the hands of the funding source, not in the mail.

11. Include a letter of transmittal which suggests appreciation for their review of the application, gives the proposal title, the number of copies included and, for federal grants sent to general receiving offices, the agency for which the proposal is intended.

12. Send courtesy copies of the proposal to cooperating agencies and consultants likely to have an ongoing part in the project if funded.

As noted at the beginning of this chapter, most federal government and some foundation funding sources have a specific format they require for their proposals. If no specific instructions or format are given, the following "universal" format may be used:

1. Summary.

2. Problem statement, including community profile boilerplate, if brief.

3. Characteristics of applicant organization.

4. Program objectives.

5. Work program including evaluation.

6. Significance, or benefits.

7. Administration.

8. Budget.

9. Appendix, including:
   —personnel resumes and job descriptions,
   —support and cooperation letters,
   —other materials if necessary, such as bibliographies, news clippings, additional data.

PROPOSAL CHECKLIST

	Yes	No	Not Applicable
PROPOSAL ABSTRACT			
Basic needs, objectives, and tasks identified briefly	____	____	____
Significance, or benefits, indicated briefly	____	____	____
Credibility of agency established	____	____	____
PROBLEM STATEMENT			
Specific target group identified	____	____	____
Specific needs identified	____	____	____
Nature of needs described	____	____	____
Extent of needs documented	____	____	____
Significance of needs explained	____	____	____
Importance to target group stated	____	____	____
Importance of *this* project stated	____	____	____
OBJECTIVES			
Logical relationship to meeting of needs clear	____	____	____
Specific *outcomes* identified	____	____	____
Degree of accomplishment stated	____	____	____
Time frame for accomplishment stated	____	____	____
COMMUNITY PROFILE			
Data indicating demographics of community presented concisely	____	____	____
Data on general needs presented concisely	____	____	____
Unique features of community described	____	____	____
Current services available in community described	____	____	____
STATE-OF-THE-ART (REVIEW OF THE LITERATURE)			
Up-to-date bibliographic references included	____	____	____
Work program alternatives reviewed and analyzed	____	____	____
Research reviewed and analyzed	____	____	____

PROPOSAL CHECKLIST (continued)

	Yes	No	Not Applicable
RATIONALE			
Explains why approach, methods, and agency are the most appropriate ones	____	____	____
WORK PROGRAM			
Logical relationship to objectives clear	____	____	____
Language suitable to funding source	____	____	____
Major activities clearly delineated	____	____	____
All relevant tasks described	____	____	____
Activities capable of accomplishment with personnel and within the time and budget indicated	____	____	____
Tasks for Activity 1 described under Activity 1, etc.	____	____	____
Coordination with other agencies described	____	____	____
Approval from other agencies indicated and supporting letters attached	____	____	____
Governing and advisory bodies described	____	____	____
Membership, selection procedures, functions described	____	____	____
Evaluation plan described	____	____	____
Measurement of objectives indicated	____	____	____
Data and collection procedures identified	____	____	____
Methods for data analysis indicated	____	____	____
Work plan timetable included	____	____	____
Major activities listed	____	____	____
Start and completion dates shown	____	____	____
SIGNIFICANCE			
Importance to target group stated	____	____	____
New knowledge identified	____	____	____
New or improved methods, materials, or models that can be used elsewhere identified	____	____	____
New research hypotheses identified	____	____	____

PROPOSAL CHECKLIST (continued)

APPLICANT CAPABILITY AND FACILITIES
AVAILABLE

Past programs described	——	——	——
Other materials indicating ability and stability included	——	——	——
Support letters attached	——	——	——

PERSONNEL

Resumés of major staff and consultants attached	——	——	——
Job descriptions or job statements attached	——	——	——

ADMINISTRATION

Project administration outlined	——	——	——
Overall agency administration outlined	——	——	——
Special factors detailed	——	——	——

APPENDIX

Letters attached	——	——	——
Civil rights and A-95 documents attached	——	——	——
Incorporation papers attached	——	——	——

FORMAT

Typed correctly and attractively	——	——	——
Agency return address on the proposal	——	——	——
Signature of authorized person in black ink	——	——	——
Transmittal letter on top	——	——	——

BUDGET

All line items are authorized	——	——	——
Salaries are comparable to others in agency and community	——	——	——
Correct and authorized matching share amount and line items	——	——	——
Indirect cost taken on authorized items	——	——	——
Computations are correct	——	——	——
Correct percentages of time and salaries for personnel	——	——	——
Reasonable administration to service ratio	——	——	——
Equipment justified	——	——	——
Consistent with all guidelines, rules, regulations	——	——	——

PROPOSED BUDGET PROJECT FOR RURAL INFORMATION AND DEVELOPMENT EXCHANGE (PRIDE)—PROGRAM YEAR 1

PERSONNEL

1 Sally Smith	Project director	100%	$16,500	
1 TBA*	Program supervisor	100%	15,000	
1 Juan Hernandez	Planning supervisor	100%	15,000	
1 Mabel Jones	Planner	100%	13,000	
3 TBA*	Field workers @ $13,000 ea.	100%	39,000	
1 Percy Begay	Information specialist @ $9.00/hr.	1,200 hrs.	10,800	
9 TBA*	Aides @ $10,000 ea.	50%	45,000	
1 TBA*	Secretary	100%	9,600	
2 TBA*	Clerk/typists 1,050 hrs. ea. @ $4.50/hr.	2,100 hrs.	9,450	
	Vacancy factor @ 1%		1,733	
				$171,617

FRINGE BENEFITS

@ 16.5% of salary and wages   28,317

CONSULTANT SERVICES

12 days @ $150/da.   1,800

EQUIPMENT PURCHASE AND RENTAL

3 Electric typewriters @ $900 ea.	2,700	
4 Executive desks @ $150 ea.	600	
4 Executive chairs @ $80 ea.	320	
3 Secretarial chairs @ $80 ea.	240	
1 Adding machine w/tape	125	
3 Filing cabinets @ $100 ea.	300	
		4,285

CONSUMABLE SUPPLIES

Desk top items @ $25 ea. 14 F.T.E.**	350	
times $100 average 14 F.T.E.**	1,400	
		1,750

*To be appointed.

**Full-time equivalent; i.e., part-time positions equal to a full-time position.

PROPOSED BUDGET PROJECT (continued)

TRAVEL

Domestic 3 trips @ $300 ea. and per diem @ $50/da. x 6 da.	1,200	
Local mileage 600 miles/mo. x 21¢/mile x 8 staff F.T.E.** x 12 mo.	12,096	
		6,573

OTHER

Advisory Committee expenses	600	
Machine repairs	80	
Books, dues, subscriptions	200	
Liability insurance $300,000/$1,000,000	1,035	
Audit contract (Ralph, Ralph & Assoc.)	2,000	
Evaluation contract (Evaluation Services, Inc.)	10,700	
Building Maintenance Contract (Janitorial Services, Inc.)	1,200	
		15,815
Total Direct Cost		243,453
Indirect Cost @ 13.2% of TDC minus equipment		32,136
Total Request		$275,589

MATCHING SHARE

Volunteer Aides @ $4.00/hr. x 5,000 hrs.	20,000	
Information Specialist @ $9.00/hr. x 800 hrs.	7,200	
Development Consultants @ $150/da. x 10 days	1,500	
3 Executive desks & chairs @ $30/mo. rental equiv. x 12	1,080	
3 Secretarial desks with pedestals @ $27/mo. rental equiv. x 12	972	
		30,752

The following two categories might appear if the application were being made to a funding source which did not allow indirect costs.

SPACE

Lease of 1,800 sq. ft. @ 45¢ sq. ft./mo. x 12	9,720

ADMINISTRATIVE COSTS

Administrative Overhead including payroll, accounting, supervision, etc.	8,000

**Full-time equivalent; i.e., part-time positions equal to a full-time position.

PROPOSED BUDGET PROJECT (continued)

BUDGET JUSTIFICATION

Consultant Services required to provide training to field staff one-half day twice a month. Arrangements have been made with college faculty in Communications, Psychology, and Community Development departments to provide the instructors. See attached letter in Appendix.

Domestic Travel trips include two to Washington for coordination with National Information Coalition and one to Albuquerque for the annual conference of the National Rural Society.

Advisory Committee expenses will include local mileage and materials for members.

Liability Insurance beyond the limits now held by the agency are required. The cost is the difference between the present rate and the increased coverage rate.

Audit Contract by Ralph, Ralph and Associates will cover items in Agreement attached in Appendix.

Evaluation contract with Evaluation Services, Inc., will cover instruments development, data collection and analysis, and reporting as detailed in proposal. Agreement attached in Appendix.

JOB DESCRIPTION:
DIRECTOR OF VOLUNTEERS

JOB SUMMARY

Responsible for administration and coordination of all volunteer activities and group programs, including supervision of staff, recruitment and training program for volunteers, establishment of volunteer and group programs in new geographic areas. Works closely with Executive Director to ensure that goals of program are being met. Initiates and prepares reports as required.

WORK PERFORMED

Supervises staff directing volunteer and group activities. Holds frequent meetings with them to determine that the recruitment, orientation, and training program for volunteers is adequate. Provides guidance and expertise as needed. Prepares evaluations of staff.

Reviews recruitment and training program frequently and makes necessary changes, additions, or deletions. Meets with Directors of Volunteers in other agencies to coordinate activities.

Conducts training programs for staff and volunteers when new community is ready for this training. Works closely with community staff on matters pertaining to volunteers and group programs.

Meets frequently with Executive Director and/or other staff members to ensure cooperation and understanding of problems and progress of program.

Makes recommendations and suggestions which will aid growth and success of program.

Initiates reports and statistics when applicable and prepares reports and statistics as required.

KNOWLEDGE AND ABILITY REQUIRED

Have demonstrated ability as a leader and organizer in the field of volunteering, preferably with actual experience as a volunteer. Be able to work well with other people. Have experience in conducting training group with an awareness of individual as well as group needs. Be able to work easily on several assignments at the same time. Be able to initiate and write reports.

JOB DESCRIPTION:
SENIOR TYPIST-CLERK

JOB SUMMARY

Does skilled typing work and performs specialized clerical work requiring a working knowledge of the clerical functions involved. Use of initiative and judgment within procedural and policy limits.

WORK PERFORMED

Types documents requiring extreme accuracy and independent judgment in selecting materials.

Types complex charts, forms, statistical and similar documents from rough draft. Requires skill in arranging tabular material and setting up forms and great accuracy in typing.

Processes documents according to a predetermined procedure.

Checks documents for completeness, accuracy, and compliance with other requirements.

Answers questions and gives information to the public.

Operates standard office machines.

Searches records and files for data where judgment and discrimination are required in selecting or abstracting material.

May exercise minor supervision over the work of others.

KNOWLEDGE AND ABILITY REQUIRED

Four years' office clerical experience involving typewriting.

Ability to type at the rate of 40 net stroke words per minute.

RESUMÉ:
SALLY SMITH

EXPERIENCE

ADMINISTRATION AND SUPERVISION

Administered program to link residents to services needed to ameliorate problems. Supervised work output of fifteen staff outstationed in Hispanic and Asian/Pacific Island community agencies. Supervised four staff in resources development. Developed proposal for refunding program.

PROGRAM DEVELOPMENT

Participated in conceptualization, planning and implementation of program for the elderly. Worked with businesses, governmental agencies, private nonprofit groups, community organizations, and general public. Developed management by objectives process for attainment of goals. Evaluated proposals for funding in fields of housing, criminal justice, nutrition, transportation, multipurpose centers, outreach, and information and referral for the elderly. Provided technical assistance to businesses, agencies, and groups involved or interested in providing services to the elderly.

Developed and implemented programs for at-risk families in criminal justice, housing, and information and referral, combining public and private sector resources.

Planned and implemented programs in art and cultural awareness for students of all ages, parents, professional staff, and low-income groups.

Developed and obtained funding for program model based on self-esteem to foster attitude changes of delinquent Mexican American youth.

Developed and implemented new procedure for welfare department for interstate transferring of client documents, including forms, controls, tracking systems, and procedures manual.

TRAINING AND TEACHING

Developed and conducted weekly seminars and annual conference for training of management, staff, and volunteers working in problem-solving capacity with handicapped persons. Emphasis on development of job-related skills and team building.

Participated in development of training program for staff and welfare recipients in methods for solving problems in landlord-tenant relationships, nutrition, child care, family planning, and health.

EMPLOYERS

1974 to date   Program Director, Project for Human Services, Inc.

1968–1973   Social Worker, County Department of Public Social Services.

1965–1967   Consultant, Dogood Foundation.

RESUMÉ (continued)

EDUCATION

1973   M.P.A., State University.

1964   B.A. with Honors, Upper State College.

PROFESSIONAL MEMBERSHIPS

American Association for Public Administration.

Southeast Family Society.

LANGUAGES

Fluent in Spanish.

REFERENCES

Provided upon request.

Developing Human Service Strategies

5

Strategies are intentional actions. They can be devised by an individual, group, agency, or government. Regardless of who the strategists are, the purpose is either to alter the *status quo* or to avoid change and preserve the *status quo*. Every strategy is based on three requisites: (1) an assumption about what is, (2) a statement about what is desired, and (3) a description of the steps that will move from what is to what is desired. The concept of *status quo* assumes at least a power balance between groups or individuals who want a situation to change and those who want things to remain as they are. A strategy can be devised for either position and the steps taken by strategists on one side or on the other may be virtually the same. The difference is the outcome they seek.

Strategy in human services is in some ways analogous to the strategy of chess players. Each seeks, at least initially, to accomplish a goal, usually beginning with a specific strategy in mind. Strategies are modified if they are not successful, but the degree and timing of a modification depend on the strategist's confidence, experience, and ability to accurately assess the alternatives.

Effective strategies depend on at least three factors:

1. DIAGNOSIS—the "apparent" strength (experience, information, and desire to win) and resources (time, money, ideas, and personnel) of each side.
2. TACTICS—alternative actions and probable opponent reactions to each alternative.
3. ASSESSMENT OF THE COST-BENEFIT TRADE-OFF—the degree of winning or losing each side is willing to accept in the short run from specific tactics and in the long run from the overall strategy.

In the real world adversarial relationships are rarely as clearcut as in chess. Rather than the one-to-one action and limitations of chess, human service strategies can, and frequently do, involve dozens of interests on all sides. There usually are more than two sides. The action of one cluster of interests can affect uninvolved persons and sometimes make it difficult to be certain whether the sought-after outcome was achieved. A further difference between strategy in a chess game and the real world is in the recognition and enforcement of rules. In chess the rules are known and accepted, as are the penalties for noncompliance. A clever chess strategist looks for advantages within the rules. In human services, playing by the rules is but one strategy. Other equally legitimate strategies include not playing by the rules. Similarly, in chess the players and the audience know the rules. The same cannot be said for all the players and observers in the arena of human services. Sometimes the strategy employed is to intentionally keep the rules and other information from the opposition and the observers. In human services, determining the winners and losers is not the sole prerogative of the players, as it is in chess. Third parties—people in the community, other agencies, special interest groups involved in the interchange—also observe and assess who are the winners and losers.

The strategies of human services raise several basic questions about strategy-making and implementation:

Who should the strategists be?

What outcome is desired (i.e., to change or not to change the *status quo*)?

What short- and long-range tactics are appropriate to achieve the desired outcome?

In most human services agencies, strategy-making and implementation take place simultaneously at different levels in the organization. These levels are illustrated in Figure 5-1. Strategists at the C level are persons responsible for supplying services directly, such as community outreach personnel in comprehensive health centers or job developers in manpower programs. At level C the strategies are usually concerned primarily with the delivery of services to clients. Level B strategies typically focus on issues internal to the organization. Examples include personnel recruitment and assignment, record-keeping, and quality assurance. Strategists at the B level are usually program managers and supervisors. In most agencies, strategies that deal with survival needs, such as how to best define eligibility criteria and where to apply for funding, tend primarily to be the responsibility of persons at the A level. Administrators and board members are generally the persons who operate at this level.

Because strategy development often takes place simultaneously in many places in an organization, strategists tend to be concerned with narrow interests. Persons at level C may be concerned with providing added services, those at level B with quality control. The result can be a vexing management problem of coordinating strategies without stifling creativity or responsiveness. Communication among levels through formal mechanisms, such as planning committees, or informal mechanisms, such as after-hours discussions in the local hangout, are useful for de-

Figure 5-1

STRATEGY-MAKING AND IMPLEMENTATON IN HUMAN SERVICE AGENCIES

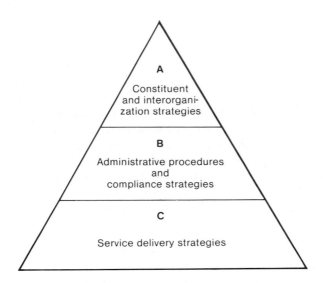

fining the issues and developing consensus about particular strategies.

Others besides board and staff members can help to shape agencies' strategies. The extent of outsiders' involvement depends on how the staff and board members of an agency see its mission. The planning activity of a small staff of an urban park is illustrative. The role of the park employees was to manage the field house, schedule athletic events, and oversee arts and crafts for senior citizen and preschool groups that met at the field house on weekday mornings.

The park was the only recreation area in a poverty neighborhood of 4,500 families, many of whom lived adjacent to the park in a public housing project. Although facilities were always in use, many residents were afraid to use the park. They feared violence from teenagers who frequented the park and also feared the drug dealers who accosted anyone venturing into "their corner."

The staff members decided to confront the problem by bringing consumers into decisions about program strategies. They publicized and held a neighborhood meeting each Saturday morning throughout the month. They chose that day and time because older persons felt safest in the morning (they rarely left their homes and apartments after dark) and because many people were at home on Saturdays. The meetings were open to everyone. Twenty persons attended the first meeting, with the last three meetings averaging about 35 people.

Each meeting began with a staff person describing the intent of the meetings and then highlighting a variety of strategies. Included in the strategies proposed was an option for developing classes and events specifically for teenagers. With the limited personnel resources this would mean a decrease in services to other groups, but could help in lessening the threat of violence from the young people. Another strategy considered was to offer less recreation and more cultural activities. Participants critiqued each of the strategies and identified alternatives.

Several positive results came from the series of meetings: (1) consumers came to realize that the park's resources were finite and that there were trade-offs associated with each strategy choice, (2) people became involved in the park, many for the first time, and (3) the staff members were able to integrate community needs and desires into their service activities.

Strategies of the federal government are developed and implemented by different categories of persons. The Congress and President develop laws based on their perception of the public will and common good. Strategy at their level takes the form of policy formulation and not direct action. The federal legislative process is used to foster particular points of view, create changes in services and service delivery systems, and stimulate private sector enterprises to move in new directions. The legislative process is not neutral or value-free.

The bureaucratic arm of the federal government—the departments, commissions, and agencies—interprets the law (in effect, deciding what the Congress or President really meant) and writes regulations to implement the interpretations. The regulations prescribe action, spelling out broad strategies to implement the laws.

Federal involvement and responsibility for human services are only about 60 years old. When the Founding Fathers spoke about life, liberty, and the pursuit of happiness, probably little thought was given to social services or health needs. The eighteenth century was quite different from our modern world. People accepted the belief that humans were born to suffer, that ill health and poverty were products of providence, and that for the most part there was little anyone could do to alter fate. With the exceptions of quarantine inspection and military hospitals, the federal government took little responsibility for services until after the First World War. Indeed, for 125 years what little governmental intervention existed in human services was at the municipal and state levels, and that usually consisted of little more than the collection of birth and death records. Human services not given by family and friends were provided by charitable persons, organizations and institutions.

In 1918 federal legislation was passed to assist the states to establish screening and treatment programs to cope with an epidemic of venereal disease. The epidemic was linked to American soldiers who purportedly brought the disease back from their sojourns in other countries. The legislation was implemented through grants based on a population formula. The larger a state's population, the more money it received. Grants were not tied to need. The use of an "objective" formula (state population), the earmarking of funds for a specific purpose (venereal disease screening and treatment), and the delegation of implementation to others (the states) are the components of federal government strategy that continue in widespread use today.

Federal responsibility for human services began gradually, accelerating as social values changed. Federal action and social values have impacted on each other. As the degree and variety of federal government intervention increase, greater numbers of people are affected. Federal interventions, therefore, have real potential for influencing how people behave and what they value. As behavior and values change, the demand and expectation for federal action increases and the federal government tends to respond with still more interventions. This cycle is depicted in Figure 5-2.

Federal intervention strategies in human services have been episodic in character. Distinct types of actions have occurred in different areas. The intent of federal interventions changed from limited single purposes in the 1920s, to employ-

Figure 5-2

FEDERAL INTERVENTION CYCLE

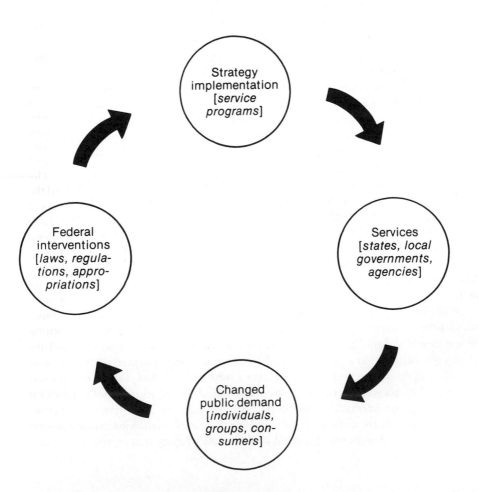

Strategy implementation [*service programs*]

Services [*states, local governments, agencies*]

Federal interventions [*laws, regulations, appropriations*]

Changed public demand [*individuals, groups, consumers*]

ment, disability, and old-age security in the 1930s, to facilities construction strategies in the 1940s and 1950s, to more comprehensive service-oriented activities in the 1960s, to serving broad groups of persons in the 1970s. In the 1980s, the trend toward services to broad groups of persons will probably continue.

An outgrowth of the deprivations caused by the Great Depression and the Second World War, one aim of public policy in the human services has been the improvement of the quality of life for all persons. The poor, the elderly, and the medically needy have benefited through income redistribution programs, such as Supplemental Security Income, Food Stamps, and Aid to Families with Dependent Children, while other persons have benefited through new and improved services or increased access to services.

The purpose of these federal interventions has not been revolution, but gradual social change. Since the 1930s and the passage of the Social Security Act, the federal government has taken an increasingly active prescriptive stance in human services. The assumption is that any movement away from poverty, illness, and dilapidated housing redresses inequities in society. The intervention strategy has been to involve other units of government and local agencies in implementing this incremental approach to change. The federal government's role generally has been and remains catalytic and regulatory.

Local government strategy historically has been to support protective services, such as police and fire departments, and human services, especially education and recreation, with public tax dollars. Some communities are wealthier than others. When they choose to, they tend to have better schools, streets, and services than less affluent places. Where there is a gross disparity among different communities or among neighborhoods in a city, persons who are least able to afford private assistance are also often least able to get services from their local government.

The active involvement of the federal government in human services since the mid-1960s has changed circumstances and strategies dramatically for local government. Choice—whether to provide services or not, the amount of services, and decisions about eligibility—has often been limited for local communities by their acceptance of federal dollars. State and local governments have increasingly had to follow federal strategies because of scarce local funds and the federal requirements for matching contributions. To be sure, there is considerable diversity. Medicaid (Social Security Act, Title XIX) is an example. Services vary from state to state depending on the extent of local contribution. Wealthier states tend to have more comprehensive services than those less wealthy. One state, Arizona, does not participate in the program.

State and local governments can consider a variety of strategy alternatives. These strategies are depicted in Figure 5-3. Until the massive federal involvement in the mid-1960s, state, city, and county governments paid for services, administered the programs, defined the population to be served, and often delivered the services themselves. This traditional approach can be described using Figure 5-3 alternative strategies.

Figure 5-3

LOCAL GOVERNMENT STRATEGY ALTERNATIVES

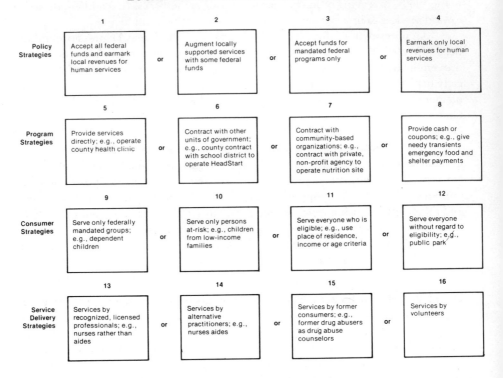

POLICY: # 4.   Earmark only local revenues for human services.

PROGRAM: # 5.   Provide services directly.

SERVICE POPULATION: #10.   Serve only persons at-risk.

SERVICE DELIVERY: #13.   Provide services by recognized, licensed professionals.

Since the mid-1960s, most urban communities employ the following combination of strategies.

POLICY: # 1.   Accept all federal grant funds and earmark local revenues for human services.

PROGRAM: # 6.   Contract with other units of government

and/or

7.   Contract with community-based organizations.

SERVICE POPULATION: # 9.   Serve only federally mandated populations

and/or

#11.   Serve everyone who is eligible.

SERVICE DELIVERY: #13.   Services by recognized licensed professionals
and/or
#14.   Provide services by alternative practitioners
and/or
#15.   Provide services by former consumers.

In many rural and politically conservative urban communities the tendency has been toward a different combination of strategies.

POLICY: # 3.   Accept funds for mandated federal programs only.
PROGRAM: # 5.   Provide services directly.
SERVICE POPULATION: # 9.   Serve only federally mandated populations.
SERVICE DELIVERY: #13.   Provide services by recognized licensed professionals
and/or
#14.   Provide services by alternative practitioners.

As an example, consider the city of approximately 100,000 which used three different service strategies before settling on a direction. When it received its first housing and community development block grant funds, in the early 1970s, it allocated the funds to operate its own departments. It spent the funds on street and sewer repair or city planning. At first the city council saw the block grant as a windfall to replace the city's own general revenues. As local special interest groups lobbied for part of the block grant funds, however, the council changed its strategy. It contracted out the funds, but used them primarily for public-works-related services. The primary consumer was again the city government itself.

After a couple of years of pressure by the community, the strategy was changed once more. The city began to use block grant funds for work outside of government, such as specialized transportation for the elderly and disabled, housing rehabilitation and redevelopment of the city's central business district. This last strategy has been retained because it achieves two important aims. First, it enables the city to encourage services, such as transportation, which would not usually be paid for from general revenue. Second, by subcontracting with community groups, the block grant dollars help build fledgling community groups into cohesive organizations.

When local revenues available for human services become more limited, dependency on federal assistance is likely to increase. Meanwhile, federal strategies have been broadening coverage and encouraging services delivered by less traditional means.

Private, nonprofit, community-based agencies have increasingly been funded to deliver services since the mid-1960s by government at all levels. These agencies may take on service responsibilities as an adjunct to their usual programming or the services may become the focus around which they operate. A church funded to operate a Headstart project is an example of the former, while a single purpose agency operating an alcohol abuse prevention program is an example of the latter.

Regardless of type of agency, multipurpose or single purpose, each has to locate and secure funding and develop strategies for delivering services. Given the scarcity of service dollars in relation to needs, agencies tend to expend an inordinate amount of effort in getting funds. The result is usually considerable competition between providers. Unfortunately, competition in this instance is sometimes deleterious to program quality. Competition takes resources away from the delivery of services and allocates it to the hunt for dollars. Despite their affiliation (county government-operated comprehensive neighborhood health clinic, private, nonprofit agency-operated manpower training program, etc.), agencies have to devise strategies to deal with the limitations of resources in relation to perceived needs. Often the issue is not who is to be served, but who is to be excluded.

The strategies for limiting services used by community-based organizations come in a variety of forms. One option is to increase the number of persons served, but decrease the quality (effectiveness) or amount of services offered. Another is to offer the services to everyone, but to restrict the publicity about the services so that few people learn about their availability. Both of these strategies have an ethical orientation that makes them less than desirable.

Strategies for service delivery are necessitated in part by the imbalance between needs, actual and potential, and resources available to meet the needs. Also, the perceptions and preferences of the funding sources and/or the service delivery agencies impact on strategy choices. One strategy commonly used at the local level is to limit a particular service project to a geographic area, called a "target" or "catchment" area. This can be done in at least two ways. The first is to define a set of boundaries within which a potential consumer must reside to be eligible for services. The second is to limit the sites at which the particular services are offered. The effect of limited sites in many cases is to limit those who use the services, as accessibility to a site where services are delivered is an important determinant of utilization. The main advantages of target areas are that they usually tend to be small enough in size to make possible seeking out the underserved and hard-to-reach and that such areas ordinarily have a population with stable characteristics on which the program approaches can be focused. The chief disadvantages of target areas are that persons of equal or greater need not residing in the area are denied services and that they can encourage agencies to monopolize pieces of turf.

Another strategy used by some agencies is to focus their service delivery efforts on a selected group (e.g., Black poor) rather than serving everyone (e.g., all poor). The rationale for this choice is to improve the sensitivity with which the services are delivered, thereby increasing both the variety and amount of services which will be accepted and their effectiveness. An Older Americans Act congregate meals program located in a local Buddhist temple and serving *dim sum* is far more likely to attract Chinese elders than a meals program serving hamburgers and french fried potatoes which is located across town. The disadvantages are equally apparent. The "political" aspects of service delivery become considerably more important as each group competes for funds to serve "its own." This consideration becomes so much the focus of attention on some occasions that the quality of, and need for, services is forgotten. A large number of small projects, each with its own administrative overhead costs, may also make this approach less cost efficient.

"Gap-filling" is a prevalent strategy today, as private, nonprofit agencies put their resources into the delivery of services not provided by other agencies. While this approach may avoid duplication and save dollars, it ordinarily creates a system of services which is disjointed and uncoordinated for individual clients. An alternative strategy is gaining momentum. Case management, or channeling, is an approach being updated in order to help clients through the frequently bewildering maze of conflicting requirements, standards, and eligibility rules. An agency assigns a primary worker who manages the acquisition of needed services for his or her clients. Through direct service provision, referral to other agencies, or the purchase of services, the worker attempts to reach a "critical mass" of services for each client. The effort is to provide enough services to make a significant difference in the client's life, rather than provide only enough to meet his or her immediate needs. In hospitals this approach is used in discharge planning. No certain knowledge about increased or decreased costs for this strategy currently exists.

Reaching out to unserved or underserved clients is another strategy and ordinarily costs more. Since these clients are harder to find and generally have more, and more serious, needs, they take more resources. If the goal is cost efficiency, clearly it is easier to adopt a strategy of "creaming." To cream is to concentrate on the easy-to-reach-and-serve populations. Agencies commonly practice creaming regardless of their stated policies because they tend to take those who apply to them for services. By definition, clients who seek out the services are not hard to reach. Considerable additional outreach and client contact time is needed to get through to those who may need the help most and are least able to acquire it on their own.

A variant of these last two strategy options relates to the acceptance of clients who are vulnerable as compared to those who are at-risk. A prematurely born infant is at-risk because the incidence of difficulties is greater with such infants than with those who are carried to full term. Many at-risk infants do very well, however, and develop normally. Therefore, only some are vulnerable and in need of continuing critical care health services. An eighty-five-year-old person is always at-risk, but not necessarily vulnerable, with respect to the need for institutionalization. Service only to the vulnerable has the advantage of saving funds, at least in the short term, since fewer persons are served. However, preventive services to the at-risk may keep them from becoming vulnerable and save the costs that the agency might otherwise have to expend.

How the choice of strategies affects service provision can be seen in the example which follows. An agency which served a general elderly population for a number of years determined that a more targeted program was needed to prevent the premature institutionalization of frail older persons. Upon investigation in the community, the agency's boards of directors learned that there were a variety of possible adult day care centers and goals. Figure 5-4 illustrates the range of day care centers based, in large measure, on the degree of frailty of the participants—that is, on their ability to participate independently in activities of daily living.

Having decided that an adult day care center providing therapeutic psychosocial services was best suited to the needs, the agency's board members faced the decision of selecting which clients they wished to serve and what goals to pursue on behalf of those clients. They were informed by a consulting gerontologist that differing client characteristics required the center to provide different activities and, therefore, to hire differently trained staff. The potential client characteristics were outlined by the consultant as follows:

1. Clients who are depressed.
2. Clients who have dementia (cognitive impairment).
3. Clients who are psychotic.
4. Clients who are in need of constant supervision because of self-destructive behavior.
5. Clients who are without apparent pathology, but who need socialization to prevent mental and social deterioration.
6. Clients whose families need a respite from their care, without regard to the clients' condition.
7. Clients who have physical impairments such as blindness or Parkinson's disease.
8. Clients who fit some or all of the above categories.

The board members were advised that depressed clients can frequently benefit from counseling activities, while those with dementia generally cannot, that older persons with no cognitive or communication disabilities do not need the reality orientation training often needed by those suffering from cognitive disabilities—to name but a few of the choices.

The board members decided they should adopt one or more of the goals in-

Figure 5-4

TYPES OF ADULT DAY CENTERS BY
DEGREE OF FRAILITY

Most vulnerable   **Least vulnerabl**

Day health/treatment centers	Day care centers	Day care centers	Senior service centers	Senior centers
(Treatment services)	(Psycho-social therapeutic services)	(Custodial, recreational services)	(Social services)	(Recreational services)

dicated in Figure 5-5, recognizing that each goal selected required the selection of a different group of clients, the collection of different assessment data, the hiring of differently qualified staff members, and the conduct of different activities. Strategies for service delivery, as this example demonstrates, have impact on agencies, clients and their families, and staff members.

Funding sources sometimes use a formula to determine the scope of service in a particular community. A typical formula is one that uses a ratio of dollars allocated to consumers. For instance, a standard for basic contraceptive services for financially indigent women recently has been $72 per consumer per year. An agency budget of $72,000 annually means 1000 persons can be served. The problem with such formulas is that they do not consider quality of service.

One rural family planning agency was faced with serious problems as a result of this formula approach. The service site located in the largest town in the county was accessible to very few of the many potential consumers. The agency found that the only way to give adequate services was to establish and staff satellite service sites throughout the county. But doing this was much too costly. The agency decided on three strategies to overcome its financial problems.

First, it decided to seek third-party payments (insurance, Medicaid) and to

Figure 5-5

GOAL CHOICE CONSEQUENCES FOR AN
ADULT DAY CARE CENTER

● Goal	● Clients	● Assessment	● Staff	● Activities
Treatment of psychological and social conditions	Depressed or in need of socialization	Level of psychological and social functioning	Broadly skilled in counseling and therapeutic activities	Therapeutic activities
Respite for families	In need of supervision for short periods	Minimum attributes of functioning	Trained in recreational activities	Recreational and custodial activities
Support for clients with specific conditions: Parkinson's disease, hip replacement, dementia	Clients with specific conditions	Level of medical, mental and social functioning	Specifically trained on the conditions	Therapeutic and health care activities
Some or all of the above				

charge a fee, when possible, to augment grant funds. Because it served an impoverished community, the agency was able to recoup only a little of its added costs in this way. Next, it broadened its intake of consumers and provided services that were not labor intensive. The agency sponsored mutual-assistance classes and group education and counseling sessions to increase the number of persons served and to justify its request for additional funds. This strategy helped to meet the cost per consumer formula, but reduced the individuality of services given. The community accepted the trade-off of less individualized service for more individuals served. Finally, the agency appealed to other funding sources for supplemental funds, something it had never done before.

Strategies not only affect agencies and consumers, but ultimately strategy choices affect the community as well.

Efficiency/effectiveness strategies should be part of the thinking of everyone connected with human service agencies. Thoughtful attention should be given to the interplay between these two factors so they both can be achieved at optimum levels. The grid in Figure 5-6 illustrates the relationship between efficiency and effectiveness in order to assess the relative value of each. A 7/1 model is one which stresses quality of service over cost. Conversely, a 1/7 model puts cost considerations first. The maximum mix, 7/7, may be quite difficult to achieve, if not impossible, and agencies are wise to seek that balance which best matches their philosophies and desired service outcomes.

Figure 5-6

EFFICIENCY/EFFECTIVENESS GRID

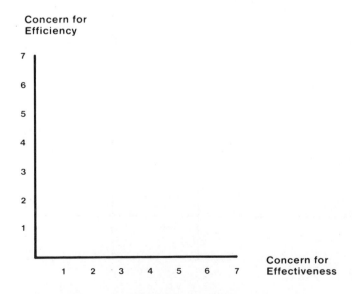

One agency providing a juvenile justice diversion program required young people referred by the courts to attend twice-weekly rap groups as well as to participate in other activities. Because of its success in reducing the recidivism rate among its young clients, the number of offenders being referred increased sharply. The staff members, recognizing that the size of the rap groups was growing too large and that each participant in the project was not getting enough attention, asked their director to accept new clients only when vacancies occurred. This approach, they felt, would ensure a continued high level of effectiveness. The director, realizing the value of keeping more young people out of the criminal justice system, decided to bring the issue to the project's Advisory Committee. The Advisory Committee, hearing that no new resources were available, faced the following choices. First, it could suggest that more clients be accepted, which would help youngsters who might otherwise not get help and who would be stigmatized by a criminal record. This would also be popular with those in the community who argued that more clients meant a lower cost per client, thus increasing the project's efficiency. Or, alternatively, the committee could suggest that the previous ratio of participants to rap groups be maintained, ensuring a high level of effectiveness, but sacrificing more efficiency.

Political or social realities may demand more "bang for the buck," regardless of the effectiveness of a service. In the late 1960s, when there were heavy political demands to reduce unemployment and underemployment, the manpower training programs translated this demand into programs that stressed vocational training. Agencies were encouraged by the federal government to seek out and train large numbers of persons. In the rush to do so, the quality of the training was sometimes overlooked as was the need to adequately prepare people who had been chronically unemployed to compete on the job with others. The result was an efficient service (divide the number of trainees by the cost), but not necessarily an effective program (percentage of persons trained who are able to get and successfully retain jobs).

On the other hand, human service agencies sometimes seek effectiveness at the expense of efficiency. For example, a family planning clinic in which physicians and allied health workers are encouraged to spend large amounts of time with patients for diagnosis, education, and treatment accents effectiveness, but ignores cost. The cost will certainly be higher than in a similar clinic where patients are seen within prescribed time limits or for prescribed services by volunteers and the lowest-paid employees possible. Comparison is made in both instances by comparing the number of patients seen by the total cost of clinic operations. Efficiency and effectiveness are tempered by the intentional involvement of consumers, the community, and other agencies. Trade-offs made between efficiency and effectiveness are indicative of a service project's "values."

The steps for developing strategies are highlighted in the following example. In sequence, the steps are as follows:

1. Identify the issues.
2. Explore the alternative actions.

3. List the probable consequences of each alternative.
4. Develop a sequence of desirable actions and the timing of each.
5. Evaluate the situation after each action to determine if changes are needed.

Betty Martin is the chief planner of a private, nonprofit agency set up by the local government to administer antipoverty funds provided by the Community Services Administration. After re-examining the needs of low-income members of the community and the resources available to them, she decided that additional funds soon to be available should be used to implement economic development projects. She concluded, further, that the projects had to provide sufficient capital for purchasing the equipment and supplies needed to run a successful business venture and, therefore, that only one or two projects should be started.

Dr. Martin realized a number of factors could impede her decision to proceed with this service program. First, the elected officials in her community were used to having the funds divided equally among the seven districts they represented, so they would probably want her agency to provide seven projects rather than just one or two. Second, the currently funded human service agencies had numerous projects of other types for which they were hoping to receive added funds, so they would probably oppose her plan. Third, some of the members of her agency's governing board had pet projects they wished to see expanded, so they probably would try to direct at least some of the funds to those agencies. Fourth, the local merchants, who might feel themselves to be in direct competition with such a commercial venture, would probably try to lobby against these proposed projects with her agency director and the elected officials.

Recognizing these difficulties, Dr. Martin weighed a variety of alternative strategies for getting her plan adopted. She could split the money into several parts, creating economic development projects in those districts in which agreement could be gained from the elected officials. She reasoned that less than half of the money was too little to mount an effective effort. However, by placing a project site on the border of two districts, she might get the support of two elected officials. Another alternative was to have one or two projects, each with satellite sites, so that all districts would be involved in the program. She decided to use this last approach.

Dr. Martin also developed other actions. She determined that the projects should consist of food markets because this would also provide a considerable amount of training to people who could then get employment in the community. To avoid the charge of competition with commercial enterprises, the projects would serve only low-income senior citizens and persons making their purchases with food stamps. In this way, she decided on a strategy that might make it possible to avoid extensive opposition.

The positive and negative consequences of each action were reviewed and modifications made. For example, she decided to place the principal site in one area and the warehouse in another in order to decrease the visibility of the project in any one neighborhood. She also developed a publicity approach that would gain support from the business community since the workers in the project could be seen as taxpayers instead of welfare recipients and, because of their training on the job, as a new skilled labor pool.

To complete her strategy, Dr. Martin developed a time plan for implementation. She would arrange for the concept to be announced first at senior citizens clubs and organizations to win their support. With their active help, she believed the project would be accepted by her agency's board of directors and the elected officials. Then she would try to get the support of the president of the largest supermarket chain in the community, thereby offsetting any opposition from the rest of the food market operators.

After presenting her project ideas and strategies to her agency's executive director and gaining approval, she realized that her planned actions might not have the results she wished in each case. On implementing the first steps in her strategy, she examined the outcomes carefully in order to be ready with changes in the tactics she had planned.

As the project proceeded, Dr. Martin also recognized that its success would change the needs in the low-income community, necessitating the development of new strategies for service.

It follows from the discussion in this chapter that strategy is a comprehensive issue. Decisions at the agency level affect attitudes and behavior of clients. They, in turn, begin to make new demands of government. Elected officials and the bureaucracy at all levels of government react with new legislation, regulations, and changes in public spending. Therefore, the possibilities for significantly altering the way in which services are delivered are quite tangible indeed.

AGENCY SELF-ASSESSMENT CHECKLIST: DEVELOPING AND IMPLEMENTING STRATEGIES

INDICATOR	STATUS OF INDICATOR			PERSON RESPONSIBLE
	Yes	No	Partial	
1. The board of directors has a service strategy for all agency projects.	____	____	____	_____
2. The agency has procedures for collaboration with other service providers in its target areas.	____	____	____	_____
3. The agency has a working relationship with its funding sources.	____	____	____	_____
4. Agency staff and board members have relationships with elected government officials at all levels.	____	____	____	_____
5. The agency involves staff members at all levels in decisions about service strategies.	____	____	____	_____
6. The agency has staff members who are responsible for analysis of legislation.	____	____	____	_____
7. The agency strategies and service objectives are reviewed at least annually.	____	____	____	_____
8. The agency develops its service strategies only after a careful review of the input from the target population.	____	____	____	_____

Implementing Human Services

6

The methods, philosophies, and styles may vary, but the process for implementing health, education, employment, recreation, social, or any other human service delivery project is the same. Every project finds clients and takes them into a program, carries out service interventions on their behalf, moving them through the program and/or referring them to other agencies and, finally, closes off the services. These activities are the basis for this chapter.

Outreach is the seeking and recruitment of persons who need, and are eligible for, the services being provided. Outreach, through one-to-one or group contact, identifies persons who need available services and makes them aware that the services exist. Outreach is a postal worker suggesting to an older woman living alone that she visit the local senior citizens center in order to "get out of the house and keep active." Outreach is an agency's "success stories" in a newspaper. Outreach is a speech to a PTA meeting by the director of a child care project. Outreach is also an alcohol abuse prevention counselor talking informally with a group of teenagers in their school hangout. Outreach has many forms, but generally consists of five different activities or combinations of them. Figure 6-1 summarizes these characteristics.

Each outreach activity has advantages and disadvantages. Using the mass news media, for example, requires a minor expenditure of staff time, but reaches many people. Because the media reach large numbers of people, however, many noneligible persons become informed. Creating demands for services when resources are inadequate can rebound to discredit an agency. The mass media are also inappropriate vehicles for reaching hard-to-serve potential clients. These persons most frequently require individual and repeated contact.

Door-to-door and telephone canvassing, on the other hand, reach out more directly to targeted areas or specific potential clients. Individual contacts obviously

Figure 6-1

OUTREACH ACTIVITIES

Activities	Client contacts	Reaching hard-to-reach	Persons contacted	Non-eligible persons contacted	Expenditures of staff time
Mass Media	General	Poor	Many	Many	Little
Service provider contacts	Specific	Fair	Moderate	Few	Little
Door-to-door canvassing	Targeted	Good	Few	Many to few	Much
Telephone canvassing	Specific	Fair to good	Few	Few	Much
Public contact	General or targeted	Poor to fair	Moderate	Many	Varies with effort

take more staff time and effort than do media presentations which may be seen by thousands of people at one time. The individual approach, however, makes it possible to answer a prospective client's questions, establish a trusting relationship, and usually provides more immediate assistance. Public contacts are more direct than reaching out through the media, but less direct than either door-to-door or telephone canvassing.

All five activities are important in the outreach efforts of any human service agency. Used with care, each can help to reach different segments of the population. Used in combination, they form a link between the providers and consumers of service.

The mass news media—radio, TV, newspapers, and magazines—provide avenues for reaching potential clients. Radio and television present numerous opportunities, such as public service spot announcements, talk shows, call-in programs, special interest programs, news shows, and community bulletin board announcements. Radio and television stations are required to provide some time for public service broadcasts in order to keep their licenses.

The major print medium for most outreach efforts is the daily newspaper. Newsletters for professionals along with employee publications also provide access to groups of persons who may have direct contact with potential clients. Special newspapers generally have smaller circulations, are closely geared to their readers' specific interests, and are read more thoroughly. Their editors are usually eager for news of local interest, so agencies may find it easy to obtain space. Such publications include neighborhood weeklies, which reach the residents in limited geographic areas; ethnic newspapers, which offer a direct link to minority groups; college and high school papers, which target the potential clients of some youth-serving agencies; and shopper throwaways, which often intersperse local features or announcements among their advertisements.

Door-to-door canvassing requires a two-phase approach to outreach. First, make a decision about which areas are most likely to contain potential clients. Divide the identified target areas block by block, or section by section in rural communities, and send outreach workers to knock on doors along the blocks or through the sections. At each stop they should provide a brief description of the services available, leave a brochure with pertinent information, and determine whether the householder knows someone who is in need of the services and might be eligible for them. During this activity the workers will also learn of any needs that cannot be met by their agency. Use this information to make referrals to other agencies and document the unmet needs for use in seeking additional funds.

The second phase is more specifically addressed to persons identified as prospective clients. Some persons known to need services require help in obtaining them. They may require transportation, translation of information, assistance in filling out intake forms, or other special help. Some may need several visits to establish the trust that will enable them to accept help. Indeed, in some cases clients will insist on help from the outreach worker only, making a transfer to other agency staff members quite difficult. By definition, these clients are hard-to-reach and serve. The door-to-door approach is the most effective with them.

Telephone canvassing usually is limited to people assumed to be in need and eligible. These prospective clients may come as referrals from other service providers or from their families and friends, as a result of inquiries from publicity, or from follow-ups to names obtained at meetings or public speaking engagements. Telephone canvassing has the personal contact element so important for many people, making it an effective means for reaching out.

Care should be exercised, however, in canvassing someone for the first time. Some people resent the intrusion of a stranger and others are frightened by the call. Establishing rapport initially is more important than asking a lot of questions, which may make the person suspicious and defensive. "I heard from Mrs. Jones that you are poor, depressed and ill," is hardly the way to begin. First, establish trust. Initial suspicions may be overcome by indicating friendship with Mrs. Jones. Listening is usually more effective than talking. Obtain information about their needs later.

Alone or in combination with home visits, telephone canvassing is a valuable outreach activity. The telephone is personalized, yet uses less staff resources than door-to-door canvassing.

Service providers from other agencies are frequently a source of clients. Since persons requesting one service often need other services as well, working in collaboration with other providers of service can help locate potential clients. If agencies and providers work cooperatively, appropriate referrals increase. Aiding with referrals increases an agency's credibility with the community. This method of outreach should not be underestimated.

Professionals in the community also refer potential clients. Clergymen have persons whom they advise and can recommend for service. Doctors and their office nurses, public health nurses, homemaker agency staff people, psychologists, to name just a few, may wish to get services for their clients or their clients' families. Teachers, librarians, and school counselors often refer young people to service programs.

Arrangements with these persons can vary considerably in the degree of formality. Presentations at meetings of professional groups help disseminate information about services. Written material on brightly colored stock cut to unusual dimensions should also be made available. Include in the written material the types of service, hours and days of service, and eligibility requirements. Include, also, the name and phone number of a specific staff person if possible.

Public contact can take a variety of forms. Some agencies make use of any place where numbers of people gather. These agencies will post flyers, brochures, posters, or whatever other appropriate written material they may have, in laundromats, shopping centers, food markets, parks, recreation and community centers, and other similar places. The posted material should look professional, i.e., not scrawled with crayon on the reverse side of a used sheet of paper. A poster, like the clothes we wear, gives others an impression of us. The impression a human service agency wants to give is one of competence, one that will inspire confidence in potential clients so they will want to initiate contact. Even "anti-establishment" providers such as free clinics have to demonstrate, along with their caring attitude, their ability to deliver a service.

The material which goes on posters, billboards, brochures, and flyers should meet three criteria. First, the material must be attractive and professional in appearance. Second, do not overburden it with information in small type so that people looking at it casually will pass it by. An agency's name, services, and phone number may be enough, although an address and hours of service are sometimes useful. Pictures and artwork, if they can be afforded, will help to attract attention to the material. Also helpful are catch phrases that stand symbolically for a much larger meaning, such as PROBLEM PREGNANCY? CONFIDENTIAL HELP. Third, adapt the material to the cultural and ethnic considerations of the persons the agency wants to reach. Sometimes the obvious is forgotten. A San Francisco agency, trying to recruit clients in Chinatown, used a poster which showed a scene from the mainland of China. This was so offensive to supporters of the government on Taiwan that many potential clients refused to accept the agency's services.

Materials translated into a foreign language should be prepared by someone who knows the idioms of the community. Incorrect, stilted or unfamiliar words and phrases can reflect unfavorably on an agency.

Using another common outreach approach, human service agencies can provide staff and board members and volunteers to speak at meetings of fraternal organizations, church groups, senior citizens' clubs, business associations, and other similar groups. The presentations usually revolve around the services the agencies provide and an explanation of who is eligible. If audience members are not potential consumers of the services, the hope is they will know persons who are in need.

Agencies also participate in community events, such as celebrations, health, job and housing fairs and service days, in order to seek out additional clients. This may take the form of distributing written materials or making presentations, or both. Many communities organize health fairs or service days at which agencies can establish booths and provide services, distribute materials, and answer questions. The possibilities for this type of activity are limited only by the imagination of an agency's staff and the circumstances in the community.

Classes and workshops present another outreach opportunity. Health-related agencies use this approach frequently. Junior high school classes in drug abuse prevention taught by an agency's drug abuse counselor can lead students into a drug treatment program. In hospitals classes for new parents can provide information which helps to meet their social service needs or provides referrals to family planning services. This form of outreach need not be costly, but does require a systematic development effort. Staff time to develop this type of outreach activity is often repaid manyfold by the resulting intake of new clients.

Outreach to minority group members generally requires added effort as these groups often have a more difficult time learning about, accepting, utilizing, and benefiting from agency-based service delivery systems. Beyond the obvious need to provide materials in the language of the potential clients along with outreach workers who speak the clients' language, consider a number of other possibilities. First and most important is staff attitude. A great many persons from minority groups have had the experience of being made to feel unwelcome by human service and other agencies. This feeling can be overcome if agency personnel understand the special concerns and fears of members of minority groups, and have the sensitivity to act accordingly.

Special attention should be given to the cultural considerations of each minority group. An unescorted male knocking on doors in a neighborhood of Mexican Americans during the day when the husbands are probably not home can expect poor results. Women in these neighborhoods will not talk to strangers. A nutrition project worker unaware of the differences in food choices between Korean and Japanese senior citizens is going to have trouble interesting these elderly persons in the program. An outreach worker for a youth employment project who does not know the geographic areas considered the "turf" of particular gangs is not likely to be very successful in recruiting gang members into that project and may inadvertently do more harm than good.

Agency personnel who are Caucasian and middle-class often do not realize that their choice of approaches for persons unlike themselves may be inappropriate. An example is the belief of middle-class agency staff members that meetings are effective in soliciting participation. Attending meetings and speaking in front of groups is a learned behavior. Many minority group persons do not have these skills and find participation in committee activities and meetings uncomfortable, if not impossible.

Also, the prospect for an embarrassing or difficult intake procedure can become a barrier to outreach. A person whose native language is not English may find filling out forms in English an unbearable burden. In some cultures, in which the disclosure of personal or family problems is not customary, the routine questions asked by an intake clerk may cause great embarrassment.

Finally, philosophical and religious beliefs can make a difference. Some minority group members hold cultural values which orient the individual to an acceptance of fate. Sometimes outreach workers find it difficult to distinguish persons with these views from people who are apathetic or even hostile toward the receipt of services. People with belief systems that keep them from easily using services require extra time and attention. Reaching out to them effectively requires that staff members exercise patience and persistence.

Outreach to members of minority groups often requires extra effort, more expense and special staff. Given the commitment, human service agencies can, if they are aware of the special requirements, reach out successfully to potential clients from these groups.

Intake and assessment are the two sides of a coin; both are intended to determine what services, if any, a person is eligible for and/or needs. In a consumer-initiated intake system, used by most human service agencies, the clients or their families first determine that they need help. Eligibility for a particular service is a different matter from need. Eligibility is most often determined by relatively objective, predetermined criteria. Assessment, on the other hand, is a judgment made by staff that needs of one kind or another do exist to some degree and can be ameliorated by a particular service or services.

Programs generally limit the type of needs they try to meet and the category of persons whose needs they seek to ameliorate. A 19-year-old youth may need summer employment, but not be eligible to participate in a jobs program limited to young people between 14 and 18. A middle-income woman with severely impaired hearing may be ineligible for a program for deaf persons with low-incomes even though the degree of her impairment falls within the program's guidelines. In the first case the eligibility is based on age, in the second on income. Another person may be the 501st person to meet the eligibility requirements of a project that is limited by contract or funding to 500 clients. Still other people may live one block beyond the catchment area of an agency or have a physical condition, such as confinement to a wheelchair, which makes them unacceptable to the agency as a client.

The intake process is frequently used as the first decision point for eligibility. The complexity of initial screening information varies among agencies. Data are collected over the phone, at clients' homes, or in an agency site. Some agencies gather a whole range of data, including such items as demographic information about the prospective clients and their support systems, medical, social, economic, and psychological histories, and perceived needs. Reports may be required from families, law enforcement and social service agencies, and physicians. Other agencies may only ask a person's name and address along with "What brings you in today?" The intake information helps to determine if services will be delivered.

Climate, or ambiance, and staff attitudes play a large role in client satisfaction and cooperation. The intake process should collect only data that are relevant and necessary and that do not demean the client. Far too frequently agencies require information from prospective clients which goes beyond the agencies' need to know. Clients should not have to surrender their privacy in order to obtain assistance. Agency procedures should be checked to ensure that only the intake data necessary for providing services to clients are collected.

In some agencies, assessment is part of the intake process. Intake consists of data collection and eligibility determination, while assessment adds the ingredients of data analysis and determination of services. In other agencies, assessment is a separate function from intake, performed by different staff members after decisions have been made about eligibility.

Assessment, in either case, depends on the services available directly from an agency or indirectly through referral. The functional relationship between an agency's program and a particular service causes staff members to concentrate on what they can do best and to focus on clients' specific needs. Certainly, service providers offer what they have available and not what is unavailable. The relationship often results, therefore, in some of the clients' needs being neglected.

To determine clients' requirements for services, information should be collected from both the clients and the people related to them, whenever possible. Usually, one outstanding difficulty is the focal point of need which has prompted a person to seek assistance. This "presenting problem" may be an emergency (life-threatening difficulty), acute (currently difficult, but temporary), or chronic (regularly difficult and long-lasting) situation. However, the presenting problem often is only the tip of the iceberg. Consequently, assessments which go beyond the immediate situation are necessary. The belief that the solution to a client's problems can be found in the provision of services is arrogant. The first issue is whether services are needed, then which mix of services is needed, and in what amounts they should be supplied.

How an agency should organize its intake and assessment procedures is determined by its objectives, the services it provides, and the staff available to perform the required tasks. For example, a medical transportation project with one dispatcher and several drivers probably will have the dispatcher collect whatever minimum intake data are necessary to determine eligibility and make assignments for service. A driver hearing concerns expressed about clients might or might not report them to the dispatcher, who might or might not know how, or be interested enough, to make a referral to another agency. In a maternal and child health medical clinic, on the other hand, well-trained eligibility workers might collect pages of economic information and social workers might collect psychosocial assessment data while the medical staff collected medical histories and did physical examinations. Thus, the range of assessment efforts is quite large and the methods diverse.

The objective should be to collect, analyze, and use the findings. In the maternal and child health clinic, for instance, social service personnel may interview a family in a group setting to determine how the family members interact, while a clinical psychologist might give one child in that family the Minnesota Multiphasic Personality Inventory to determine specific items of assessment data. An intake worker, while filling out forms, may discover that the father in the family is presently unemployed, while a nurse might learn from a casual conversation that the mother is anxious about becoming pregnant again.

Assessments are for the purpose of assisting individual clients and helping to establish needs for services generally. Based on the assessment data from this and a number of other client families, the clinic could arrange with other agencies to locate employment for unemployed fathers or provide tutoring for the school-age children in need of such assistance. It could itself conduct educational sessions on parenting, birth control methods, and nutritional meal preparation.

The ethical issues related to implementing a service delivery program are basic to any human enterprise. The responsibility for delivering on promises is as serious in human service programs as in personal relationships. Agencies sometimes raise expectations that needs will be met without making a sincere effort to accomplish that end. Unfortunately, it often happens that agencies put their survival and the needs of their staff members ahead of their clients and in the process reduce their efforts to provide the services they have promised.

It is an inviolable rule that the agency should do no harm to clients in its effort to aid them. The interventions on behalf of clients are supposedly designed to assist them, but sometimes service providers do not realize the harm they cause. One of the most insidious forms of harm, because it often goes unrecognized by both clients and agency, relates to dependency. The line between enough service given long enough to improve the circumstances of a particular client and too much service or service extended over so long a period that it reduces the client's independence is very thin. Help is not always helpful and service providers must be alert to the impact of their services on the clients they serve.

Sometimes agencies engage in the unethical practice of using clients to meet agency needs rather than the agencies serving clients' needs. To meet service quotas, agencies sometimes coerce clients into taking part in activities which have no benefit for them. Or agencies may parade clients in front of governmental officials or funding source personnel in order to help the agency gain something which is of no benefit to the clients. This demeans the clients and robs them of their privacy and dignity. Great care must be exercised by agency administrators and other staff members to ensure that respectful treatment is rendered clients and that their benefit remains the paramount concern.

For experimental and demonstration projects funded by the federal government, agencies are required to submit their plans to their peers for a review of the risks to human subjects. This procedure is to help ensure that the rights of participants are protected and that they are made aware of any risks involved.

Information and referral (I & R) services are provided by nearly every human service agency because no agency can meet all the needs of each person it serves. Giving information about services provided by other agencies is a legitimate activity for any agency. For some agencies I & R is their only activity. I & R services are provided by projects designed exclusively for this purpose, handling requests by phone only. Other agencies may have one or more drop-in locations available in the community. However, agency staff members, in the course of providing other services, generally render the most I & R services.

Information and referral services depend on several factors for successful implementation. To make appropriate referrals, a client's requests for help must be understood and his or her status determined. It will not do to send a runaway teenager who has not eaten for several days to a senior citizens meal program site, since the site staff would be obliged to turn the young person away. Likewise, an elderly person requesting help for her sick dog should not be told that she is foolish. The dog may be her only companion and her best motivation to remain outside an institution. For providers of I & R, "treating the whole person" is more than a slogan. Referral methods must be related to each client's resources, needs, and ability to cope. Ensure (1) that the information provided is correct, (2) that the clients are eligible for the referred services, and (3) that the clients can manage to obtain the service.

To give adequate information and refer clients properly, the service person must have available an up-to-date resource directory which indicates the agencies, their services, hours, locations, phone numbers, and eligibility requirements. A list of contact persons for each agency is helpful in facilitating the I & R process. Referrals to agencies can have a devastating effect when clients do not receive the services they requested, they cannot make contact because phone numbers have been changed or they are not eligible. Many potential consumers have trouble reaching out for help and are quickly turned off when their efforts are aborted by incorrect or inadequate referrals. Others, more persistent and able to cope with the service system, may eventually get assistance, but the extra effort is an unwanted and unwarranted burden.

All providers of referral services must concern themselves with the quality of services received by the clients they refer. This is a sensitive issue among human service agencies. Service providers who think poorly of an agency sometimes deny their clients access to the services of that agency. Relationships between the two agencies are involved as well as the impact on clients. On the other hand, to send clients to an agency believing they will be ineffectively served also impacts negatively on the providers and clients. How aggressively to pursue a referral once it is made or to follow up to see if mutually satisfactory contacts have been established is a policy that each agency must determine. Some agencies have found it useful to follow up on referrals not only to track their clients, but also to ensure that appropriate persons are being referred to each agency. Figure 6-2 shows the ingredients and criteria which comprise the typical I & R service.

Figure 6-2

INFORMATION AND REFERRAL SERVICES

Service	Criteria
Reception of requests	• Proper understanding of information desired • Helpful attitude toward caller exhibited • Correct determination of client status
Resource directory	• Comprehensive listing of agencies available • Complete data available • Up-to-date data available
Referrals	• Appropriate referral for requests made • Appropriate referrals for clients' capabilities made • Correct information provided • Qualitative judgments of agencies' services made
Follow-up	• Satisfactory relationships established • Inappropriate referrals identified

The informal support system is by far the major resource for services in the United States, although the amount of formal agency services provided has increased substantially in the past two decades. Far too frequently, and often despite agencies' policies to the contrary, individual service providers and volunteers see their clients' support networks as bothersome, time-consuming, superfluous, or, worst of all, competitive. To avoid making use of the informal support system as an adjunct to agency services is foolish and irresponsible. After all, the optimizing of resources on behalf of its clients is, or should be, the primary consideration of every agency.

An informal support network of people operates on behalf of all human beings during some part or all of their lives. A wife who does her husband's laundry provides support. The clothes press operator in a laundry who listens to her co-worker's troubles is providing support. The co-worker who visits her grandmother on Sundays provides support. A social club whose members volunteer to work in the nursing home in which the grandmother resides provides support. The homeowners association which helps the family of one of those volunteers to move into its new house provides support. Support is rendered by families, friends, neighbors, and organizations in the community.

Family, or kinship, networks, which can be immediate (mother, father, and siblings) or extended (other relatives) are usually the principal source of assistance for younger and older people. They frequently provide financial support, transportation, household help, meal preparation, personal care, and socialization, to name but a few of their functions. The cost to provide all these services by substituting formal human services through agencies would be staggering, even if it were possible to organize the services on such a scale at all.

Linking, or friendship, networks consist of friends, neighbors, ministers, coworkers, and fellow club members. Organizational and community networks include churches, tradespeople, and community organizations. Far more counseling and health care, for example, are provided by network members than by psychotherapists and nurses; more transportation and meals are provided than by government-sponsored projects. One solid friendship can be more stabilizing to a recently divorced woman than a host of trained service providers. For a great number of people there is no substitute for these support networks and the attendant benefits even though the networks may not always be able to provide total support or expert assistance.

The following action steps are necessary in order to take full advantage of the supporting network of any client. First, identify the client's support system and the significant gaps, if any. This step is easier to state than to accomplish, as considerable trust between client and helper is often necessary before the required data can be obtained. With the information available, then inform the support persons about the nature of the assistance needed to help the client and obtain their consent to the roles they will play. This reinforcement of network members' roles can be crucial, as there is always a tendency for them to step aside or defer to professional agency personnel.

Support should also be sought from other network persons who are not helping currently, but would with the proper encouragement. A physically disabled client who cannot shop may have a neighbor who, if asked, would bring groceries once a week. A relative of the client's, in addition, might agree to come by and prepare some meals. If the agency paid for the materials, a volunteer member of the local carpenter's union might install grab bars in the client's bathroom. To solidify the client's ability to live independently, services provided through agencies could fill the remaining gaps. For example, through referral another agency could arrange for a homemaker to attend the client twice a week, cleaning and running errands.

A service provider in an agency serving persons newly released from prison discovered in the course of a routine investigation prior to one prisoner's discharge that his former wife had never remarried. The service provider also learned that the prisoner's best friend still lived in town and was anxious to help his friend regain a responsible status in society. While the friend found him a job, his former wife located an apartment for him and decorated it as she knew he would prefer. The service provider arranged a small loan to help him get started and involved his parole officer in the process. The prisoner's informal network and agency supports, working together, effected a smooth transition from the prison to the community and provided him with a stable environment in which to rebuild his life.

However much human service agency personnel may be tempted to provide the services and not bother with the informal support system, they should remember the great value of any client's networks to the client and to the provision of services generally.

Referral, follow-up, and discharge are planned activities in a complete service system.

The requirement for referring a client from one agency to another is obvious if the patchwork nature of most human service delivery systems in the United States is kept in mind. Rarely does a single agency have the variety and depth of resources necessary to meet all the needs for services. The most viable approach, and the one most often used, is for an agency to seek out and refer its clients to other agencies for one or more of the needed services.

Referral from the original to the referral agencies is not always smooth, however, even when the staff members of each agency cooperate with one another. Clients may not meet the eligibility requirements of other agencies or may not wish to utilize their services. A referral agency may not be accessible, convenient, or affordable. Clients may intend to accept the services suggested, but fail to initiate the contact. Some clients, when placed on waiting lists, may become discouraged and give up. Other clients may be physically or psychologically unable to go once more through intake and assessment procedures or the development of relationships with new staff members. The percentage of clients who receive the services for which they were referred is far below 100 percent.

The more positive answers an agency can give to the following questions about its referral system the more likely it is that its clients are receiving services from appropriate referral sources.

Have each client's needs for services not available from this agency been adequately assessed?

Does this agency have a resource directory which fully identifies the services available in the community?

Are the agencies to which clients are referred routinely called to check eligibility requirements, days and hours of operation, location, and availability of services?

Are clients' physical, social, psychological, and financial conditions considered in selecting the referral agencies?

Does this agency ensure that each client and family, where appropriate, understands and accepts the necessity for a referral?

Does this agency make sure that all clients can get to the referral agencies?

Are referral agencies routinely notified when clients are being sent to them?

Does this agency determine that clients have received, and are satisfied with, the services of the referral agencies?

Follow-up, the continued assessment of the status of inactive and former clients, is a practice that varies widely among human service agencies in method, quality, and amount. Some case management-oriented agencies do routine periodic checks of their inactive client needs and accomplishments as part of their standard operating procedure. Other agencies manage their follow-up by the principle of exception—that is, the agencies check on their former clients only when some difficulty is brought to their attention for which they feel a remedy is available. Still other agencies make no effort, once a service is completed, to contact the client to determine either the effect of their intervention or the current needs of the client.

The determination to look after clients or to evaluate the results of services is in part a philosophic choice, but may also be determined by the nature of services rendered or the funding available to support such activities. Some agencies feel a sense of obligation to the persons in whose lives they intervene. The staff members get to know the clients well enough during the delivery of services to determine the range of their needs and are able to keep track of their whereabouts. Other agencies do not feel this responsibility. Some agencies cannot exercise the option to follow up because of limited resources or inability to track their inactive clients. For some agencies, especially those with a single service focus, such as transportation, the services rendered may not lend themselves to the type of involvement which makes follow-up valuable.

Agencies generally follow three guidelines in cases where they decide there is merit in follow-up activities. First, they limit follow-up activities to a reasonable time period. Second, they carry out services which increase the independence of clients and decrease dependence. Third, they respect their clients' right to be left alone when the clients choose not to continue their association.

Discontinuing services is not always easy for clients or staff members. Agencies often have a tendency to hold clients too long. This is particularly true of individual service providers in social service agencies. The reasons may vary from their lack of knowledge about how and when to effect a termination of services to an unwillingness to seek closure because of the satisfaction derived from serving certain clients. Sometimes the power-dependency relationship is the attraction, while at other times staff members may wish to keep their caseloads filled with old, familiar faces rather than to work with new and uncertain problems.

A termination procedure that keeps clients from feeling abandoned and works on their behalf requires several explicit and implicit ingredients:

1. The client, and family if appropriate, and staff member agree that the discontinuation of services is in the client's best interest.
2. The amount of time devoted to closure, a feeling of satisfaction at the ending of the relationship, is adequate.
3. The staff member is aware of the conditions in which the client will function and is confident that the client can manage.
4. The client is aware of how services can be reinitiated should the need arise and what follow-up activities can be anticipated.
5. Records are kept accessible for use at a later time.

SERVICE INTAKE RECORD
(CONFIDENTIAL)

Date _____

Name   _____

Address _____ City _____ Zip _____

Social Security _____-_____-_____   Telephone _____

Male _____   Female _____   0–18 _____   19–64 _____

CLIENT STATUS: New client _____   Former client _____

TYPE OF CONTACT: Office _____   Telephone _____   Residence _____

ETHNIC
CLASSIFICATION: Asian/Pacific _____   Black _____   Caucasian _____
                 Latino _____   Native American _____   Other _____

MARITAL STATUS: Single _____   Married _____   Widowed _____
                 Divorced/Separated _____

FINANCIAL STATUS: Below poverty level _____   Above poverty level _____

EMPLOYMENT: Full time _____   Part time _____
              Unemployed _____   Retired _____

RESIDING: Alone _____   With spouse _____   With family/relatives _____
            With friends _____

RESIDENCE: House _____   Apartment _____   Hotel _____
             Nursing home _____   Residential care home _____
             Other _____   Specify:

SERVICES REQUESTED BY CLIENT   COMMENTS:

_____

_____

_____

Client's signature _____   Intake signature _____

OPEN-ENDED INTAKE/ASSESSMENT FORM
(CONFIDENTIAL)

Name _____ Date _____

Age _____

Marital status _____

Sex _____

Race/nationality/ethnicity _____

1. How are things going for you?

2. (a) Do you live alone or with others?

    If living with another person, is this a satisfactory arrangement?

    (b) Do you rent or own your home?

    Is this a satisfactory arrangement and is the cost reasonable? If not satisfied, how would things have to be different to feel comfortable? (If appropriate, discuss community resources that may be of help.)

3. Are you presently working?

    If Yes, is the work part- or full-time? Are you happy with your current employment? (If appropriate, discuss community resources that deal with job training and placement.) If No, would you be interested in being employed? If Yes, what type of employment? Part- or full-time? (If appropriate, discuss community resources which deal with vocational planning.)

4. How do you usually spend your day?

    Would you like to have more to do and would you like to have more contact with other people? (If appropriate, discuss community resources that deal with leisure time, etc.)

5. What kind of transportation do you usually use?

    Are you happy with your transportation situation? If No, what type of help could you use?

6. Is your income enough to meet your regular needs?

    If No, what are your sources of income? Do you have any supplements to your income, such as food stamps, living in public housing, etc.? (If appropriate, discuss eligibility for an income source such as Public Assistance, Social Security, Veterans Benefits, etc.)

OPEN-ENDED INTAKE/ASSESSMENT FORM (continued)

7. How is your health?

    When was the last time you saw a doctor? (If appropriate, discuss how to obtain help in receiving and paying for health services.)

8. Is there anything we haven't talked about which is a personal problem for you?

9. Do you have any relatives or friends you are concerned about?

AGING INFORMATION & REFERRAL FORM

A.

| mo | date | year | day | 1-su 4-w 6-f / 2-m 5-th 7-sa / 3-tu | time | 1-am 2-pm | social security number |

INTERVIEWER _____

initial contact by: 1-phone 3-walk-in 5-other / 2-mail 4-outreach / specify

B. IS CALLER SAME AS CLIENT? 1-yes 2-no   IF NOT, FILL IN CLIENT & CALLER SPACES.

CLIENT
last name / first / m i / facility/organization / branch

address number / nsew / street name / st,bl,etc. / apt. no. / ltr.

city/community / zip code / dist. / client phone / sex 1-m 2-f / client 1-individual 2-agency

CALLER
last name / first / m i / facility/organization / branch

address / city / zip code / caller phone / relationship to client

C. INCOME 1-social security 2-ssi 3-both 4-other _____ specify

MEDICAL 1-medicare 2-medicaid 3-both 4-other _____ specify

AGE 1-under 60 2-60 to 75 3-over 75

LIVING ARRANGEMENT 1-alone 2-w/family 3-w/unrelated persons 4-other _____ specify

ETHNIC BACKGROUND 1-black 2-white 3-native american 4-latino 5-asian _____ specify 6-other _____ specify

HEARD OF I&R SERVICE THROUGH 1-radio 2-tv 3-newspaper 4-flyer 5-friend/family 6-agency/facility 7-club/organization 8-nutrition program 9-other _____ specify

D. 1- YES   2- NO

HAS CLIENT CONTACTED I & R CENTER BEFORE?   POSSIBLE SSI-ALERT

ESCORT NEEDED   RIDE NEEDED   FOLLOW-UP INITIATED   ssi client agency

E. INQUIRIES   SERVICE CATEGORIES

category / sub- / sub-
category / sub- / sub-
category / sub- / sub-

01-animals
02-communications
03-consumer
04-counseling
05-death related
06-education
07-employment
08-financial
09-health
10-homemaker/chore
11-housing
12-legal
13-leisure/recreation
14-mental health
15-nutrition
16-transportation
17-volunteer

FOR SUB-CATEGORIES, REFER TO SERVICE CATEGORY MANUAL.

SERVICES UNAVAILABLE   EXTENT: 1-COMPLETELY 2-PARTIALLY

category / sub- / sub- / extent / category / sub- / sub- / extent

F. ROLE OF I&R SERVICE

1-help caller clarify problem
2-verify what caller already knew
3-give reassurance to caller
4-mediate between caller & facility
5-make a referral
6-give information only
7-call inappropriate for I&R
8-other _____ specify

REFERRAL FORM

This person is being referred to your agency for service. Please complete the attached form and return it to our office in the enclosed stamped self-addressed envelope. Thank you.

Date of referral _____

Person's name _____

Address _____ Phone _____

Reason for referral

Employment _____   Legal _____

Financial _____   Personal/social services _____

Health _____   Transportation _____

Housing _____   Other _____

Home help _____   Other _____

Name of referring person (print) _____

(signature) _____

- -

Send to: COMMUNITY MENTAL HEALTH CENTER
1877 No. Barnes Place, Northvale
555-6789

_____

REFERRAL RESPONSE

Date _____

Person's name _____

Address _____ Phone _____

By the date above, this person had contacted our agency. Yes _____ No _____

This person has been seen or is scheduled by our agency. Yes _____ No _____

Name of respondent (print) _____

(signature) _____

Agency _____

Address _____

Comments:

_____

AGENCY SELF-ASSESSMENT CHECKLIST: FINDING CASES (OUTREACH)

INDICATORS	STATUS			PERSON RESPONSIBLE
	Yes	No	Partial	
1. The agency has an identified strategy for outreach to eligible persons in the target area.	____	____	____	_____
2. Personnel assigned to outreach activities are, as appropriate, bi-lingual and/or sensitive to the cultural beliefs of the target population.	____	____	____	_____
3. Publicity for outreach is written in language suitable to the potential consumers.	____	____	____	_____
4. All service sites are accessible to potential consumers.	____	____	____	_____
5. Outreach staff are provided with training that covers program services, the agency's role, outreach methods, and the target population.	____	____	____	_____
6. The agency has a procedure for routinely surveying its target community to identify places, such as churches or the homes of clients, events, or persons, such as doctors, that can be used for outreach activities.	____	____	____	_____
7. Outreach procedures include casefinding through the other agencies in the target area.	____	____	____	_____
8. The agency routinely seeks volunteers to assist outreach workers.	____	____	____	_____

AGENCY SELF-ASSESSMENT CHECKLIST:
MANAGING CASES

INDICATORS	Yes	No	Partial	PERSON RESPONSIBLE
1. The agency participates in information and referral exchanges with other agencies that serve the target area.	___	___	___	_____
2. Bilingual personnel are available for intake and assessment as appropriate.	___	___	___	_____
3. The agency has an intake procedure, appropriate forms, and adequately trained personnel.	___	___	___	_____
4. The agency has a written procedure for client assessment, appropriate assessment devices, and adequately trained personnel.	___	___	___	_____
5. Client assessment devices are designed with the background of potential clients in mind.	___	___	___	_____
6. The agency has an adequate system for tracking all cases referred to it and all cases referred by it to other agencies.	___	___	___	_____
7. The agency routinely reviews the status of clients to determine when they are ready for discharge.	___	___	___	_____
8. The staff members keep appropriate case histories, including identification of the potential informal support network available to each client.	___	___	___	_____
9. The agency record-keeping system provides adequate available data for reporting.	___	___	___	_____

STATUS

Supporting the Delivery of Services

7

Requirements for supporting the delivery of human services fall into five categories: (1) adequate site or sites, (2) competent staff and volunteers, (3) necessary equipment and supplies, (4) record-keeping system which serves staff members, and (5) a sound fiscal system. These are practical considerations with which agencies wanting to deliver human services effectively and efficiently must concern themselves.

Sites are important to clients if services are to be delivered there. This obvious statement is reiterated here because agencies sometimes ignore it. In their desire to save money on rent or their emphasis on pleasing personnel, agencies often choose sites which are not in the best interests of their clients.

Sites which are intended for the delivery of services to clients should meet a number of conditions. First is consumer convenience. Rental opportunities and finances necessarily play a role in site selection, but it is clear that sites located near potential clients and/or accessible by public transportation are most desirable. Studies of service centers indicate that the closer the potential consumers are to a center the more likely they are to use it. Firsthand knowledge of a center's location is a factor along with ease of getting there. Several sites located throughout the areas with the most potential client population could ordinarily be expected to provide the most convenience.

What is most desired is not always possible, however. Some agencies have insufficient funds to obtain the best site locations or not enough staff to handle all the facilities. In some communities the better locations may be inappropriate. If, as in the case of persons with physical disabilities or elderly persons, walking even moderate distances is difficult, a site on a bus line, although farther away, may be preferable to a closer site that cannot be reached easily. A site for a criminal justice diversion project consisting of recreation and socialization programs for youth gang members had best be on neutral "turf" if all the possible consumers are to use it. The nearest neutral area may be blocks away from the most convenient location.

In some cases one site or location, although inconvenient, may be preferable to another location for programmatic reasons. A project located in a building with other projects to which clients are frequently referred may save its clients time and energy over a project located away from other service agencies.

A second criterion is the physical layout of the facilities. Are there adequate doors and windows to meet fire safety regulations? Are there sufficient and workable toilets? Is there enough space for storage, client and staff activities indoors, and parking outdoors? If interviewing or counseling is part of the program, is space for privacy available? Are there barriers such as flights of stairs, narrow bathroom stalls, or revolving doors which will keep physically disabled and older people from using the facility?

A third criterion, ambience, or general atmosphere, is harder to identify, but equally important. An outside sign that is large enough to read from a distance may not be essential but it does help clients find the project facility more easily. Are the hours and days of service prominently displayed? Are the interior and exterior clean and neat? Are there informative materials available for waiting clients and comfortable places for them to sit? Is smoking allowed and, conversely, will nonsmokers be comfortable? Are drinking water and coffee available? Can clients who bring their children with them find areas where the youngsters can play safely? Is the waiting room furniture moveable so that people can cluster to converse? In other words, is the facility a place which people can get to easily and in which they can feel comfortable?

In addition to the sites that house programs, equal attention should be given to sites which are used for meetings and educational events. For the most part, the criteria stated above also apply to these. Be sensitive to the attitudes and feelings of participants. Some adults are uncomfortable in schoolrooms, others feel awkward in city hall, a court building, or a church. If schools, municipal buildings or religious centers are not suited to a particular group, consider alternative settings, such as recreation centers, fraternal halls, homes, or even meeting rooms in banks and businesses.

Competent, caring staff and volunteers are among the most important factors which make a human service delivery program function effectively. In this section we will discuss a procedure for hiring new staff members, since hiring is a shoal on which many agencies founder.

A constant dilemma in hiring is whether to insist upon a person who has the abilities to fit an available position or alter the job to fit the person whose attitude appears to be good, but who does not have all the needed skills and/or knowledge. Hiring practices which result in effective staff members joining an agency are not always easily adopted by all human service agencies. Sometimes board and staff politics get in the way as board members try to influence the hiring of their favored candidates. At other times the very factor which makes those agencies providing human services so valued—caring—is a barrier to their hiring competent people.

A person who needs the job is not always a person who can do the job. The motive may be noble, but the result is that clients receive less than effective services.

An important consideration in establishing criteria for employees and volunteers is the extent to which age, sex, ethnicity or disability are attributes to be sought after. An agency's ability to relate its services to clients may be enhanced by workers who reflect the demographic characteristics of the target population.

The following process describes a reasonable hiring practice used by many agencies. First, prepare job descriptions and salary schedules. Second, recruit candidates through posted job announcements, advertisements in professional journals, newsletters and newspapers, and by word of mouth. Third, ask initially for resumés and then follow with a form that requests references, specific education and training, and employment data if not provided. Fourth, establish an applicant review committee which has a board member, a client or potential client, and a person who does a similar job for other agencies. In agencies with several projects, a project director or head of a division often participates, as well. Fifth, provide training to this committee. Sixth, based on criteria like those indicated in Figure 7-1, screen the applicants down to those the committee members wish to interview. Seventh, conduct the interviews and select three persons, possibly in rank order, to recommend. Finally, the executive director selects the person to hire from the three who have been recommended.

Figure 7-1

CRITERIA FOR SCREENING JOB APPLICANTS

Criteria	Score	Comments
1. Knowledge of client group and their needs	(15) _____	
2. Knowledge of community and resources	(15) _____	
3. Formal training/education	(15) _____	
4. Relevant experience and competence	(25) _____	
5. Ability to communicate orally and in writing	(10) _____	
6. Attitude	(10) _____	
7. Other specify:_____	(10) _____	
TOTAL:	(100) _____	

Equipment and supplies, mundane as they may seem, are nonetheless an important part of almost any program. One shortcoming of many fund requests is the underestimation of the need, and cost, for supplies and equipment, resulting in inadequacies during the life of the projects. Program implementation usually involves two categories of equipment and supplies—those that support the staffs and operations of the agencies and those needed by or for the clients.

A number of agencies, by virtue of their funding sources, qualify for federal government surplus property. Any agency can apply to the regional office of the General Services Administration (GSA) for this purpose. Eligible agencies will receive GSA credit cards allowing purchases of equipment and supplies at considerable discounts.

Most agencies find ways to beg and borrow equipment. Retailers, manufacturers, corporations, and private individuals should be approached for donations of used or new desks, chairs, and other furniture. Purchases may be coordinated with other agencies in order to buy at wholesale prices.

Whatever approach is used, including routine purchases, mark the equipment with a recognizable identification number and keep an inventory list. For equipment purchased with grant funds, the funding source will wish to check the list during an audit to determine that all items are accounted for. When inventoried items are lost or stolen, report the items to the police and keep a copy of the report. Once a project ends, depending on the rules of the funding source, purchased equipment may have to be returned to it or to another agency of its choosing.

For a project which will last only a short while, some agencies prefer to rent the necessary equipment or obtain it on a lease/buy option. This latter approach will enable an agency, assuming the funding source has previously agreed to the procedure, to pick up the option and, by paying the remaining costs, take possession of the items.

Supplies can sometimes be obtained from other enterprises in the community. One agency arranged to have a large insurance company headquarters nearby do most of its photocopying. Another agency negotiated with a department store for old file folders which could be inverted and used satisfactorily for case records. An agency serving the elderly petitioned a bank in which many older persons kept their savings and received funds for enough recreation supplies to keep its center's activities operating for a year. The extent to which such savings in supply costs can be made through donations is usually limited only by the staff members' time to pursue it and their imagination.

A record-keeping system that serves staff members' needs for information will partially overlap the type of management and results information described in Chapter 9. Often, service providers have data needs that go beyond those required by the agency or funding source. There is little danger that staff members will attempt to record and store too much data, as record-keeping seems to be a chore to most service providers. Indeed, the danger is that information which may be needed will not be recorded, stored, or used even if available.

The largest category of data required by staff members and nobody else is that which relates to their daily contact with clients. They usually collect this information in narrative, rather than numerical, form. An example is social workers' progress notes which describe their impressions, judgments, and decisions on actions about each of their clients. Despite the antipathy to recording evidence by many service providers, these and other similar notes are important. Should a staff member resign or be temporarily unavailable, another person can, by using these progress notes, pick up the relationship with a client without going through the entire information-gathering process again. In the event of lawsuits or other legal proceedings, these notes are valuable evidence. Also, since few people have perfect memories, the notes are useful reminders of past and planned actions to the social workers themselves.

Experience suggests that regardless of any particular procedures or policies, not all staff members will be equally diligent in recording their activities and those of their clients. Four requirements by the agency will make record-keeping satisfactory to a reasonable degree. First, there should be a clear policy of insistence that adequate records be kept. Adequacy of record-keeping should be one criterion for performance appraisal. Second, a standardized format for recording should be provided. If everyone collects the same data and records them in the same way, supervisors are better able to judge them. Third, training should be provided when staff members are hired and during their tenure in the job. And fourth, each service provider's records should be sampled periodically to demonstrate the serious intent of management in this area and to aid staff members in their performance of this important task through corrections and refinements of their work.

Agencies vary considerably in the amount and nature of the records they require their staff members to keep. Some require more data than anyone can reasonably be expected to use, while others literally keep no records at all. The nature of an agency's services, its staff resources, and the demands made upon it determine what is a reasonable amount of record-keeping. One of the most productive ways to accomplish this is by examining all the categories of information collected and decide item by item which are needed, which are nice to have but not necessary, and which are superfluous. Data not used should not be gathered. A written policy stating who will be responsible for collecting, storing, and retrieving which items of information should be developed in all agencies. Finally, the question must be answered about when each item will be gathered and recorded. Following these steps will provide a workable system of record-keeping that any agency can manage.

The data used by service providers are not the only information needed. The information gathered from intake forms, assessment instruments, outside reports, and so forth, along with the information described above will give a full record of each client. The formats for recording this information combine with an agency's need to report data to external sources as well. A systematic and efficient system which staff members will accept and use is possible. Figure 7-2 illustrates how all the data can be combined to make one system.

Figure 7-2

SAMPLE AGENCY RECORD-KEEPING SYSTEM

Type of data item	Collected by:	Stored in:	Available for:
1. Client intake form	Eligibility Worker	Master & client file	Quarterly report
2. Assessment instrument	Case Worker	Client file	Case management
3. Counseling session report	Counselor	Activity file	Monthly report
4.			
5.			

A sound fiscal system which works in support of staff members and not as a barrier to their efforts is a valuable asset to any agency engaged in the delivery of human services. Any person who works for, or with, a service agency will come into contact with the financial aspects of its projects. Although everybody does not have to be an accountant, each person should know enough to ensure that funds are spent efficiently and effectively.

Agencies have *income* from five sources: clients' fees, donations and endowments, grants, contracts, and third party reimbursements. Income is allocated for various *expenditure* categories, allocations typically being made for personnel and fringe benefits, space, supplies and equipment, travel, consultants, and such other costs as are necessary to sustain each agency and enable it to carry out the tasks necessary to the accomplishment of its objectives. This allocation of funds to categories of expenditures is called a "budget." Portions of the monies allocated in the budget to one category of expenditures can be transferred to another should that become advisable, as long as the rules of the funding source are followed or special permission is received in writing.*

The responsibility for approving a budget, including all the specific line items and dollar allocations to those line items, is the responsibility of an agency's board of directors. The executive director of an agency is responsible for seeing that the budget is adhered to or that modifications get the necessary approvals *before* they are made. The financial officer, accountant, bookkeeper, or whoever is given the task of keeping the books (the financial record) is responsible for seeing that all money due an agency is received and properly recorded, that all expenses are paid correctly and promptly, and that an adequate record of both income and expenditures is kept.

The exact recording of all financial transactions is imperative since an agency's financial records are frequently subject to scrutiny by a variety of government

---

*Many funding sources allow a 10 percent variance among categories. Some allow any amount of changes among categories as long as they do not exceed 10 percent of the total budget. Most funding sources require specific authorization for equipment category modifications. None allow more money to be spent than has been authorized.

auditors as well as by many other funding sources. Each transaction is part of an "audit trail," an examination of documents and calculations surrounding each financial action. Many an agency has lost its funding, been denied opportunities for new financial support or been required to make restitution of funds because of the poor quality of its fiscal system.

The board members of an agency have the role of ensuring that the fiscal system at least meets the standards of the funding source, the IRS, and any other agencies with whom they must deal. They must see to it that fiscal controls are adequate to ensure that funds are being properly expended. Staff members also play a part by containing costs in those areas where their activities result in the expenditure of money, such as phone calling, use of supplies, and travel. The final burden for control of the financial resources, however, usually falls on the executive director of an agency.

Based on the budget allocations of funds and the expenditures at any given point, the executive director has to determine if the rate of expenditures in any category should be increased, decreased, or held constant. A wise director prepares, or has the person in charge of finances prepare, a periodic summary of expenditures. Some directors do a review monthly, others quarterly. In larger organizations with many programs there may even be weekly reviews. Figure 7-3 shows a useful expenditure report format. Reports such as these often form the basis for financial reports to funding sources and boards of directors.

Column 1 is the actual amount of the funds expended in each category during the most recently completed month. Column 2 is the amount of funds which were incurred in addition, but not yet paid for—that is, unpaid bills. Column 3 is the total of columns 1 and 2, the amount of money spent or committed to be spent during that month. Column 4 is the total of all the column 1's for the months since expenditures on this budget began—that is, the actual amount of the funds expended in each category since the beginning. Column 5 is the total of all the column 2's since the beginning and column 6 is the total of all the column 3's since the beginning. The final figure in the TOTALS line under column 6 is all the money spent or obligated to be spent since the expenditures on this budget were begun.

Column 7 is the budget—that is, the amount available to be spent during the life of the project. Column 8 (which is column 7, the total budget, minus column 6, the amount of the funds already spent or obligated) equals the amount of money still left to be spent.

If the executive director sees, as in Figure 7-3, that at the end of the sixth month of a twelve-month project 75 percent of the funds for travel (local mileage) have been expended, he or she might reason that the monthly rate of expenditure is too high and must be cut back, or that there was an unusually high expenditure during the period because of a special circumstance that will not be repeated and no modifications need be made, or that the monthly rate of expenditure is high but necessary, and funds must be transferred from some other category to make up for the anticipated deficit. Since most, if not all, equipment is ordinarily purchased at the beginning of a project, the lack of available equipment funds is understandable.

MONTHLY SUMMARY OF EXPENDITURES

CHART OF ACCOUNTS	COST CATEGORY	EXPENDITURES January 1 to June 30						CONTRACT BUDGET	BUDGET AVAILABLE
		Last Month			To Date				
		Actual 1	Unpaid Obligations 2	Total 3	Actual 4	Unpaid Obligations 5	Total 6	7	8
100	Personnel	9,500	500	10,000	52,000	1,000	58,000	120,000	62,000
200	Building Space (rent)	1,000	-0-	1,000	6,000	-0-	6,000	12,000	6,000
300	Travel	1,400	600	2,000	7,450	1,550	9,000	12,000	3,000
400	Consumable Supplies	250	-0-	250	1,100	400	1,500	3,000	1,500
500	Communication & Utilities	200	50	250	1,600	200	1,800	3,000	1,200
603	Equipment	-0-	400	400	1,650	400	1,950	1,950	-0-
710	Liability Insurance	-0-	-0-	-0-	965	-0-	965	1,000	35
900	Other Costs	400		400	1,600	400	2,000	8,000	6,000
	TOTALS	12,750	1,550	14,300	72,265	3,950	86,215	160,950	79,735

Figure 7-3

Exercising this degree of budget monitoring regularly keeps income and expenditures in balance.

Other aspects of sound fiscal policy relate to risk managment, a technical name for insurance, and daily expenditure control. Needless to say, operating without all required types of insurance, including fire, theft, liability, worker compensation, and others which are relevant, is foolish. Likewise, the levels of coverage must be kept high enough to minimize the risk to agency funds.

Expenditure control on a daily basis includes those procedures and forms which enable the financial personnel to keep track of how much is being spent and for what line items. Included might be such forms as travel authorizations and petty cash vouchers. The latter are frequently used for things bought by staff members that are under a certain dollar amount, perhaps five or ten dollars. Some agencies require specific signatures to authorize any purchase, others permit small expenses to be incurred by identified staff members. The prime requisite is that the policy and procedures be clearly written out and that all staff and board members know them.

Human service agencies also use several other budgeting formats. A *functional budget* in accordance with the *Standards of Accounting and Financial Reporting for Voluntary Health and Welfare Organizations* is one that requires expenditures to be presented in three functional categories: management, fund raising, and program. *Program budgets* show expenditures by activities or service categories, reflecting the fields of service in which an agency is engaged. *Performance budgets* distinguish measurable program outcomes, or costs for units of service, within service categories.

Almost all human service agencies use an *incremental budgeting* process which presupposes a basic budget that is increased or decreased line item by line item each year. Contrasted to the gradual approach is the *zero-based budgeting* process, which, in theory at least, requires an agency to justify the inclusion of each line item each year.

Fiscal systems can be complex and technical when requirements of the funding source demand stringent accountability. In such cases agencies should seek the assistance of a trained accountant to establish effective systems. Below are the basic steps, or procedures, which development of a proper system requires.

1. Determine who will authorize budgets and approve fiscal policies.
2. Establish the process by which budets and policies will be developed.
3. Determine who will direct the expenditure of funds, maintain records, and develop and supervise procedures.
4. Develop policies on sources of income, including procedures for applying for and accepting grants and contracts.
5. Establish the procedure by which budget changes will be recommended and approved.
6. Develop a system for financial record-keeping and the authorization and payment of expenditures.
7. Establish adequate insurance coverage to meet legal requirements and preserve the agency's assets.

8. Develop *written* procedures and staff training for financial operations, including such activities as issuing petty cash, bonding for those handling funds, and authorizing travel.

9. Organize a system for inventorying and maintaining equipment and supplies.

10. Establish the procedures by which these activities will be monitored, how often and what kind of summary reports will be prepared, and how often audits will be conducted.

SAMPLE EMPLOYEE PERFORMANCE EVALUATION REPORT

Last Name	First Name	Initial	Social Security #	
Classification		Department		

Outstanding: Performance definitely superior.
Above Average: Performance well above required job standards
Average: Performance satisfies required job standards
Improvement Needed: Performance below required job standards.
Unacceptable: Performance is such that employee is considered a liability.

RATING: Outstanding
Above Average
Average
Improvement Needed
Unacceptable

Comments: Describe strengths or weaknesses.
Give examples of both good and bad accomplishments
Explain reasons for ratings. (Use attachments if necessary)

Job Knowledge
Has strong knowledge of job, keeps abreast of developments in job field, growth in job, understands operational procedures.

Quality of Work
Accuracy, completeness, thoroughness, neatness, in keeping with job standards.

Quantity of Work
Volume and speed, keeps up with work assignments in a normal work day.

Dependability
Meets deadlines without close supervision, accepts responsibility, attendance.

Attitude
Accepts supervision, conforms to established policies and procedures.

Cooperation
Works well with others.

Accepts responsibilities for and makes conscientious efforts to comply with equal opportunity policy and affirmative action program requirements.

continue for
Supervisory Personnel

Supervisory Ability
Effective in planning, organizing and controlling work activities, motivating and developing subordinates, improving work methods and making decisions, fairness, impartiality, leadership.

Overall performance evaluation (in comparison with other employees with same length of service on this job and with your standard of what is required of the employees).
Unacceptable ☐   Improvement Needed ☐   Average ☐   Above Average ☐   Outstanding ☐

Evaluation prepared and discussed with employee by:

Signature (Rater)   Title   Date

Employee's Acknowledgement: This evaluation has been discussed with me. Comments: (Use attachments if necessary; if no comments, enter "none".)

Signature (Employee)   Date

Signature (Reviewing Officer)   Title   Date

AGENCY SELF-ASSESSMENT CHECKLIST: PERSONNEL SYSTEMS

INDICATORS	STATUS			PERSON RESPONSIBLE
	Yes	No	Partial	
1. The agency has written personnel policies.	____	____	____	_____
2. The procedures for personnel promotion, compensation, and disciplining action are in use.	____	____	____	_____
3. The agency procedures for recruiting, selecting, and supporting staff members are in regular use.	____	____	____	_____
4. The personnel recruitment and selection system uses criteria to identify potentials for conflict of interest.	____	____	____	_____
5. Documentation shows that all persons employed by the agency devote the percentage of time for which the personnel budget account is charged.	____	____	____	_____
6. Work effort forms are filed weekly or monthly and maintained for regular reporting.	____	____	____	_____
7. Positions are routinely filled as described in a staffing plan and timetable approved by the agency's board of directors.	____	____	____	_____
8. Written job descriptions exist and are updated annually.	____	____	____	_____
9. Qualifications stated in job descriptions include only those skills or prior education necessary for performance of the duties indicated.	____	____	____	_____
10. A recruitment program informs the target community and larger community about agency personnel requirements, job availability, qualifications, and, as appropriate, examinations.	____	____	____	_____
11. Agency procedures and practice are based on the Civil				

AGENCY SELF-ASSESSMENT CHECKLIST:
PERSONNEL SYSTEMS
(continued)

Rights Act, as amended on the
Rehabilitation Act, as amended
and assure nondiscrimination
in recruitment, employment,
and promotion.   ___   ___   ___   _____

12. The agency assesses an
    employee's performance in
    writing at least annually.   ___   ___   ___   _____

AGENCY SELF-ASSESSMENT CHECKLIST:
CONTROLLING EQUIPMENT, SUPPLIES, AND FUNDS

INDICATORS	STATUS			PERSON RESPONSIBLE
	Yes	No	Partial	
1. The agency has written procedures governing the management and operations of grants and contracts which are in keeping with laws and regulations.	____	____	____	_____
2. The agency has up-to-date documentation to support its nonfederal cost-sharing contributions.	____	____	____	_____
3. The agency has procedures to assure complete financial records of all activities undertaken with grant or contract funds.	____	____	____	_____
4. The agency's internal fiscal accounting system assures separate accounting for each grant or contract administered by the agency.	____	____	____	_____
5. No illegal commingling of funds is permitted.	____	____	____	_____
6. Records are maintained for all line item expenditures in the budgets of each grant or contract.	____	____	____	_____
7. All financial transactions are approved by an authorized person.	____	____	____	_____
8. All receipts of funds are recorded and deposited in the bank promptly.	____	____	____	_____
9. The agency has a procedure for ensuring the proper disbursement of funds and ensuring the integrity of all bank accounts.	____	____	____	_____
10. The agency's accounting system provides for consistent identification of direct and indirect costs, and is reviewed at regular intervals.	____	____	____	_____

AGENCY SELF-ASSESSMENT CHECKLIST:
CONTROLLING EQUIPMENT, SUPPLIES, AND FUNDS
(continued)

11. The accounting system provides information for completion of all financial status reports required by funding sources, and reports are prepared in a timely manner.   ____   ____   ____   _____

12. Written procedures regarding the purchase of equipment and supplies exist.   ____   ____   ____   _____

13. Records are maintained of all existing property and are inventoried periodically.   ____   ____   ____   _____

14. All property is insured against casualty loss, and the agency against liability.   ____   ____   ____   _____

15. The agency employs competent outside auditors to perform financial audits on a regular basis.   ____   ____   ____   _____

16. Fiscal records are maintained in a form suitable for audits by funding sources.   ____   ____   ____   _____

Boards of Directors and Advisory Councils

8

Governing boards and advisory councils are among the most frequently mis-used forms of consumer and citizen involvement in agencies providing human services. Some boards and advisory councils exist for no other reason than compliance with government regulation. Far better reasons exist, however, and will be explored throughout this chapter. An effective board of directors and often advisory councils are needed for the successful operation of human service agencies.

Roles of boards of directors and advisory councils must be clearly defined for these groups to be effective. Agencies, in general, are made up of two categories of people who have entirely different functions. One group is responsible for deciding policies, for governing, and the other (usually a far larger number) is responsible for operating programs based on those policies. In virtually all private, nonprofit human service agencies the making of policy rests with the board of directors. In most government agencies, such as a county health department or a city community development department, the policy-making role is the responsibility of appointed or elected officials, such as the county health commission or city council. In these instances the relationship between policy-makers and those who carry out policy (the staff members of the organization) may be somewhat different than for private agencies. However, many of the problems are the same.

Policy-making boards of private, nonprofit agencies have different titles. Sometimes they are known as the board of directors, sometimes as the board of trustees, and sometimes as the governing board. The title is not important, but their role is. They are the legally constituted body in which final responsibility for the agency's funds and services resides. The primary job of such a board is to make choices about the direction their agency is to take. In other words, they establish goals and decide where to spend the human, financial, and material resources of the agency. Once they make the decisions and create the rules by which the agency will operate, the staff will implement the policies, carrying out the board's directives.

An advisory council, on the other hand, has no legal corporate authority and generally is associated with programs or projects. Their advice can be tantamount to a directive or ignored. They can be a link between community and staff members or a barrier. They can provide support or pressure. The degree to which any advisory council controls what a program or project does is based on the abilities of that committee's members, the traditions within the agency, the behavior of staff members, and/or program regulations. The role of an advisory council tends to be programmatic and not organizational.

The board and advisory council ordinarily meet monthly to review progress toward achieving the goals they have set forth, determine new policies, decide on fiscal and programmatic courses of action, and make major decisions about organizational structure and personnel. Both board and advisory council members have as their first duty making their agencies accountable and responsive to the client communities. A board or advisory council can move toward this objective, in part, by recruiting consumers of the services to become members of the board or council, by fully orienting new members to the board's or council's roles and to the agency's mission, and by ensuring that all board and council members have adequate information from a variety of sources. Although initially this role may be performed by staff members, once the board of directors or advisory council is established, two of these tasks — recruitment and member orientation — tend to be taken over by the board or council themselves.

Every board of directors has responsibilities appropriate to its agency, but generally the responsibilities involve the following:

1. Review agency budget and approve fiscal procedures.
2. Determine agency policies, goals, and plans.
3. Review and approve reports of the staff and board committees.
4. Identify funding sources and raise money.
5. Publicize agency activities.
6. Review and revise (as needed) board bylaws.
7. Hire (and dismiss) the agency's executive director.
8. Obtain and assess information from persons in the community about needs for services.
9. Evaluate and assess agency services.

In the case of an advisory council fewer roles are involved and the corresponding responsibilities and authority are less broad, though the contribution is no less significant. The council's role includes the following:

1. Recommend policies and practices to the board of directors and the project or executive director.
2. Evaluate agency services and recommend improvements.
3. Assist in determining the needs of consumers.
4. Publicize agency activities.

Every board of directors faces a major task in the management of personnel, the employees who are hired by an agency to carry out its work. The board is concerned, naturally, with personnel, since effective services depend heavily on having a staff which functions well. However, board members must limit themselves to matters related to personnel policies; they do not become involved in daily personnel decisions. That is the job of the executive director. Ordinarily they do not become involved in hiring either, except for the executive director or, sometimes, project directors.

Board members must be aware of two major difficulties. The first is patronage. Some members of a board find that they have old friends who want help in getting a job. All that these friends want the board members to do is "to put in a good word" for them. These are not harmless requests, however, and may affect the integrity of the board as well as staff morale. Should a board member "pull strings" to get a friend a job, the friend may turn out to be a poor worker, embarrassing the entire board and hindering its effectiveness.

Sometimes board members try to obtain jobs in agencies for themselves. Certainly these members should be asked to resign from the board before being considered for the positions. This will remove any possibility of conflicts of interest.

A second danger is that of becoming involved in personnel administration. A board's involvement in personnel management should be at the policy level only. A board sets policy, but the executive director manages the staff. As an individual, no board member has the authority to instruct the executive director to take any action. Board members, therefore, should never give orders to staff members or attempt to publicly evaluate a staff member's performance. Instead, any difficulties that are observed should be reported to the executive director.

The proper role of a board of directors is to ensure that personnel policies and practices are relevant to the needs of the agency and clients, sound fiscally and programmatically, and that they comply with funding source requirements. Here is a summary of the personnel matters the board should be involved in:

Personnel policies. Boards must approve agency personnel policies and see that they are published and given out to board members, job applicants, and employees.

Recruiting. Board members can help the staff in recruiting applicants for jobs in the agency. They can suggest places to post announcements in the target communities, get referrals from public and private agencies, and use their own resources, such as people they know in other organizations.

Selection. Selection of staff can create problems unless a board sets very clear policies. The executive director is responsible for the selection of staff, but the board has to decide how much authority the director will have in this matter.

Training and career development. Many human service agency board members take a special interest in the career development of staff members, particularly paraprofessional aides. The executive director is primarily responsible for judging the training needs of the staff, but board members can assist. A board of directors can be particularly helpful if the members use their prestige and personal contacts to enlist the help of educational institutions and other community resources in providing training.

Civil rights. The board members are responsible for making sure that the agency complies with civil rights legislation. Even more important, they set up and are responsible for overseeing the implementation of an affirmative action plan for their agency.

Job classification, salaries, and employee benefits. The board always approves, and sometimes participates in designing, the agency's position classifications and pay scales which outline how much salary will be paid to employees for doing different kinds of work. The board also approves all policies related to pay plans, including such fringe benefits as vacation, sick leave, and health insurance. Board members should not become involved in questions concerning an individual's job classification, salary, or benefits, however, unless they are brought to the board formally through the grievance procedure.

Employee-management relations. The board of directors should set up procedures to encourage good employee-management relations and provide grievance procedures for solving any problem which may arise. The personnel committee of the board may become involved in cases in which employees appeal a suspension or firing, or some other personnel action which they feel is unfair. Board members should not become involved in disagreements between an executive director and a staff member until there is a request for a hearing. If board members start taking sides in a staff dispute, they can create serious problems for everyone.

While the relationship between the board of directors, advisory council, and staff members is important in all agency functions, the effective coordination of efforts becomes particularly crucial during planning and budgeting periods. These times require a large amount of work and cooperation. Success often depends on board, advisory council, and staff members not only doing their own work but also working closely with each other. The board of directors has the responsibility to become involved in the ongoing decisions that are being made in each step of the planning process; determining the mission and goals of their agency, the needs of their agency's constituents, programs that can best meet the identified needs, and the resources which should be made available. Because board and advisory council members volunteer their services, they usually do not have time to be involved in gathering all the information needed. The staff members therefore bear the responsibility for providing the board and advisory council members with the ideas and information they need to make decisions.

The outline which follows is intended to distinguish responsibilities of the board of directors, advisory council, and staff members in the planning and budgeting process. It does not cover all the decisions and actions they will engage in, but is intended, rather, to highlight the type of involvement the board and advisory council members can have as compared with the staff members.

IDENTIFY NEEDS

Board and Advisory Council Members

Review the community's problems and resources, including services.

Review studies which relate to the needs of the target community.

Review list of needs prepared by staff.

Board Members Only

Direct staff to organize meetings of target area groups at which board members will be present to discuss needs.

Staff Members

Provide a list of problems and current solutions, including institutional, political, technical, legal, and administrative.

Conduct studies of needs and present analyses, findings, and recommendations to the board.

Hold hearings or meetings to obtain community input.

Evaluate current efforts with data from program participants as well as from professionals working in the programs.

ESTABLISH GOALS AND OBJECTIVES

Board and Advisory Council Members

Define goals or redefine existing goals relating agency mission and funding considerations.

Explore how objectives, if accomplished, will affect needs of clients.

Agree on objectives and inform staff and consumers of them.

Staff Members

Review legislative and funding requirements as needed.

Provide interpretations as requested.

Provide information as requested.

Develop detailed objectives, taking into consideration decisions of the board members.

Prepare appropriate publicity releases and presentation materials for use of board members in talking with other groups.

REVIEW RESOURCES

Board and Advisory Council Members

Determine what resources are available and which (finances, personnel, facilities, equipment, materials) are needed to achieve the objectives.

Staff Members

Explore new funding sources, changes in guidelines of existing funding sources, volunteer potential, and other resource mobilization possibilities.

Determine which resources could be put to greater use or redirected to more adequately serve the target community.

Prepare appropriate material which states agency resource needs and proposals for meeting them.

DEVELOP PROGRAM ALTERNATIVES

Board and Advisory Council Members

Review and analyze preliminary plans, taking into consideration agency goals, current program operations, and available resources for one-, three-, and five-year periods. Such plans should be comprehensive enough to include relevant services, coordination relationships, and budget estimates.

Staff Members

Prepare plans and budget estimates as requested, consulting with other agencies or groups involved and with consumers.

Develop alternative approaches, activities, and resources, relating each approach to the objectives and resources available for meeting it.

Develop strategies for reaching the unserved and underserved.

CHOOSE PROJECTS FOR IMPLEMENTATION

Board and Advisory Council Members

Request staff to develop projects based on the alternatives chosen by the board.

Provide mechanism for review of projects by the target group for whom each program is intended.

Request changes in projects based on feedback from these groups and on board's own consideration of such items as budget and staffing.

Board Members Only

Vote to implement projects and adopt budget.

Staff Members

Prepare proposal documents, budget documents, and other materials.

Ensure that review by all groups is carried out, making appropiate changes.

Implement projects.

The size of a board of directors and advisory council is an important variable which affects their ability to effectively and efficiently carry out their functions. The size of any board often depends upon an agency's mission. In a health systems agency that serves half a million people, a five-person board cannot provide representative membership to the dozens of health care provider groups and the thousands of health care consumers. However, a thirty-person board is probably the maximum number for an active, workable group, regardless of other considerations. Probably nine to twenty-one members is optimum in most situations for a working board of directors. All the members can become involved and the size of the group will permit individuals to know one another. This size range generally provides an ample number of positions for the divergent interests among constituents, but is not unwieldy for making decisions.

Advisory councils need not make efficiency as important a criterion in considerations of size. With a membership between seven and fifteen persons, the advisory council will find it easy to function. However, where many representatives of constituent entities — such as nationality groups, geographic areas, clubs, or type of disability — are desired, councils with 100 members and more are not unusual. One city with a variety of Central and South American nationality groups as well as a dozen Asian nationality groups decided to form an advisory council for a human service program consisting of 150 members. A small executive committee acted routinely as an official body to take timely action necessary between meetings of the entire group.

One way to spread opportunities for participation, especially of potential consumers of a service, is through the use of special interest advisory councils which identify needs and make those needs known to the board of directors. A large metropolitan area antipoverty agency, to illustrate, established ten neighborhood councils, each with a representative on the board of directors. An advisory council on the handicapped was created in one area by selecting a representative from each of a number of established organizations (deaf, blind, spinal cord injury, etc.) to serve as members. The form and size of membership of such councils are not vital factors in their success as long as there is a clearly established way for the feedback from their members to be recognized and used.

Large boards and advisory councils in agencies generally create smaller work groups in order to achieve an efficient use of their members' time and abilities. These groups, called "standing committees," are permanent, and may even be designated in an organization's bylaws. The following are typical standing committees:

Planning and Policy	Personnel
Budget or Finance	Board Training
Publicity	

Boards and advisory councils also put together temporary, or *ad hoc*, committees to handle special problems. *Ad hoc* committees perform such tasks as fact finding, police-community relations, or bylaw revision. The areas in which these committees work and the length of time they exist depend on the extent of their assigned task.

Because their composition is ordinarily made up of members of the parent body and their focus is the accomplishment of specific tasks, standing and *ad hoc* committees are of smaller size, usually three to seven persons. Their role is to develop concepts and policy positions and to gether data that the board or advisory council will use for its deliberations. The committees meet more frequently than the board or council — as often as needed to accomplish a particular task. In most organizations, the chairperson asks for volunteers and/or appoints members to serve on the *ad hoc* as well as on the standing committees. Agency personnel and outside experts hired specifically for the purpose may act sometimes as resources to standing and *ad hoc* committees.

The proper membership composition of boards and advisory councils can be an important ingredient in the success of an agency. A wag once said that there are three categories of potential board members: those who are rich, those who have rich friends, and those who should not be selected. However, federal legislation often makes this advice impossible to follow. A good example is the Community Services Administration, the poverty program administrative agency which ensures that at least one-third of a poverty program board is composed of low-income persons or their representatives. The federally designated health systems agency in any community must have at least half its board members representing consumers of service rather than providers. Similar requirements are found in program areas such as education and housing. Community politics also militates against boards of directors on which the sole criterion of membership is wealth. Racial, ethnic, and nationality groups, women, the disabled, homosexuals, youth, and the elderly all demand representation on the governing boards and advisory councils of agencies which serve them.

To the extent that people truly "re-present" the opinions and beliefs of the groups of which they are a part, their representation makes for greater effectiveness in programs. Taking into account client constituencies when board and advisory council members are selected makes sense. For example, one advisory council in a county human service program is composed of ninety members. Some are appointed by elected officials, which ensures geographic representation from each district. Some committee members are appointed by the chief administrator, which ensures policy support. The remainder are selected by the other members of the council, with an equitable balance of age, sex, income, ethnicity and race, and consumer representation given the highest priorities for selection. This helps to ensure broad community support.

Board and advisory council members who are dedicated to the ideals of the agency, who represent a significant segment of the community, who are knowledgeable about service delivery methods, and who have the time and interest to serve as well as meeting the criteria for selection, such as age or income, are not easy to find. At times only extensive recruiting efforts will result in finding persons who meet the criteria and who will accept the responsibility.

Issues concerning criteria for selection can be troublesome. For instance, imagine the process for selection of board or advisory council members of a drug treatment project. Suppose that such a project serves PCP users. The decision as to who is or is not an appropriate consumer member of the board can be crucial to the board's functioning. Is it reasonable to expect persons who may literally be under the influence of drugs to work coherently and rationally with others in board decisions? On the other hand, are nonusers or ex-users good judges of services when they are not currently and may never have been a consumer of the agency's services?

Another disagreement is on the issue of how many consumers of services should be involved. Many a community-based organization operates on the basis of having at least 51 percent consumer representation on its board of directors. The intent is to make certain, insofar as possible, that a board is representative of the agency's potential client population. However, in the case of the drug abuse treatment program cited above, can a board of 51 percent active drug consumers be expected to effectively provide services designed to end the abuse of drugs? Should all the members of the board of an agency with a program designed to serve the elderly be older persons? How old is old? Social Security recipients are generally 62 or 65 and over, but persons 60 plus are eligible for services under programs funded with Older Americans Act dollars. An older worker in employment programs can be someone over age 45. These issues are but a few of the representation problems which arise in the selection of board and advisory council members.

There are no universal criteria or methods for board and advisory council member recruitment. Choices vary with agency history, mission, and funding source requirements. Generally, there are six methods for selecting policy board and advisory council members, as follows:

1. Selection of residents in the agency catchment area to represent the potential consumers.
2. Nomination by community organizations and voluntary associations to represent them.
3. Nomination by professional associations to represent them.
4. Nomination by local units of government to represent elected or appointed officials.
5. Selection by current board members because of group membership, such as ethnicity, age, or physical disability, or because of client status.
6. Election by residents of a community in a competitive election process developed by the agency.

The chief advantage of *selection* is that the process allows an agency to obtain the person whom it wishes to have. The major disadvantage is that there are frequently unwanted political consequences. *Nomination* is a useful process with groups which have a history of being involved in the delivery of services. They tend to choose people who want to serve and who are capable. *Elections*, on the other hand, are often popularity contests and while their motives for wanting to serve may be noble, candidates may not know much about the workings of a human service agency. Elections do have the advantage of resolving some political problems. However, the process may create ill will on occasion among the forces supporting the losing candidates, thus creating other concerns.

Making boards and advisory councils function effectively is the responsibility of both members and staff persons. Just about everyone connected with a human service agency is responsible for ensuring it has a competent, effective board and advisory council or councils. At least initially that responsibility may rest with the staff members, who have a primary role in orienting and training board and council members in a new project. The role may even be expanded to include advisory council recruitment. The paradox is that the staff members assist the board

and council members in readying themselves for their jobs, yet remain subordinate to them in authority.

Staff members have the potential for creating weak or strong boards or advisory councils. The intent and competence with which staff members provide support can make or break boards' and councils' abilities to cope responsibly with opportunities and problems facing their agencies. In the final analysis board and council members are usually dependent on the staff for information about the services provided, for technical help in interpreting regulations and legislation, for answers to budget questions, and for assistance in accomplishing routine but necessary tasks, such as preparing minutes of meetings and typing correspondence.

Since agency and project directors set the tone for their staff members and usually have the closest relationship to board and advisory council members, the attitude and behavior of directors is a major factor in determining how effectively boards and councils will carry out their responsibilities. Sometimes the relationships among board or council persons are so bad that even an experienced director cannot help them to function effectively. However, it more often happens that an ineffective board can be traced to an ineffective director or to one who does not wish a strong, capable board.

A director or other staff member who does not want a board or council to succeed can frequently sabotage its efforts. Members of boards and councils and volunteers are part-time and, no matter how sophisticated they may be, tend to depend on staff members for information. Volunteers ordinarily cannot devote the time and energy to an agency that staff persons can. By withholding information or providing false data, staff members can create confusion and make effective operation of a board or council difficult. A manipulative director or staff member can also create disharmony and disarray by fostering jealousy and distrust among board and council members.

The board and advisory councils, however, can overcome even the most virulent efforts of staff persons to ruin the members' effective functioning by seeing to it that all of their members are properly oriented to their roles and procedures and the missions of the agency. The board and council must ensure that all members are kept informed, that each person receives information at the same time, that rumors are quickly dispelled, and that cliques and small coalitions of board or council and staff members are not allowed to dominate the agency's activities.

Another reason a board or advisory council may fail to function effectively may be its inability to resolve internal political disputes. Members representing special interest groups or other agencies or who show personal animosities toward particular staff persons or other board or council members can be most troublesome. These members must have their disruptive behavior brought to the attention of the full board or council so that action can be taken to prevent harm to the agency and its programs. The guidelines about conflicts of interest and internal quarrels must be stated clearly and enforced by the full board or advisory council.

In one case, a neighborhood development corporation collapsed despite firm support from an economic development agency because the board of directors of the neighborhood corporation was split among several special interest factions. One faction wanted to aid local small businesses run by black entrepreneurs, another faction felt that new housing for the elderly was the most important need in the community, and the third faction wanted to use the funds to create cooperatives. Board meetings were chaotic. No faction was willing to compromise. After nearly a year of ill-will, the economic development corporation withdrew support and the community agency collapsed leaving many dissatisfied people. Unfortunately, this situation is not unusual.

One successful solution for a similar circumstance was found by a criminal justice agency. The funding agency wanted a community-based organization to operate a juvenile diversion project. The funding agency encouraged neighborhood people to incorporate, and assigned two staff persons with considerable community organization and group process skills to work with the fledgling service agency. The staff worked many hours with the group prior to incorporation. They helped "brainstorm" group member interests and helped in the drafting of bylaws that incorporated the different special interests of the membership. These interests were then developed into program components for the diversion project. For instance, some board members thought that a diversion project should provide employment to its clients. A standing committee on youth employment was created and planning was begun to staff an employment component for the project. Another faction thought that recreation should be an important aspect of a diversion project. Their interest was translated into a board committee and into a program component. This procedure recognized differences among the membership and institutionalized those differences at the policy level as board committees, and at the service delivery level as program components of the project.

One kind of board or advisory council conflict results from a lack of understanding of parliamentary proceedings. Most Caucasian, middle-class homes provide opportunities for learning these procedures through church clubs, Girl Scouts, etc., but not all ethnic groups can, or even wish to, learn how to behave in this way.

Representatives of each Indian tribe in a Southwestern state, for instance, were brought together to form an intertribal "umbrella" board for an organization that was to oversee several federally sponsored off-reservation adult basic education project sites. The representatives were selected by local federal officials, most of whom were themselves Native Americans. The organizing problems of this board were exacerbated by the differences in culture between the consumers and the funding agency. Board members were not familiar with the traditional board/staff division and once they understood it, most rejected the concept. They were uncomfortable with parliamentary procedure. After a few frustrating and stilted attempts to contribute at meetings in which parliamentary procedure was used, they lapsed into silence. A few meetings later they returned to their reservation, in effect resigning from the board. The board rarely met officially because the board members seemingly refused to accept the quorum requirement of the bylaws. Members would come and go without regard to procedural requirements.

From a traditional agency perspective, this behavior is deemed unacceptable.

The federal agency funding the project insisted that the Indian group perform like "any other organization." When they did not, the federal officials sought another organization to oversee the project. The funding agency could have taken two alternative, and perhaps preferable, courses of action. It could have helped the group to modify their bylaws to allow the preferred decision-making style of the members or it could have solicited new members who would be comfortable with the funding agency's way of operating a board of directors.

The most common causes of failure to function effectively as a board are apathy, lack of knowledge, and confusion about roles and functions. Although board members have to know about many different types of services and community needs, few people have the necessary background. Therefore, most members of boards and advisory councils need comprehensive orientation prior to assuming their positions and ongoing training thereafter. Even though agency staff members may have responsibility for providing both orientation and ongoing training for board and council members in some organizations, the board or council needs a standing committee with the responsibility for board member training. This approach keeps the members involved and independent.

The training of board and council members should focus on four areas, with the priorities depending on the sophistication and needs of individual members. These training topics can be listed as follows:

1. Role, including discussions of those areas outside the jurisdiction of members.
2. Agency programs and community needs.
3. Planning and budgeting.
4. Skill development, such as service monitoring techniques and parliamentary procedure.

To facilitate their work between full membership meetings, boards of directors and, to a lesser extent, advisory councils often form executive committees. Typically, executive committees are composed of the board or council officers. The general responsibilities of the executive committee members are as follows:

Chairperson
Prepares each agenda, often with the help of other officers and the agency or project director.
Speaks publicly for the group, signs contracts, and keeps the organization growing and moving toward its goals.
Develops other members so that new leadership is constantly being built.
Leads interesting, orderly meetings by encouraging each new member to talk, and tactfully keeps the group moving forward and making decisions.
Appoints committees to carry out special tasks of the group.
Does not usually take sides in discussions, but serves as moderator.

Vice Chairperson

Conducts meetings and handles the group's business when the chairperson is absent.

Serves as an *ex-officio* member of all standing committees.

Helps plan the agenda.

Secretary

Takes the minutes of each meeting and keeps a permanent record of what has taken place. Some agencies have a staff person take the minutes for review and approval by the Secretary.

Sees that each member learns about the actions of the last meeting by copying the minutes and distributing them in advance or by reading the minutes aloud at each meeting.

Receives and handles letters sent to the board or prepared by the board.

Treasurer

Handles all financial matters for the board including working with the agency's accountants and other fiscal personnel.

Makes regular financial reports to the board.

Is usually a signator on agency checks, loan or mortgage agreements, and other fiscal documents.

Meetings which are well planned and conducted can assist a board and advisory council to function well. Meetings which drift from topic to topic are usually less effective. When meetings are dull or disorganized, members do not attend and since the bylaws of most boards call for a quorum, an agenda that stimulates member interest is quite important. In preparing an agenda the chairperson and the other officers should do the following:

1. Check the report of the last meeting, looking for unfinished business.
2. Include committees which have to make reports on the agenda, making sure the people who are to report will attend the meeting.
3. Review correspondence that has been received since the last meeting, summarizing important letters.
4. See that a financial report is ready for presentation.
5. Check on all the new business which has come up since the last meeting, placing on the agenda everything upon which members must take action.
6. Include plenty of time for new business from the floor and for general discussion at the end.

A chairperson must see that important items are not crowded out of a meeting. An agenda is a guide for timing the action of a meeting and establishing the order in which items will be considered. A chairperson calls for one item at a time and completes the discussion and action on that item before moving to the next item on the agenda. The agenda should not be used as a tool to push people around, however; members must be allowed time to express their ideas and views. By following an agenda, a chairperson helps the members organize their thoughts and decide on the action they want to take. Agencies which are adhered to help keep meetings from going on endlessly, reducing frustration and increasing attendance.

The following is an example of an agenda for a board of directors meeting of a community-based comprehensive health center:

COMPREHENSIVE HEALTH CENTER BOARD AGENDA

Call to order

Minutes

Correspondence

Treasurer's report

Executive Director's report

Committee reports (executive committee, standing committees, *ad hoc* committees)

Old (unfinished) business:
   Arrangements for community health symposium
   Plan to establish advisory councils at each clinic site

New business

Adjournment

Many boards use a parliamentary procedure, such as *Robert's Rules of Order*, but parliamentary procedure is only one way to run a meeting. Because they do not have corporate responsibility as do boards of directors, advisory councils are often less formal. However organized, members have to feel comfortable at meetings. They need the opportunity to share in decisions and to know their ideas are important. The purpose of parliamentary procedure is to give members a chance to listen and speak so they can decide wisely on the many policies and actions needed to make an agency effective.

Another device which can help to make boards and councils function more effectively is the establishment of goals and objectives for committees. Each committee needs to state a broad, encompassing goal that it hopes to achieve on behalf of the persons for whom its services are intended. Long-range (2 to 5 years) and short-range (up to 2 years) objectives should be enumerated. The more specific the short-range objectives are, the better. Finally, action steps should be identified which, when completed successfully, will move the group closer to the accomplishment of its objectives.

GOAL, OBJECTIVES, AND ACTION STEPS
FOR COMMITTEE ON TRANSPORTATION

Goal: An accessible transportation system in all areas of the community which meets the mobility needs of the elderly at a reasonable cost.

LONG-RANGE OBJECTIVES

1. To be an effective advocate on behalf of the elderly in the field of transportation with local government and other public and private bodies.
2. To maintain an up-to-date record of the needs of senior citizens for transportation.
3. To develop and maintain an up-to-date record of efforts being made nationally to provide senior citizens with low-cost, accessible transportation.
4. To monitor the progress of various local and state transportation plans and legislation to ensure that the needs of the elderly are met.
5. To increase the knowledge of the Transportation Committee members about transportation.

SHORT-RANGE OBJECTIVES

1. To assist the agency staff in monitoring this year's transportation project and in developing proposals for next year by having at least one-half the committee members provide twelve days of service a year.
2. To develop a plan for increasing accessible transportation for two priority geographic areas for the elderly population with very limited mobility within the first three months of the grant period.
3. To develop a position on the county rapid transit ballot measure and to advocate for that position by October 1.

ACTION STEPS

1. Interview resource persons from various governmental/operational areas to obtain data.
2. Develop a needs/priority list for each area of the community and select the two highest priority areas.
3. Develop a stand on the rapid transit ballot measure, get it adopted by the full council and hold a press conference.
4. Organize a study/action subgroup to begin work on a plan for the two priority areas.

GOAL, OBJECTIVES, AND ACTION STEPS FOR COMMITTEE ON HOUSING

Goal: Every senior citizen is entitled to housing which provides comfort, dignity, and security.

LONG-RANGE OBJECTIVES

1. To be an effective advocate on behalf of the elderly in the field of housing with government and other public and private bodies.
2. To maintain an up-to-date record of the needs of senior citizens in the field of housing, adult day care, and nursing home care.
3. To develop and maintain an up-to-date record of efforts being made locally and nationally on behalf of senior citizens in the field of housing, adult day care, and nursing home care.
4. To monitor the progress of various local and state housing, adult day care, and nursing home care plans and legislation to ensure that the needs of the elderly are met.
5. To increase the knowledge and skills of the Housing Committee members about housing.
6. To increase by 50 percent the number of housing units available to senior citizens for purchase, rental, or rehabilitation.

SHORT-RANGE OBJECTIVES

1. To advocate with local government departments for specific housing requirements in two priority geographic areas for the population over 75 years old.
2. To monitor the progress of the housing subsidy programs in the community to ensure equitable participation by the elderly.
3. To develop a plan for an increase within 18 months of 350 housing units for the elderly for purchase or rental.

ACTION STEPS

1. Interview resource persons from various governmental/operational areas to obtain data.
2. Develop a needs/priority list for each area of the community and select the two highest priority areas.
3. Organize two subgroups to develop plans for the increase of housing units for rent, purchase, or rehabilitation in the two priority areas.
4. Organize a study group to develop a plan for monitoring local adult day care and nursing home facilities.

BOARD/STAFF RESPONSIBILITY QUESTIONNAIRE

For each of these duties, does the direct responsibility belong to the Board of Directors or to the Executive Director?

RESPONSIBILITY	BOARD OF DIRECTORS	EXECUTIVE DIRECTOR
Decide on long- and short-range goals.		
Hire and fire staff members.		
Supervise the staff.		
Determine community needs.		
Order equipment and supplies.		
Evaluate the work of the staff members.		
Monitor projects.		
Plan the development of new projects.		
Approve program plans and priorities.		
Promote members of the staff.		
Approve the agency budget.		
Approve specific requests for spending funds.		

ROLE OF THE INDIVIDUAL BOARD MEMBER QUESTIONNAIRE

Is it proper for either an individual member or the chairperson of the Board of Directors to do these things?

ACTION	INDIVIDUAL	CHAIRPERSON	NEITHER
Make a suggestion to the Executive Director.	_____	_____	_____
Issue an order to the Executive Director.	_____	_____	_____
Issue an order to staff members.	_____	_____	_____
Follow the advice of the Executive Director.	_____	_____	_____
Take orders from the Executive Director.	_____	_____	_____
Get information about community needs.	_____	_____	_____
Make a proposal to the entire Board of Directors.	_____	_____	_____
Ask the Executive Director for assistance.	_____	_____	_____
Ask staff members for assistance.	_____	_____	_____
Make public statements.	_____	_____	_____
Question recipients about the program.	_____	_____	_____

AGENCY SELF-ASSESSMENT CHECKLIST:
WORKING WITH BOARDS OF DIRECTORS AND ADVISORY COUNCILS

INDICATORS	STATUS			PERSON RESPONSIBLE
	Yes	No	Partial	
1. Clients or their representatives are on the board of directors in satisfactory numbers.	___	___	___	_____
2. Clients are on all advisory councils in satisfactory numbers.	___	___	___	_____
3. A complete list of all board and council members with addresses and phone numbers is kept current and is easily accessible.	___	___	___	_____
4. Board of directors and advisory council memberships reflect the demographic makeup of the community as a whole as well as of the client service population.	___	___	___	_____
5. There is a plan for in-service training for board and council members and orientation training for new members.	___	___	___	_____
6. Advisory councils are involved in program review and long-range program planning.	___	___	___	_____
7. Each member of the board of directors has a procedure manual that clearly describes roles and responsibilities.	___	___	___	_____
8. There is a procedure for providing standing and *ad hoc* committees with staff assistance.	___	___	___	_____
9. The board of directors meets regularly and fully carries out its roles.	___	___	___	_____
10. The agency's bylaws are routinely reviewed at least annually.	___	___	___	_____

Providing
Training
and Technical
Assistance

9

Adults develop their job-related attitudes, skills, and knowledge from trainers, experts, experience, and each other. This chapter concentrates on the process of training, as practiced in most human service agencies. We will also look briefly at its counterpart, technical assistance. Five phases are involved in the training process:

1. assessing training and technical assistance needs,
2. setting objectives,
3. developing a plan,
4. implementing the plan,
5. assessing the results.

Why bother with training? "After all, training takes the time of staff and volunteers that might be better spent working!" "Training costs too much money." "Most people don't change their basic work habits, anyway." "Change is scary and uncomfortable, so nothing is likely to result from training." "We hired them on the basis of merit, therefore they must be competent—they don't need any training." "People go to training sessions to kill time and to complain; they never learn what they are sent to learn." At one time or another nearly everyone involved with training has heard these statements. The comments are not fair, however, since they generally refer to experiences with poor or ineffective training.

Comparing ineffective workers with ineffective training is fairer. Ineffective workers do not get much work done no matter how many hours they are on the job. They do not have the ability or flexibility to improve their work habits, and they find change so frightening and uncomfortable that they do not desire to change.

Effective training, like effective staff members, is an end that all agencies desire. Good workers are constantly coming up with improved ways to get things done, just as good training makes time spent working at services more productive. Productivity and caring about clients increase most when personnel from an agency know what to do, how to do it, and feel confident of having support for their efforts. Effective training results in improved work performance. Training may cost money, but it need not cost more than the achieved gains in quantity and quality of services which result. Finally, good training encompasses not just the persons to be trained, but the entire setting that influences their work. As a consequence, changes are planned and supported, reducing fear, stress, and resistance.

Training can result in more effective and efficient services carried out with more sensitivity. It can decrease problems. Training can assist staff persons and volunteers with their professional and personal growth, and with job and life satisfaction. It can remedy deficiencies in knowledge, skill, and attitudes among agency personnel. So, why *not* bother with training?

Assessing training needs can be accomplished by several methods. Unfortunately, one common approach is to determine what training is available without cost. Free training should not be scorned as long as the content is necessary and the presentation is effective. However, to abandon the need determination process in favor of getting something for nothing can lead to getting nothing for nothing, to wasted time, and to a continuing inability to do a job well.

Examining agency objectives provides a better basis for assessing staff member and volunteer training needs. A good start is to list the major objectives of a project. Suppose, for example, one objective is to help persons who are suicidal to overcome their self-destructive behavior or thoughts. The attitudes, skills, and knowledge needed by the staff counselors, aides, and volunteers to help the clients reach this objective should be identified. The areas to be covered by training should be determined by subtracting the attitudes, skills, and knowledge already possessed by the staff from those which are needed.

ATTITUDES, SKILLS, AND KNOWLEDGE NEEDED	minus	ATTITUDES, SKILLS, AND KNOWLEDGE POSSESSED	equals	TRAINING NEEDS

The most rigorous method for assessing training needs requires the analysis of the tasks of staff members and volunteers. The full range of specific tasks which must be done should be detailed. For example, "Child abuse counselors will be able to administer the XYZ questionnaire to clients in 20 minutes and correctly interpret the findings from the chart." Each counselor's attitudes, skills, and knowledge can then be evaluated in relation to the specified task. The differences between what the counselors have to do and what they can do indicate their training needs.

Staff members' and volunteers' perceptions of their own and each other's needs form another frequent source of assessment data. Their views can be gathered from interviews (individual and/or group) and written questionnaires. The perceptions of supervisors can be used as a check on the training needs identified by staff persons and volunteers. The methods for collecting the data can be the same as before.

The responding persons should put their needs into priority order regardless of what method is used to gather the information. One method is to distribute a composite list of identified needs for staff members and volunteers to rank in priority order. Another method is to use a committee of representative people to do the ranking. Priorities are important because usually not all the desired training can be provided and, even if all the needs could be met, they are not likely to be met all at once. Priority setting has the added value of increasing the involvement of the trainees in the development of the training and their willingness to participate actively in the training sessions.

A variation called "modified Delphi" is an approach for obtaining people's perceptions of their training needs and priorities that is becoming more common in larger agencies which have a tradition of using representative committees to work on tasks. The group is assembled at one table, if possible, and each member gets a stack of 3 " x 5 " cards. They each write one training need on a card and put the card in front of them on the table, repeating the process for 15 to 20 minutes or until no one can identify any additional needs. Next, each person in the group prioritizes his or her own cards or the cards are exchanged and then prioritized, or all the cards are mixed, divided into equal piles and prioritized by subgroups of three or four persons. To obtain a collective priority listing, the entire group can rank the items until a consensus is reached. Any combination of these methods can have good results and the data derived from different approaches when compared may lead to insights about the needs that will greatly enhance the actual training.

Training needs assessment activities are carried out with the underlying assumption that an agency will meet its identified training needs in some systematic way. This means that it will establish objectives and a training plan which it will implement based on the needs determined.

The training needs assessment should lead directly to the attitudes, skills, and knowledge that each group requires. To the extent possible, individual needs should be accommodated. Generally, the areas in which individuals require help are common to many. These common topics then become the basis for establishing the content of the training.

The people to be trained and the content areas might look like this:

TRAINEES	CONTENT AREAS
Supervisors	Planning and organizing work and time, delegating work, handling discipline, providing job instructions.
Information and Referral Workers	Handling persons threatening suicide, record-keeping, referral sources.

Service Specialists and Volunteers	Coping with emergencies, small group counseling skills, keeping progress notes, discharging clients.
Office Staff	Public relations, office procedures, record-keeping.

For the benefits of training to have impact on an agency, the managers, especially the executive director, must provide support for the learning which takes place and the changes which result from that learning. Therefore, the assessment results and the proposed content for training must be seen and approved by those who have major responsibility for agency activities and procedures.

Developing a training plan, once a needs assessment is completed, provides the basis for a systematic results-oriented training program. A plan which will serve the needs of most agencies consists of seven parts.

Part 1   describes staff/volunteer training needs:
- (a) How needs were determined.
- (b) Needs identified for the agency generally, for each group of employees or volunteers, and for individuals.
- (c) Outcomes, or benefits, to the agency expected when the needs have been met.

Part 2   states overall objectives of the training:
- (a) Priority content areas for training that were selected.
- (b) Objective(s) for each priority content area.

Part 3   details objectives and content of individual training sessions:
- (a) Measurable objectives for each session.
- (b) Specific training session content areas.
- (c) Materials to be used.

Part 4   indicates the arrangements for training activities and scheduled times of those activities:
- (a) Training activities, general content areas, and persons for whom the activities are intended (e.g., workshops for all supervisors on caseload management).
- (b) Blocks of time when each activity will take place (e.g., one-half day a week for ten weeks).
- (c) Locations for training sessions.
- (d) Special benefits attached to the training, such as the offering of college credit.

Part 5   lists the resources available to carry out the training:
- (a) Institutions, businesses, or individuals who agree to conduct the training.
- (b) Volunteers and/or staff who will provide coaching or other instruction.
- (c) Resources for materials.

Part 6   identifies the evaluation methods and reporting:
    (a) Data collection forms and techniques.
    (b) Methodology (e.g., pre-post testing for each training session).
    (c) Data to be reported, frequency of reporting, format for reporting, persons who will get reports.

Part 7   states the costs for training:
    (a) Payments for instruction, materials, space rental, refreshments, etc.
    (b) Items which are being donated that would ordinarily cost money, such as free instruction or space.

Preparation of training plans is done by agency training coordinators, hired training consultants, training committees, volunteers, and by any combination of these. Regardless of who prepares them, plans are important because they identify an agency's overall strategy for satisfying its training requirements.

Setting objectives is an important phase of the training process, because objectives are the end products which become the criteria, or standards of measurement, when the evaluation of the training is done. Therefore, objectives for training plans and individual training sessions should be specific and measurable.

Preparing training objectives is not difficult once the parts of an objective are understood. The principal parts can be summarized briefly in the following form.

1. The attitude, skill, or knowledge to be learned, task to be accomplished, end to be achieved; e.g., lay out a weekly work schedule, indicate differences between two methods of outreach, name laws affecting children in foster care placements.
2. The evidence of accomplishment; e.g., identify at least five, with no more than two errors, as indicated by successful completion of the sample task.
3. The time frame in which it is to be accomplished; e.g., by December, in six weeks, by the end of the training session.

The following illustrations are instructive.

TRAINING PLAN OBJECTIVES

1. By December (*time*), at least 50 percent of the health aides will complete three college credits in a course of study related to their job (*end*) with a C grade or better (*evidence*).
2. In six weeks of training (*time*), the Planning Unit staff members will acquire the ability to write proposals (*end*) as evidenced by a proposal they have produced and submitted for funding (*evidence*).
3. Within two months (*time*), an ongoing training program will be established for volunteers that provides at least two hours of task-related training a month (*end*) and is attended by at least 80 percent of the volunteers (*evidence*).

TRAINING SESSION OBJECTIVES

1. By the end of the training session (*time*), each community aide will be able to name three methods for establishing an advisory board meeting agenda and identify at least one advantage and disadvantage of each (*end*) without using notes (*evidence*).

2. By the end of the training session (*time*), all of the supervisors will be able to complete a work scheduling simulation exercise (*end*) with a score of at least 90 percent (*evidence*).

3. By the end of the training session (*time*), the drug abuse counselors will be able to identify at least ten harmful drugs from a list of 25 substances (*end*), with no more than two errors (*evidence*).

4. By the end of the training session (*time*), the volunteers will show improved attitudes toward the client population (*end*) by their responses on a pre- and post-test (*evidence*).

In both the training plan and specific training sessions, generalized objectives should be avoided, such as "The staff will learn more about human relations" or "The relationship between staff members and volunteers will get better" or "Supervisors will do a better job of supervising." These statements do not make specific the behaviors to be learned, just as they do not cite the evidence of accomplishment which can be measured to see if the objective was met, or specify when completion can be expected.

One problem in dealing with many college instructors and consultants is their tendency to set teacher-oriented objectives, the success of which cannot be measured. Objectives should relate to what the learners will accomplish, not to what the teachers will teach. "To teach about record-keeping" is a frequently found but poor statement of an objective.

Once objectives have been developed to give training direction and substance, the remainder of the training plan and the training designs for individual sessions are needed to make the objectives a reality.

Scheduling training requires a balancing of available time and opportunities. Depending on the purpose of the training and the number of people involved, a variety of formats and settings are usually possible. Short one-hour to four-hour sessions done regularly have the advantage of allowing personnel to try out what they have learned at one session before the next session. These can be conducted on an agency's site, on a campus, in a church social room, or even in someone's living room.

Retreat sessions, which last two or three days, provide a nondistracting, intense learning period with a change from daily routines and tensions. They allow time for in-depth coverage of material, with ample opportunity for discussion, review, and team building. In other words, this means leave the usual work site and meet elsewhere: a retreat can be held in a park recreation center room, library meeting room, junior college campus, or a conference room. The purpose is to get away from day-to-day distractions and meet in a setting conducive to learning. An informal atmosphere, and yet a place in which serious discussion can take place, will need comfortable chairs, movable tables, a blackboard or chart stand, and nearby restrooms.

Federal grants do not ordinarily permit expenditures for food, so agencies sometimes have the entire expense at hotel sites, including meals, billed as a single conference cost. If a trainer or institution, such as a college, is involved, agencies will often contract to pay a conference fee per person. This single fee includes the costs for instruction, space, and meals. If the staff of an agency stay in an expensive hotel, this can make an unfortunate news item, so care needs to be exercised in making arrangements. Other facilities are frequently better for public relations and also less expensive, such as college dormitories, vacant summer camps, and religious retreat centers.

Can an agency afford to give time off during working hours to send staff members and volunteers to a class? Can an arrangement be worked out to utilize part work and part personal time? How about a Friday and Saturday retreat? Should everyone take part and the agency close down or should some people be asked to take charge while the others participate in training? Raising all these questions will ensure that the training plan will include a schedule that balances the numerous demands on personnel time with the need for continued personal and professional growth.

Another consideration relates to the mixes in training sessions of persons with different roles and ability levels. In one community, most of the private, nonprofit agencies delivering human services agreed to bring all their advisory committee members together for a joint training session on the role the committees could play in advocating more funds for services. This approach has the advantage of commingling members, thereby reducing organizational jealousy and competition. The approach facilitates members' learning from each other's experiences, a much richer resource than any committee has by itself. The main disadvantage of this approach is that the content has to be general and not specific to the capabilities, sophistication about advocacy, and other needs of a particular committee.

A number of issues should be reviewed before adopting a final schedule. Here are some of the questions that will have to be answered.

Are volunteers and staff members to be trained together all or part of the time?

Should supervisors and their subordinates go to training sessions together?

What effect does the participation of a project director or members of the board have on the training of staff members?

When personnel from different agencies train together, where should the training be conducted?

What times of day and days of the week are least disruptive to the agency's operation?

When do people learn best?

Another difficult task is ensuring that everyone who is scheduled takes part and that he or she starts with a positive attitude toward learning. Staff members can probably be ordered to attend, but cannot be forced to cooperate. Volunteers may be forced to attend by insisting that they cannot continue with the project unless they participate. Coercion, however, rarely puts people in the best frame of mind for learning. A better method is to give the potential trainees a stake in deciding what the training will be, when it will be held, and who will conduct it. The ways in which the clients, the agency, and the trainees themselves will benefit should be pointed out. Finally, it should be made clear that the training is not a judgment of the trainees' ability to perform their jobs and will not be used to "evaluate" them. This will help to relieve any anxiety and increase their willingness to participate in the program.

Approaches to training used by the persons conducting the training sessions will significantly influence what the trainees will learn. Training covers a variety of philosophies, strategies, and materials. Some approaches are better suited to assisting trainees to improve their work-related knowledge, skills, and attitudes than are others. Agencies with a staff person who can make informed judgments about the effectiveness of learning and teaching methods generally get better training.

To be efffective, training must take place on several levels at the same time, just as the individual in the real world (as opposed to the hypothetical situations presented in so many classroom settings) experiences events on several levels at once. Therefore, training sessions should develop skills, provide knowledge, and modify attitudes by combining new information, group interaction, and task experiences. Group interaction (or group process) refers to the way individuals relate to one another as they go through various experiences together, and task refers to getting work done, a problem solved, or activity completed. A teaching/learning situation in which participants improve their functioning with people and enhance their ability to do their job is usually the most effective.

Adults learn best by doing. Lectures are not always bad, but neither are they always good. Therefore, adult learners should not be put in situations that make them passive receivers of information, rather they should be participants in activities. They need to practice what they learn and must have time to integrate their learning, to make it part of themselves. They need opportunities to give, and get, nonjudgmental assessments of what they are doing well and what needs strengthening.

Training sessions based on the following assumptions are most likely to be effective:

1. Training based on "reality," enabling participants to work with the contents of the sessions in terms of their on-the-job experiences.
2. Training based on the intended achievement of specific results, including improvement in job performance.

3. Training techniques varied to fit the content of the sessions and the level of information and ability of the trainees.
4. Trainers expecting the participants to do well, and knowing enough about the trainees and their jobs to provide training that matches needs and abilities.

Such a training session based on these assumptions should include the following segments:

1. Provision of background information and concepts.
2. Development of a job-related task for the trainees to experience, including interpersonal interaction.
3. Analysis of the experience by the trainees, including a review of the task, group processes, and personal feelings involved.
4. Provision of feedback by the trainer.
5. Exploration of ways for the trainees to apply learning to their jobs.
6. Reinforcement of modified attitudes, improved skills, and knowledge acquired.

In the training session depicted in Figure 9-1, centered on the role of the chairperson of an advisory committee, the objectives are modest and measurable. Thus, either the participants can list the required amount of information or they cannot. The session involves an inductive approach to training as opposed to the didactic method common to traditional classroom instruction. This approach helps the trainees to develop their ideas about the role of a chairperson through a sharing of knowledge with others in the group. At appropriate points in the discussion, the trainer may add information not offered by the group.

This approach to training assumes that participants are adults who have experience and some relevant information and skills when they enter a training session. The trainer fosters sharing of information available among the participants and gives new information when they are ready for it. Trainees are ordinarily ready for new information and ideas only after they have had an opportunity to discuss their own ideas. Participants who have an opportunity at the beginning of a session to feel at ease and get to the point of readiness for learning will usually receive and retain more of the content of the training. These techniques illustrate our overall view of training; namely, that participants be involved in and responsible for their own learning and that the responsibility of the trainer is to facilitate that involvement.

The information trainees receive and the attitudes and behavior of other persons in the group influence trainees' attitudes. Skills grow from practice in a setting which provides nonjudgmental feedback. The interaction format makes it difficult for anyone to go through the session without some participation. The final segment ensures that trainees consider how to apply their learning on-the-job. Mailing the participants a summary of the items and implementation methods will further reinforce the learning in their work with their own committees.

When trainees do not know one another, brief "get acquainted" tasks may be in order, such as either having each person introduce himself or herself or briefly in-

Figure 9-1

SAMPLE TRAINING DESIGN

Advisory Committee Training Session IX: Role of the Chairperson

Objectives: At the conclusion of this two hour session participants will be able to:

1. list at least five specific roles of a chairperson
2. list at least one activity a chairperson can do to carry out each of the roles identified in objective #1

Time	Content	Task	Methods	Materials
5 min.	Welcome and introduction	Review goals for the session	Discuss and modify list of goals	Goals listed on newsprint
45 min. (15 min. each segment)	Role of chairperson	List at least six specific roles that a chairperson must carry out to have a functioning committee	Committee chairpersons and their vice-chairpersons work to make a list	Paper and pencils
			Group pairs to make units of four; chooses six top priority items	
			Each unit of four lists its items on newsprint; post lists and compare items	Blank newsprint and marking pens
20 min.	Priority roles	Identify three most important roles	Total group discusses items and chooses top three	Newsprint lists
5 min.	BREAK			
30 min. (15min. each segment)	Methods for carrying our roles	List activities to accomplish the three priority roles	Divide into three sub-groups. Assign each to list three activities for one of the priority roles	Blank newsprint and marking pens
			A representative from each sub-group reports its assignment to total group	
10 min.	Summary of learning	Review what was learned and how it can/will be applied	Trainer leads a general discussion with total group	
5 min.	Evaluation	Assessment of learning	Distribute questionnaires and get responses	Evaluation questionnaire

terview another person and then introduce that person. Similarly, during an infor-
mation-giving period, such as a lecture, panel presentation, or film, participants
will need an opportunity for active involvement. One technique, for example, is to
give assignments, such as asking several subgroups of the trainees to each watch a
different aspect of a film for later discussion.

Training methods are crucial to effective training. Unfortunately, not all
trainers have skills and experience in using a variety of training methods. Too many
tend to use the same method each time with little awareness of how the method affects the outcome. As a rule of thumb, it is best to vary methods within a training
session and certainly to vary the methods used in the several sessions that make up a
training program.

One objective of a health care agency's training plan may be to improve the
knowledge of its professional, paraprofessional, and volunteer clinic personnel in
ways to identify and work with physically abused children. Suppose that this training plan calls for seven weekly three-hour sessions. The content of each session must
be relevant to trainees with different levels of education and experience. One problem that will confront the training coordinator is how to introduce a variety of learning opportunities to a group with such diverse levels of professional sophistication
and keep the attention and involvement of this group over a seven-week period.

The following program description is an illustration of how methods can be
varied in a series of training sessions to account for the diversity and to sustain involvement.

Session 1.   Field trip to observe interviews with abused children.
Session 2.   Case study analysis in five-person heterogeneous groups (paraprofes-
             sionals, professionals, and volunteers mixed).
Session 3.   Counseling demonstration using role-playing.
Session 4.   Lecture by a physician on the physical signs of abuse.
Session 5.   Panel presentation by experts—between session "at-home" assignments.
Session 6.   Problem-solving by homogeneous groups (volunteers only, paraprofes-
             sionals only, etc.).
Session 7.   Reports on "at-home" assignments.

A training design is the curriculum outline which a trainer follows in a training session. The training design is usually time limited in scope, covering one training session (an hourly time block or perhaps a full day of training). Each training
design has specific objectives which detail what the group should know or be able to
do as a result of that single training session. The design ordinarily lists the content to
be covered and the methods and materials the trainer will use during the session. A
training design prepared by a professional trainer might look like that depicted in
Figure 9-1.

Evaluating the outcomes of training is important for several reasons. First,
evaluations of training can provide data about the extent to which objectives were
accomplished; i.e., the degree to which the attitudes, skills, and knowledge of the

trainees changed in a positive direction. Second, the assessment process, when it involves the trainees, can increase each participant's stake in future training. This creates a more favorable climate for learning to take place. Third, evaluation findings are a form of feedback to the instructors that enables them to more closely meet the needs of the trainees by altering content and methods if necessary. Finally, evaluations of training can provide an agency training coordinator with the information needed to plan and schedule the most appropriate training.

The evaluation procedures should be linked to a training plan. If the plan calls for job readiness training of twenty community health aides, for example, use the assessment methods which best determine the degree to which the objectives in the plan were accomplished. The plan objectives, as noted earlier, will have indicators of accomplishment. Suppose 90 percent of the health aides were expected to earn enough credits in two years to qualify for an associate of arts degree at the community college. Checking their records would no doubt provide all the data required. Suppose, further, that they were to be knowledgeable about the community's resources, as indicated by their ability to use the agency's resource directory. An exercise can be developed in which a hypothetical client with myriad problems is presented to each aide, who then must determine which resources are most appropriate to meet the client's needs.

Training plan evaluation requires a variety of data. To collect the data, a variety of methods should be developed to ensure the most accurate and helpful findings. Comparing the record of sessions held, persons trained, and content areas covered with the plan will show if what was proposed was carried out. The opinions of the trainees about the quality, effectiveness, and amount of training they received can be surveyed through interviews and questionnaires. The opinions of supervisors and co-workers should be sought about changes in the performance of trainees. Clients' opinions about changes noticed in services will help determine if any of the changes that occurred are related to the training. These sources of data can be tapped without great cost or sophisticated data collection methods and the data, when analyzed, can provide a reasonable accounting of the program's strengths and weaknesses. Many parallels exist between the assessment of training and of services.

The assessment procedures most appropriate to the measurement of objectives should also be used for evaluating individual training sessions. For example, one of the training objectives may have required the community health aides to learn enough medical terms in Spanish and Japanese to be capable of working with persons in the community who do not speak English. A variety of techniques could be used to measure the degree to which an aide can handle the two languages. A simple paper and pencil test which requires matching English, Spanish, and Japanese terms could be developed. Or persons fluent in each language could rate each aide in conversations with clients. Or tape recordings of terms could be prepared, and each aide required to translate between English and the other two languages.

To measure attitudes without the use of standardized instruments is more difficult. Probably, the most valid results can be gained by getting the trainees' responses to relevant statements of value or judgment before and after a training session. Such statements might be along the following lines for social service workers.

There are occasions when a husband should hit his wife.

People who are poor do not mind their poverty as long as they know others also are poor.

I am looking forward to growing old.

The Vietnamese who emigrated to the United States should not be allowed to collect welfare payments.

Young people are rowdier and less respectful of others today than in past generations.

Other techniques for gathering data on individual training sessions include the sampling of training-related work performance, the collecting of trainees' perceptions about the training, and information testing.

Pre- and post-testing, if specifically related to a session's objectives, is both an assessment device and a learning tool. In a training session for outreach staff members designed to develop skills and information in giving resource information to clients and their families, questions such as the following were given to the trainees at the start.

What three agencies can a teenager who drinks excessively be referred to?

It is never okay to telephone a client's spouse without first obtaining the client's approval. True or false?

The answers to such questions can be used as a basis for discussion during the session and then as a post-test to determine what was learned.

Assessment of training should never be used as a judgment (good or bad) of the trainees. People find it hard enough to be honest and contributing members of a group in training without being made to feel that as a result of their participation they will be judged, embarrassed, or punished. To be effective, trainers must be seen as nonjudgmental, safe to talk with, fair, supportive, and helpful. They should report accurately what the trainees accomplished or still need to learn, but should never be made to evaluate a trainee. When trainees mistrust their trainers or fear judgment, they do not learn as well.

Free and low-cost training opportunities are available to human service agencies. Large urban areas have more institutional resources from which to get free or low-cost training, but even in remote rural areas resources can be found. Among the possible providers are federal, state, and local governments, charitable agencies, and commercial and industrial companies.

Many federal programs which fund local agencies to provide human services, either directly or through block grant subcontracts, also provide funds for training. Getting these funds may require writing a proposal or working with a local university or community college. In other cases, training can be obtained without cost from an agency or business that specializes in providing training and technical assistance under a federal grant or contract. The legislation, regulations, and guidelines will provide information about the requirements for training support.

State and local governments frequently provide training services to agencies they have funded for community projects. Government agencies at all levels provide training to their own personnel and sometimes let staff members of private, nonprofit agencies participate. Nearly all offer basic orientation and supervisory training, as well as job-instruction training. Large governmental jurisdictions usually have training departments for special personnel, such as police and firefighters, social workers, and public health personnel. All of these represent potential resources for free training.

Charitable organizations, such as the Red Cross and United Fund/United Way, offer low-cost training programs to persons from other agencies. Banks, manufacturers, retail chain stores, and other commercial enterprises have training programs for their personnel and will sometimes include human service agency staff members in their general programs. They will also lend their training or technical assistance persons to agencies for specific tasks, such as providing training for supervisors or setting up a better payroll system. Many professional organizations, such as the American Society for Training and Development, have local chapters whose members will often donate their time as a community service.

Working with universities, colleges, community colleges, and adult schools can be an effective strategy for meeting training and technical assistance needs because the cost is low and many added benefits can often be obtained. For example, students can be recruited for later employment and for volunteer work. Instructors, with special competence in fields related to an agency's programs, can often be induced to volunteer as technical assistants. Academic or extension programs can provide the requisite learning opportunities and certificates and/or academic credits for agency personnel.

Extension, or continuing education, divisions of community and four-year colleges and universities, as well as adult schools of the public school systems, have several different ways to provide training. They offer regular academic classes in the evening, such as basic accounting or communication skills. They may design courses specifically to meet an agency's needs on topics such as planning or employment counseling. And they may offer credit for training developed and conducted by an agency if they approve the content and the instructor. The academic credits and certificates which these institutions give provide a strong motivation for learning for some staff people.

Whether educational institutions call their programs "education" or "training" should make no difference so long as the "students" or "trainees" get what they need. Generally the difference is in the degree of specific job applicability, with training the more specialized and applied.

It works the other way as well. Educational institutions benefit from the liaison through increase in real-life attributes which agency staff members bring to campus. Instructors get to see the end results of their efforts and this helps them to sharpen their teaching. Also, if there has been an agreement to pay for the educational program, the school or college may make a profit. Since community colleges and adult schools generally receive tax funds based on the number of student classroom contact hours they provide, called "average daily attendance," offering programs for agencies increases their budgets. Therefore, an agency can usually drive a hard bargain and ensure that agency personnel get a program to meet their needs and not just the training the educational institution wants to provide.

When necessary or desirable, an agency can do its own training. Many people, who are not teachers by training or experience, can develop the ability to facilitate the learning of others. Thus, a staff member or volunteer who knows the subject to be taught (interviewing skills, supervisory techniques, budgeting), has patience while people learn, and is willing to do the work can learn to teach. Teaching is as hard as learning. With the help of a professional trainer or local adult education teacher, agencies can often train their own trainers.

Regardless of whether training is provided by the agency itself or by an outside source, every agency needs a training coordinator. In a large organization there may be several people responsible for coordinating and conducting training, and this may be their only function. In a small agency, a designated person, along with other duties, can be responsible for helping to assess needs, set objectives, develop a training plan, obtain resources and trainers, and evaluate results. Only an agency's director or a supervisor, however, can be responsible for seeing that staff people attend the sessions for which they are scheduled.

The difference between training and technical assistance is not always

clear, although persons calling themselves trainers, consultants, or technical assistants have been trying to define the distinction for years. Trainers focus on learning, whereas technical assistants focus on accomplishing tasks. Trainers are experts in the teaching/learning process, while technical assistants are experts in content areas, such as management, planning, program, or evaluation.

Technical assistance generally follows the same process as training, but technical assistants ordinarily tend to carry out more of the task themselves than do trainers. An effective technical assistant would not complete a task, such as preparing a funding proposal, without ensuring that agency staff members increased their capacity to prepare their own proposals. Also, a technical assistant would not leave an agency until the proposal was completed. Likewise, effective trainers would not consider their training complete until staff members had developed the capability to write a fundable proposal, but most would not feel obligated to complete the proposal themselves.

Technical assistance by consultants with the same knowledge and attitudes of those of a trainer is the most likely to be effective. One difference, however, is that the trainer may know quite a bit about something in theory, but may not have the skills or experience to perform tasks in that area. Effective teachers of program administration, for example, may never have administered anything. The better technical consultants are generally those who have had practical experience doing the tasks which they are being hired to assist. Consultants who "know the ropes" are better able to see what needs to be done and often know short cuts to getting it done more efficiently.

All training is technical assistance, but not all technical assistance is training. For our purposes, the differences do not make much difference since technical assistance and training follow a similar process in assisting agencies to reach their objectives.

Surprisingly, however, many program administrators have found it difficult to use the services of technical assistants effectively. There are several reasons for this. First and foremost, the agency staff usually does not have a clear idea of what to expect from the consultants and are never quite sure if they got what they wanted or needed. Sometimes, the consultants fail to communicate what they can do, will do, and/or have done. Although the consultants may do what is asked, they may not do what is needed or, conversely, they may do what is needed, but not what was requested. Occasionally, consultants are more interested in seeing that the agency staff members learn to do the tasks for themselves than they are in accomplishing the tasks. Or the technical assistants are so interested in getting the tasks completed that they push all the agency personnel aside and admonish them to stay out of the way. It happens, too, that staff members, hurt by the agency's distrust of their abilities, will occasionally ignore or sabotage the efforts of unwary technical assistants.

The steps outlined below will help overcome these difficulties and make effective use of technical assistants and trainers.

1. Make sure the services acquired, the tasks to be accomplished, and the training to be conducted meet identified needs and clearly stated objectives. Accept only services that fit these objectives even if the services are free.
2. Develop a clear contract that defines what and how much the consultants will do, and what and how much the agency will do. Write out the specific tasks and the indicators of accomplishment.
3. Involve staff members who will be involved later in the initial planning with the consultants, so that they will want to participate in, and not obstruct, the effort.
4. Ensure that the consultants get the information they need.
5. Stay flexible. The consultants may have helpful insights into agency needs that will require a rethinking of the "contracted" tasks.
6. Determine what follow-up, if any, will be needed by the agency's personnel, the consultants, or others to ensure the best results are obtained from the effort.

Training and technical assistance help the staff members and volunteers of human service agencies to develop personally and professionally. This growth can have positive effects on services to clients.

METHODS OF DETERMINING NEED FOR TRAINING AND TECHNICAL ASSISTANCE

Method	Advantages	Disadvantages
Interview	Affords maximum freedom for expression of opinions, suggestions and feelings, as well as facts.	Time-consuming and results may be difficult to interpret; may make interviewees feel threatened.
Questionnaire	Reaches many persons in short time; inexpensive; data easily categorized; may be given anonymously.	Structures, therefore limits range and freedom of responses.
Job analysis and performance review	Produces specific information about tasks, performance; increases chances that some training needs will be correctly identified.	Time-consuming; reduces chances that some training needs of the organization will be correctly identified; difficult to do without training in job analysis techniques.
Tests	Provides easily compared results about specific strengths and deficiencies of individuals.	Results may not be conclusive; valid tests difficult to find or develop; reduces chances that some training needs of organization will be correctly identified.
Group problem analysis	Affords discussion of differing views; helps build support for needed training.	Time-consuming and results may be difficult to interpret; may make interviewees feel threatened.
Records study	Provides evidence of problem areas.	May not provide wide enough scope to show needs clearly; may not reflect current needs.

Figure 9-2

TRAINING EVALUATION FORM

Your comments on the training you have just participated in will help in planning future sessions. Please answer the questions frankly. You need not sign your name.

1. Did you understand the purpose for which this training (session) (program) was held?

    Not at all _____ A little _____ Somewhat _____ A lot _____ Completely _____

2. How much information have you gotten from this training that will be useful to you?

    None _____ A little _____ Some _____ Quite a bit _____ A lot _____

3. Have any of your opinions or attitudes changed in the course of this training?

    No _____ Yes _____ If yes, in what way?   _____

    _____

4. Do you think your effectiveness on the job will increase because of your participation in this training?

    Not at all _____ A little _____ Somewhat _____ Quite a bit _____ A lot _____

5. What did you like *most* about this training (session) (program)?   _____

    _____

6. What did you like *least* about this training (session) (program)?   _____

    _____

7. Compared to others with whom you have participated, how would you rate the (trainer) (speaker) (facilitator) (instructor)?

    Ineffective _____ Poor _____ Fair _____ Good _____ Outstanding _____

TRAINING EVALUATION FORM

PARTICIPANT EVALUATION

Program Title: _____ Date: _____

1. Over all I rate this training experience:

    (Please circle the number that best reflects your feeling.)

    | 1 | 2 | 3 | 4 | 5 | 6 | 7 | 8 | 9 |

    Very Poor   Poor   Average   Good   Very Good

2. I rate each of the following:

	Very Good	Good	Average	Poor	Very Poor
(a) Organization of the subject matter was:	____	____	____	____	____
(b) Presentation of information was:	____	____	____	____	____
(c) The trainer's ability was:	____	____	____	____	____
(d) Compared with other training, what I learned was:	____	____	____	____	____
(e) The meeting facilities were:	____	____	____	____	____

3. In addition, I felt that the training experience was:

    _____

    _____

    _____

4. Things that need improvement in future training are:

    _____

    _____

    _____

QUESTIONNAIRE FOR ASSESSING SUPERVISORY TRAINING NEEDS

Dear Supervisor:

Please fill in each of the blank spaces with the letter from the Table of Responses that best describes your capability at this time. *Be assured that all answers will be held in the strictest confidence.*

Thank you for your cooperation.

TABLE OF RESPONSES
A   Need considerable learning in this area.
B   Need some additional learning in this area.
C   Feel confident in this area.

I.   Planning and implementing work.
   1.   Setting goals _____
   2.   Controlling costs _____
   3.   Clarifying job roles _____
   4.   Delegating responsibility and authority _____
   5.   Understanding organizational structures _____
   6.   Implementing procedural changes _____
   7.   Assessing and evaluating program and employees _____
   8.   Managing one's own time _____
   9.   Providing job-instruction training _____
   10. Understanding job tasks _____

II.   Communicating
   1.   Getting information _____
   2.   Reporting information _____
   3.   Conducting staff meetings _____
   4.   Keeping records _____
   5.   Following personnel practices _____
   6.   Giving orders _____
   7.   Interviewing skills _____
   8.   Writing memos and reports _____

III. Relating to subordinates
   1.   Providing an environment of security _____
   2.   Preserving individual uniqueness _____
   3.   Supporting cultural differences _____
   4.   Developing empathy _____
   5.   Listening _____

QUESTIONNAIRE FOR ASSESSING SUPERVISORY TRAINING NEEDS
(continued)

    6. Checking for comprehension _____

    7. Understanding feedback _____

    8. Observing nonverbal behavior _____

    9. Providing personal encouragement _____

  10. Exhibiting personal concern _____

  11. Assisting in clarifying goals _____

  12. Bringing out potential qualities _____

  13. Involving employees in creative process _____

  14. Involving employees in decision-making, as appropriate _____

IV. Solving problems and making decisions

    1. Identifying problem areas _____

    2. Analyzing causal factors _____

    3. Identifying obstacles and constraints _____

    4. Establishing criteria and objectives _____

    5. Identifying resources _____

    6. Developing alternative solutions (creative) ____ (rational) ____

    7. Developing a plan of action and alternative implementation strategies ____

(Do *not* sign your name.)

AGENCY SELF-ASSESSMENT CHECKLIST: TRAINING AND TECHNICAL ASSISTANCE

INDICATORS	STATUS			PERSON RESPONSIBLE
	Yes	No	Partial	
1. The agency has adequate documentation of all requests for training and technical assistance.	____	____	____	_____
2. Training plans reflect objectives developed in collaboration with staff and volunteers.	____	____	____	_____
3. The agency's annual training plan reflects agency goals and funding source requirements.	____	____	____	_____
4. The agency has procedures to assess the value of training for the participants.	____	____	____	_____
5. The agency maintains a written record of all training and technical assistance provided.	____	____	____	_____
6. The agency has a procedure for scheduling and notifying participants of in-house and non-agency training opportunities.	____	____	____	_____
7. All training events have written training designs that include a statement of objectives, description of content and methods, and list of resources.	____	____	____	_____
8. The agency has developed written policies for staff and volunteer participation in training.	____	____	____	_____
9. The agency has identified training and technical assistance resources within the agency and the service community.	____	____	____	_____
10. The agency has a person who is responsible for ensuring that adequate training is provided.	____	____	____	_____

Monitoring and Evaluating Human Service Programs

10

Travelers cannot know if they have arrived at their destination unless they know where they want to go. Knowing where they intend to go and having guideposts to indicate the way greatly increases their chances of getting to the destination safely and with an efficient expenditure of resources. In this sense the delivery of human services is much like travel. The more clearly stated are the objectives and the more knowledge they have about the best methods, the more likely service providers are to accomplish their aims.

The processes for assessing the degree and nature of the delivery of services are clear. But the methods of assessment are often not only unclear but may also be expensive and sometimes disruptive. Explaining the processes for finding out how programs "are doing" is the purpose of this chapter. The examination is from the perspective of funding sources and human service agencies because both have need for information about the programs in which they are involved.

The purposes of performance assessment depend upon the needs and desires of the consumers of the information. Congress and state legislatures use performance data analyses to help determine public policy. Local elected officials use the assessment material to assist in determining what programs and which agencies they should fund. The research community uses evaluations to determine relevant factors in social service delivery approaches, and professional organizations and individual service providers use performance assessment to decide which strategies and techniques work best for particular clients. Allied agencies, as well as the general public, are interested because of the desire to know the progress and results of programs in which they have a stake. Clients and potential clients wish to know whether to trust their well-being to a particular program or agency, the effectiveness of which may be indicated by evaluation data. Members of the board of directors and the agency's staff want to know the available information about their performance so they can improve their efforts. An agency can use performance data to persuade funding sources to provide added funds, and funding sources can use the data to determine if such additional money is warranted.

A human service agency uses performance assessment to determine what modifications in the service delivery systems, organizational structure, and/or methods are needed. Data collected from all stages of a project can tell which approaches are most likely to give the best results. However, the use of assessment information is ordinarily weighed against other factors of an organizational, programmatic or political nature before changes are made. Thus, a "better" program may cost too much for its potential increase in effectiveness. A change in methods suggested by assessment data may please the evaluator and project personnel, but may displease clients.

Congress needs less to know how a particular project is performing than to have the aggregated knowledge about all similar projects. Conversely, while the collected data about a particular program may be of some use to an agency, data about its own performance are most likely to aid it in improving its services. Generating, collecting, analyzing, and reporting data from many sources takes time. Not surprisingly, Congress or a government agency may not receive adequate information about program performance for a long period after the agencies have begun providing their services. What is surprising, however, is how often a human service agency will not get assessment data on its own performance until long after the chance for making improvements based on that data has passed.

Who is to receive assessment information, when, and for what purpose, usually determine the type of performance assessment which will be conducted.

Definitions of the types of performance assessment vary considerably, depending upon who is using the terms and the context in which they are used. We distinguish among *monitoring, contract compliance*, and *evaluation* by the focus of each. The focus of monitoring is on the process of service delivery. Monitoring is concerned with measuring the degree to which *process* objectives stated in a proposal or contract are achieved. Monitoring is the systematic observation, assessment, and reporting of performance, usually done by funding sources. It is an attempt to determine *efficiency*. Contract compliance is concerned with contracts and the assurance that all of the contractual obligations, the legal requirements, have been met. A useful distinction can be made with the metaphor of a glass of water. Monitoring views the glass as half full, concentrating on the accomplishments and aims at improving services. Contract compliance views the glass as half empty. It concentrates on shortcomings, deviations from contract requirements, and aims at correcting these deficiencies.

Evaluation has its focus on the *product* objectives of service delivery, rather than the process. Evaluation seeks to discover how much *impact* programs or agencies had on clients in those areas where services were supposed to have an effect. It tries to ascertain, through a variety of scientific and quasi-scientific approaches, the degree of *effectiveness* services had in ameliorating the needs of clients as specified in product objectives. As used here, evaluation refers to research-oriented data gathering and analysis, and to the description and understanding of cause ⟶ effect relationships. Evaluation is usually carried out either by agencies or by professional researchers and evaluators hired for the purpose. While funding sources often pay for evaluation studies, they do not often do them.

To meet people's needs, human service agencies develop plans (proposals/contracts) which are the bases for their projects. The projects, when implemented, lead to "results," or "impacts." Not all the clients' needs are likely to be met by the agencies providing services, nor do all the agencies' efforts go into serving clients. Some proportion of the efforts to meet the clients' needs is redirected into agency-oriented activity. The proportion of effort directly related to client services is a function of the *efficiency* with which the agencies provide the services. The results are a function of the *effectiveness* with which the agencies ameliorate the needs of the client group.

Monitoring is essentially concerned with the relationship between the proposed and the actual services delivered. Evaluation, as used here, primarily seeks to discover the relationship between needs and results. That is, evaluation attempts to discern what impacts on clients' needs were achieved as a result of the services provided.

To do monitoring, contract compliance, or evaluation requires three basic steps, regardless of the degree of sophistication in application. First, the establishment of measurable objectives, which are criteria of performance or outcome. Second, the development of measuring devices which can elicit data that measure the actual accomplishment, or performance, against the objectives. Third, the analysis of the data in order to determine ways of improving services.

Monitoring can be thought of as a measuring stick laid against performance. The measure is a standard of quality or quantity against which performance is compared. Figure 10-1 shows that time is a factor as well, since the comparisons are made at specific points in a project. The standards may be items such as units of service delivered or number of complaints received. Time is most often indicated at regular intervals, such as monthly, quarterly, or annually.

Monitoring begins with measurable objectives. As indicated earlier, correctly stated objectives lend themselves to the procedures for monitoring. An objective which clearly states what will be accomplished, the degree to which it will be accomplished, and the time frame in which it will be accomplished becomes a standard (criterion, indicator, yardstick) that can be measured. The following process objective from a maternal health project is an example. "An average of one hundred pregnant women each month will be provided with at least three one-hour edu-

Figure 10-1

THE MEASUREMENT OF PERFORMANCE

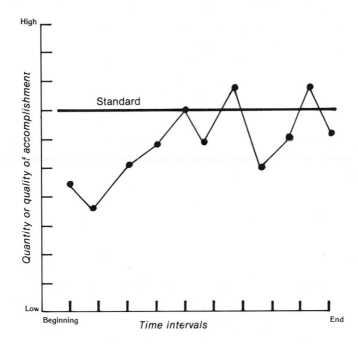

cational sessions on topics related to pregnancy and childbirth." A monitor can with little difficulty determine if an average of one hundred pregnant women received the appropriate sessions each month.

On the other hand, the following criteria items from the monitoring review form of a state agency hardly lend themselves to easy determination—if an objective judgment is possible at all.

1. The executive director exercises capable leadership at all times.
2. Personnel authorized to receive personal information and to store and retrieve it are skilled and reliable.
3. The agency plans for future needs.
4. The family members attending the counseling benefit from each session as much as the clients do.

Monitors may be interested in a variety of activities for which the agencies have no measurable objectives. Monitors may explore many performance attributes related to the agencies' improving their delivery of services. However, the monitors should inform the agencies of the standards in advance. Agencies can only be expected to work toward standards of which they are aware. For example, a monitor might wish to know about some or all of the following items for which no objectives may exist.

1. The project offers training at least two hours monthly to all volunteers.
2. The project has toll-free telephone services available from all points within its catchment area.
3. At least two announcements are made weekly about the availability of services through civic, labor, religious, business, social, or other organizations.
4. The project maintains a resource file which provides the name, hours, and types of services provided by other agencies located in the catchment area.

Monitoring depends on the collection of data which measure progress toward the accomplishment of objectives.

Data should be carefully planned since gathering them is never free. There is always at least the cost of expended resources. When appropriate, data should be collected on a periodic sampling basis. Only data which are required for regular reporting or which serve some specific routine purpose should be gathered regularly. Far too many funding sources require frequent reporting of data which they never analyze or use. Many human service agencies expend considerable effort to collect data about their clients which they also do not use to improve their services.

Data for the assessment of performance have important uses. Many consumers of data with legitimate uses for them do exist. Appropriate information provides a history called an "audit trail" that ensures funding sources of legitimate expenditures of funds by agencies. Data can indicate not only the quantity of services but also the quality and can point the way to trends and future options. Information about service delivery and the operation of an agency may determine whether that agency is doing well enough to be re-funded. In this instance, the data take on political overtones that will be considered later in this chapter. Information about services is collected to meet reporting requirements imposed from the outside and to provide internal management with guideposts to their accomplishments.

Usually agencies collect four categories of data:

1. Administrative activities, such as staffing, training, and reporting.
2. Service activities, such as the number of clients served, the demographic characteristics of the clients, the quantity of units of service delivered.
3. Ancillary activities, such as the number of advisory committee meetings, the accessibility and safety of a site.
4. Fiscal activities, such as income, expenditures, cash balance.

The following are among the sources from which agencies collect data about their activities:

1. Interviews with clients and their families, staff members, experts, board members, representatives of the community, and staff members from other agencies.
2. Systematic observations by evaluators.
3. Agency statistics from record-keeping documents.
4. Questionnaires, tests, examinations, ratings.

The usefulness of the data will increase to the extent that these data sources accurately reflect the perceived realities of a project.

Ordinarily an agency will collect data for its funding source first, its management second, and for any other entity, such as an other agency, last. Since these data will tell the agency's story, how and how often the information is gathered are important. A typical process of data collection can be seen in Figure 10-2.

The forms provided by a government department or other funding source are usually for monthly, quarterly, and/or annual reports and are not designed for the data needed by the service providers. Agencies ordinarily prepare their own forms for intake, case files of individual clients, activity reports, and such financial forms as travel reimbursement requests or purchase orders. Since many agencies have more than one source of funds, they need a uniform data collection system that is consistent and avoids repetition.

The criteria for determining the usefulness and efficiency of any form for data collection are straightforward. One criterion requires listing items of data only once and in a format that makes it easy for staff people to fill out and later to tabulate. Obviously, data not required should not be used. Unfortunately, forms used by one project in an agency are sometimes adopted for another project even though the information to be collected may have little relevance in the new context. Another criterion requires making a category of items discrete, not overlapping one another. Is

Figure 10-2

TYPICAL DATA COLLECTION SYSTEM

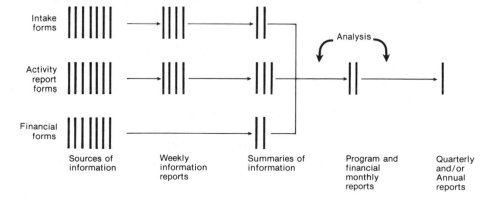

thirty minutes on the telephone with a client listed as a phone contact or as a counseling session? A third criterion requires the clear definitions of terms. If staff members are unclear about the type of data to put in each category, the information will be meaningless when aggregated. One agency, for example, which had persons from the Philippines as part of its client group, had some staff which listed them under Spanish surname and others under Asian. Consistency is perhaps more important than "correctness," since the title of a category can always be changed, but misplaced data units cannot always be recovered.

The establishment of the data items before a program begins is vital, since data are ordinarily the basis for monitoring and evaluation. The sooner a staff begins to collect the information, the more accurately a picture can be drawn. Data about services given but unrecorded are hard to recover, if they can be reconstructed at all. Experience suggests that staff members will resist filling out forms less when the forms have been part of their job from the beginning.

Data verification of financial records is frequently done, usually in the form of an audit by accountants representing a funding source. Some governmental bodies will use their own auditors, and others, including foundations that require financial audits, will provide their contract agencies with funds to hire an independent accounting firm to review fiscal procedures and records.

When financial irregularities are suspected, comprehensive audits may be done. Agencies have been defunded or had expenditures disallowed as a result. Considerable care and attention have to be given to the proper documenting and recording of all financial transactions. Verification of program data, on the other hand, is infrequently sought by the federal government and hardly ever by foundations. However, local and state governments have monitoring and/or contract compliance staffs which usually do at least periodic checks.

Since performance measured by indicators of workload (e.g., one hundred clients will receive counseling per month) is most often a major factor in deciding whether a program has been "successful," data are sometimes manipulated by agency personnel to show accomplishments greater than those actually achieved. One agency, for example, was required to provide cultural awareness and job interview skills training to teenagers. When the agency could not reach the numbers of clients needed in a month, both training subjects were covered in a single session and the number of client contacts claimed was doubled. Monitors have a responsibility to see that information submitted is consistent with reality for the sake of fairness as well as for decision-making purposes.

The two most common verification techniques are site visits and data sampling. Site visits are usually made at regular intervals by either a single monitor or a team. One governmental office sends two people, a staff member and a person serving on that office's advisory committee. In addition to two heads being better than one, the extra person can serve as witness if a dispute arises later about anything that was said or done. Some funding sources make only one site visit, usually just before a decision about re-funding an agency is due. The visit may be complex, using a structured site visit report form, and include talks with clients as well as board and staff members. Sometimes, tours of off-site service locations in the community are included, too. Other site visits may consist of little more than the recorded subjective impressions of a monitor.

Data sampling, which may or may not be done at the time of a site visit, is generally handled in one of three ways. A few clients' cases may be followed from intake to discharge. This approach enables a monitor to learn a good deal about the procedures of the agency and to check the forms and systems for data recording. It has the obvious disadvantage of not showing how other clients and possibly other staff have fared. To the extent that the few cases are not typical, the monitor may miss valuable generalizations.

A second approach is to take either a random or a selected sampling of various stages of the service activities. Both methods of selecting the instances to be reviewed are designed to give a wider perception of the activities and effects than the approach using only a few cases. In exchange for the broader view of the second approach, the monitor has to expect to lose some of the depth of perceptions offered by looking at only a few cases. The third approach is to review all records for a particular week or month. This has the advantage of enabling the monitor to compare the findings with the report of the agency for the period. Of course, if the time period selected is not typical, a distorted picture of the more usual events may be obtained. The third approach is probably the most time consuming. Clearly, being able to use all three approaches would yield the best results. For reasons of finances and time utilization, however, funding sources do not often make an effort of this magnitude.

The reporting of data, like the collecting of data, depends to a large extent on whom the data is for. Funding sources frequently provide their own reporting formats for financial reports. With human service agencies that receive their funds periodically, financial report forms may require monthly and year-to-date expenditures, fund requests, and account balances. Some foundations require nothing to be reported or ask only for an end of year financial position statement. In these latter instances, an agency will, no doubt, develop its own internal reporting system in order to ensure sound fiscal management and the appropriate expenditure of funds.

Agencies report program activity data in a variety of ways from a simple count of numbers of activities or clients to a complex narrative detailing quality as well as quantity elements. They report the quantity of service activity in one or more of three ways. The amount of time spent by one staff person in contact with a client or clients is one measure. One-half hour of counseling a battered wife or one hour of physical therapy in a health care center are examples. A second measure is the number of contacts, such as the number of persons attending an educational session on birth control in a planned parenthood project, the number of persons contacted as part of an outreach component of a child abuse prevention project, or the number of older persons attending a senior citizens center on one day, regardless of the type or quantity of services they receive.

The third common measure is a unit of service. A lecture on birth control methods counts as one unit no matter how many participants attend. Staff and other resources are the same regardless of the variation in attendance. Units of service can be difficult to define, but are more and more being used. They provide convenient pegs on which to hang costs. A unit in a transportation project might be a one-way trip for one person, regardless of time or distance. Theoretically, long and short, expensive and inexpensive trips will average out over a large number of units. Each medical examination in a health screening project for low-income children might be one unit, while each specialized follow-up examination, health education session, or individual referral assistance might be another unit. The unit of service measure is an effective management tool for assigning resources and controlling costs.

Numbers of any type tell only about quantity, rarely about quality. To overcome this difficulty, some funding sources seek qualitative measures that go beyond the usual data collection approaches. An area agency on aging (AAA) in the Midwest attempts to get a measure of "complaints" by providing a central telephone number for that purpose. The number and nature of the complaints reveal something of the quality of the efforts of the agencies funded by the AAA. A similar agency has a team of staff and volunteers who call a sampling of senior citizens it serves to check on the service, the follow-up, if any, and the clients' satisfaction.

Commonly used client satisfaction studies may provide some clues to the quality of services, but care must be taken in conducting them. One agency found from such a study that 96 percent of the clients were "very pleased" with the services provided. Only later did it realize that the views of former clients, who may have left because they were unsatisfied, were not obtained. Also, some clients may have been afraid to give negative answers for fear of losing the services.

Should the funding source require a periodic or annual report, but not have a reporting format, the following format might serve.

1. Narrative description of project services and special accomplishments or activities.
2. Statistical data on clients, staff, and services.
3. Problem areas and steps taken to overcome them.
4. Financial summary of income, expenditures, and balances.
5. Changes in need and proposed new or expanded services.

The role of a monitor is difficult, since monitors are often called upon by their organizations to play two conflicting parts. On the one hand, monitors are required to be evaluators and judges, a role that makes agencies reticent to reveal their problems. On the other hand, monitors are also supposed to develop technical assistance relationships that can help agencies overcome these same problems. The helping relationship requires trust rather than suspicion and a revealing, not a hiding, of problems. Few monitors can bridge these opposing parts easily. To succeed, monitors must effectively carry out the four major aspects of the relationship: entry, interventions, sanctions, and closure.

Entry into an agency is usually a time for mutual anxiety and suspicion, especially if the staff members of an agency have had an ineffective relationship with a previous monitor or consultant. To facilitate effective relationships, monitors need initially to establish a "contract," a set of generally unwritten, but clearly understood and mutually agreed upon, expectations. A relationship without surprises is the most helpful.

In the evaluator role, monitors are not consultants serving at the pleasure of the agencies; therefore, this aspect of the beginning relationship cannot be ignored or trivialized. A monitor's deeds can convince an agency's staff members that the evaluations will be objective and serve the purpose of identifying shortcomings only in order to improve inappropriate activities. Having set this tone in the "contracting" process, the behavior of the monitors must always be trustworthy.

The monitor must also establish the technical assistance, or helper role, if it is relevant, during the entry period. At this juncture, an individual monitor's style and his or her organization's practices and policies influence the helping process. Monitors who have little technical knowledge about services should not offer to provide assistance. Not only can ineffective or erroneous advice make agencies wary but it also will negatively affect the monitor's credibility. Monitors who are not seen as credible or trustworthy will have a most difficult time getting information or giving assistance in any area. Monitors who have considerable information and experience with the services run the risk of making agencies dependent on them and/or threatening staff members of lesser competence. How much help any agency needs and wants should be settled as early as possible, with a monitor making clear how much help he or she will give.

Interventions by monitors vary considerably in nature and amount. As already indicated, some funding sources do no monitoring at all. Others permit their monitors to intervene so often and in such crucial ways that they, and not the directors, appear to be running the projects. Some monitors limit their contact with agencies to desk reviews of monthly or quarterly reports. Others visit the agencies frequently, taking a role that is far more active. Some give advice only in response to questions from agencies or when required by their organization, while others never stop meddling with staff and board members, clients, and community resources. Monitors who are most effective appear to be those who consciously decide what interventions to make and when they should be made, based on the following criteria.

1. Will the intervention enhance the effort of the agency without creating disruption or dependency?
2. Will the intervention aid a monitor's credibility with an agency?
3. Will the intervention be made in such a way and at such a time that agency personnel will welcome it rather than resist?
4. Have the appropriate people been notified? (Monitors should never go to board or staff members without the knowledge of the agency's executive director.)
5. Do the organization's policies and practices allow for this type of intervention to be made at this time and is the information given in accord with those policies?

Sanctions—approval or disapproval of past, present, or future activities—are a form of intervention. Many monitors make the threat of disapproval the keystone of their relationships with agencies. Not only is this unfortunate but it also usually reduces morale and the willingness of agency staff members to try innovative ideas. Many threats to defund or to intervene in the services of an agency often cannot be carried out for legal or political reasons in any case. Monitors should note and offer recommendations for changes, but should do this in a positive, and not a punitive way.

Monitors can extend their approval too far as well. Some literally fall in love with agencies they are assigned to monitor. Because of the close relationship which often develops between monitors and agencies, behaviors may result which have a deleterious effect on efforts to improve services. Because reports glow from positive comments, difficulties are ignored or excused. A positive approach and an effective relationship does not mean that monitors must put aside their objectivity, overlook problem areas, or serve as apologists for agencies.

One funding source rotates its monitors every eight or nine months to ensure that a detrimental relationship does not develop between monitors and agencies. This procedure has the added advantage of giving the monitors more experience with the many different services funded by that organization. However, the constant rotation has disadvantages as well. It prevents monitors from getting to know the personnel and circumstances at the individual agency. It also creates difficulties in the agencies, which must go through the "contracts" about relationship over and over again with monitors of varying knowledge, abilities, and styles.

Closure is the ending of a relationship in a manner satisfactory to both monitor and agency. Monitors need to plan an effective closure of their relationship with an agency for which they have been responsible. To make an effective transfer, monitors should give notice of their departure in advance so that unfinished business can be completed, appropriate farewells given, and a transfer of records made to a new monitor. The entry of the new monitor starts the process over again.

Evaluation research is used to assess impact, or effectiveness. Earlier in this

chapter, we said that the term *evaluation* is sometimes used by others to mean assessment of both product and process outcomes. The latter we called "performance assessment." Evaluation, as used in this book, provides data about products, or impact. It is research that seeks not only to know the nature and degree of effect a program has had on those it was designed to affect but also tries to determine those program activities or factors which were important in determining success or failure.

Suppose a project to find jobs for ex-convicts results in 87 of 100 participants being placed successfully in the first year. Suppose, further, that such projects generally average about 50 percent of successful placements. Naturally, other agencies and the funding source would want to know why this project was more successful than others. Performance assessment would indicate that it was successful, but not necessarily why. Evaluation deals with causality.

Evaluation research plans are called "designs." The design, statistics, and methodology for evaluation of human services are becoming increasingly technical and are usually best left to experts. However, there are several basic elements of evaluation research it is useful to know about. This understanding leads to better judgment in selecting and working with expert evaluators, improved ability to interpret their findings, and broader opportunities to use the results in the improvement of services. Below is a brief examination of the classical experimental design and then of some less rigorous quasi-experimental and non-experimental methods which are commonly used for evaluation of human service programs.

Classical experimental designs properly carried out enable evaluators and consumers to have the most confidence in evaluation results. Experimental designs assume that there are one or more program factors, called "variables," we wish to know about and to measure. *Dependent* variables are factors whose outcomes are influenced by, or dependent upon, other factors. *Independent* variables are those factors which are free from a controlling relationship. Imagine an ideal situation in which the number of unwanted pregnancies (dependent variable) in a large group of female teenagers decreased directly in proportion to the number of counseling sessions attended. The sessions are an independent variable because their number does not depend on the number of unwanted pregnancies. We should be able to assume with confidence that there is a cause $\longrightarrow$ effect relationship between the number of unwanted pregnancies and counseling sessions attended.

However, the world of human behavior is not ideal, and numerous other factors, called "*intervening* variables," may account for decreases in pregnancy as well. Perhaps, just the simple attention and caring the teenagers get, and not the counseling, influences their behavior. Another group of females given attention only and no counseling might show a similar decrease. Maybe the availability of contraceptives for some but not for others influenced the result; or perhaps some of the male partners of the participants in the study left home, causing a physical separation. Suppose that different counselors are used or different methods of counseling, or that a new group of teenagers from a different community is studied. What will these changes do to the results of the study?

To maintain the purity of relationship between the dependent, or outcome, variables and the independent, or causal, variables in a human services program, evaluators who use classical design methods try to exclude all other variables through the special use of at least two groups. All the females potentially eligible for the program cited above, or a sample of them if the total group is too large, are placed by the technique of randomization into either the first group, which receives the counseling services, called the "experimental" or "treatment group," or into the second group, which receives no services, called the "control group." Those persons assigned to the experimental group are called "subjects," the others called "controls."

If the two groups are of sufficient size, the laws of probability will produce a similar distribution of characteristics in each group. The interventions, or counseling activities, can now be given to one or more experimental groups and withheld from the control group. For example, one group of teenagers may be given counseling treatment type A, a second type B, and a third group no treatment. The last is the control group.

Without a proper control group, no cause —→ effect can be shown to probably exist. The probability that a particular action will result in a certain outcome is determined statistically by weighing the outcome against the probability that it occurred by chance. A remedial reading class, for example, cannot be said to have helped poor readers more than a regular reading class might have unless a control group is involved. Improvements might justifiably be ascribed instead to special attention from the teacher, the hour at which the class was given, or the increased physical maturation of the students in the experimental group over the time span of the class.

The classical experimental method is depicted in Figure 10-3. If the changes between X1 and Y1 are significantly different from the changes between X2 and Y2, the intervention is believed to have had an effect on the subjects.

Another example may help. Suppose an experiment is established to determine if medical care at a clinic for low-income mothers and their young children has an effect on the mothers' attitudes toward health care. The device for the measuring of attitudes, called an "instrument," will consist of brief medical situations and multiple choice responses. A sample follows:

Mrs. Gonzalez' child has had a fever for two days. Should she:

(a) call the clinic doctor?

(b) ask her neighbors for advice?

(c) do nothing as the fever will go away?

(d) bathe the child in lukewarm water?

Figure 10-3

CLASSICAL EXPERIMENTAL DESIGN

	Before the intervention	Intervention	After the intervention
Experimental Group	X1	Yes	Y1
Control Group	X2	No	Y2

The measuring instrument will be given to 100 mothers randomly selected as they enroll their children in the clinic and again six months later to the same mothers. These persons will be the experimental group. The test will also be given at a six-month interval to another randomly selected group of 100 enrollees, whose children will not obtain services from the clinic. The interventions (independent variables) will be the utilization of the clinic for six months by the experimental group mothers and their children. The dependent variables will be changes in attitude toward health care found by the researchers. This explanation is abbreviated and simplified, but the basic elements are those that would require the attention of research-oriented evaluators.

Quasi-experimental designs lend themselves to somewhat less rigorous evaluations of programs. These alternative approaches have their uses, since the classical experimental design presupposes that evaluators are able to set up and carry out all the methods necessary to ensure validity and reliability, and that they will know what potentially important variables are involved.

COMPARATIVE STUDIES, based on a quasi-experimental design, are frequently used when a random distribution of participants into experimental and control groups is not possible. A control group in the classical experimental design sense requires randomization. Comparative studies, as their name implies, use individuals or groups not benefiting from the particular program interventions under study for comparison, rather than for control. Otherwise, the basic idea is much the same as with the classical design, with the experimental and comparison groups being measured before and after the planned intervention.

The major concern, of course, is how to make the comparison groups so much like the experimental groups participating in the program activities that no variables other than the planned interventions themselves influence the results. Such comparisons are nearly impossible to arrange exactly. Some factors such as educational level, criminal records, age, sex, income, or home ownership might be matched, but nobody could guarantee in advance that these would be the critical factors. Therefore, post-program results must be interpreted very cautiously. Still, a comparison group of reasonable likeness to the experimental group is better than no comparison group at all.

TIME-SERIES designs are based on making multiple measurements of the participants before, during, and after their involvement with a program. Since no control group is used, it is possible to include all clients in the sample. Figure 10-4 represents a typical measurement pattern. There, the increase in desired results over the course of the program *suggests* that the program has had a positive effect. This cannot be known for certain as some unexpected event may intervene. One study of senior citizens, for example, found a large increase in positive scores on a life satisfaction scale during their participation in a project designed to provide them socialization and recreational activities. The biggest increase in positive scores, however, came during the measurement period in which many of the participants received substantially larger Social Security checks. Despite such difficulties, repeated mea-

Figure 10-4

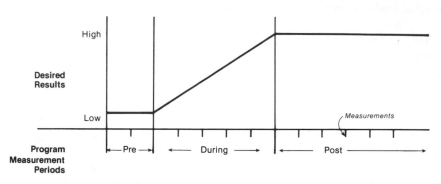

surements do help to establish a degree of confidence in the validity of the evalua-tion results. In a sense, the early measurements are a baseline against which the later measurements can be compared.

Nonexperimental evaluations include descriptive, post-planned, and con-textual studies, which are three commonly used types of evaluation research. Some-times the use of experimental and quasi-experimental designs is not possible be-cause little money is available for evaluation or perhaps the decision to try to evaluate the impact of the program is not made until after the program has begun or even has been completed. The degree of confidence that can be placed in the results of these studies is less than for more rigorous research, but they have the advantage of being less intrusive to staff and clients.

DESCRIPTIVE RESEARCH involves the development of case studies, which do not use pre- and post-measurements of groups of participants. A case study can look at the relationship of clients to services in depth, examining it from many perspec-tives, including those of staff members, families, community and board members, and other agency personnel as well as clients. Well-designed, systematically gathered case studies can provide valuable data about features of programs or pro-jects that seem to influence the nature and extent of impact on clients. Although results from individual case studies may not be generalized to others, they can pro-vide useful insights for internal improvements within a project.

POST-PLANNED EVALUATIONS of program effectiveness are by definition begun after programs have concluded or occasionally while they are ongoing. Some-times this method is called "retrospective research." Post-planned studies may try to recover much of the same data as quasi-experimental research would use. Pre-program data and randomized assignments of subjects to experimental and control groups are not possible, of course. However, reasonable amounts of available data can be the basis for fairly sophisticated analyses from which important inferences can be made about the possible impacts on programs or clients.

THE CONTEXTUAL EVALUATION method treats human services programs, not as laboratories in which specific program activities are expected to result in specific changes in clients, but rather as activities which involve multi-dimensional interactions. Instead of isolating specific causes and effects, contextual evaluations try to comprehend larger systems and relationships and to place them within a social context. A mental health project aimed at assisting homosexuals, for instance, cannot be adequately assessed contextually unless the prevailing community attitudes about homosexuals are described.

The first stage in contextual evaluation is descriptive—that is, the question "what is happening in this program?" is answered. The second stage analysis determines how "what is happening" is related to both formal and informal goals and understandings of staff, clients, and others. It details what internal and external pressures are factors of importance and how the various pieces of data fit together. The final stage examines the multiple activities and multiple results to see how they are linked. Success, or effectiveness, is judged in terms of a range of interrelated goals and multiple outcomes.

Contextual evaluations do not *prove*, but rather point the way to insights which can lead to project or program improvements. They also identify areas of study or even specific hypotheses which may provide the basis for experimental approaches.

The problems with evaluation research are widely recognized, although not always clearly understood. They bear repeating. First, constraints are imposed by the realities of organizational life. There is a decided lack of incentive by some researchers to tell agencies their services to clients show little in the way of benefits. As a corollary, agencies with few accomplishments ordinarily are not inclined to let their funding sources know. Evaluators and agencies alike are mindful of the supposed need to maintain good relations with potential sources of future funding. Some non-staff advocates of an agency, though not concerned about employment, may for other reasons wish to see negative findings suppressed. Sometimes even funding sources, which may not desire to have their wisdom in distributing funds challenged, will seek to keep negative or controversial findings from being distributed.

Second, not everyone who claims the title of evaluator is of equal or even sufficient competence. Agencies need to set standards for evaluators to ensure that there are objective findings, the analysis of data is adequate, the methodology for data collection is appropriate, and that the selection of a control or comparison group is correctly accomplished. Otherwise the results will be essentially meaningless. Methodological choices are usually the responsibility of evaluators, but the best-laid plans of evaluators have been sabotaged by an uninformed, rapidly changing or uncooperative staff. These latter shortcomings are sometimes laid at the door of the evaluators as they are "supposed to know better," despite their lack of control.

Sometimes evaluators do not know the community in which the program they are evaluating operates. This can have dramatic consequences on the cooperation given by staff and clients as well as on the results. Questions or ways of asking questions which make sense in one culture or community may not have the same meaning in another. To ask some groups sexual orientation questions may cause offense. Information about citizenship status is a matter of grave concern to undocumented Mexican nationals working in the United States. If this information were important to a study, their resistance could well complicate or disrupt the study. An unwillingness by subjects to participate may be caused by factors beyond an evaluator's control, but is sometimes the result of unintended racial or cultural biases in the methods or materials of the evaluators.

Third, methodological issues can make a difference. For example, when a lack of sufficient care has been taken to protect the validity of information obtained during administration of a data collection instrument, researchers can justify their skepticism about generalizations made from such data. The shortcomings of the administration of evaluation research in human services programs are legendary and call into question some of the "proof" we now accept about how to do things in this area.

A fourth problem is the cost, complexity, and distraction which evaluation research may cause in agencies or funding sources. An adequate comparison group can be an expensive proposition, especially if participation must be purchased. Evaluation experts in the social services field are not always easy to find nor are they inexpensive to hire. Staff time devoted to collecting research data can detract from time necessary to serving clients and can be costly. Evaluation research is often worthwhile, but frequently expensive.

There are nonfinancial costs as well. One of the most detrimental is goal displacement. The requirements of research designs can sometimes cause staff members to forget that their purpose is services to clients. One community-based halfway house, with a history of providing free drug abuse treatment to clients without regard to their background, started referring program participants who did not fit the design of an experiment to fee-collecting, hospital-based programs. Some clients, despite their ability to pay, did not choose to obtain help in a hospital setting and remained without services.

Evaluation, even with the most willing of agency staffs and clients, can create complexities and distractions within agencies that must be weighed along with the benefits.

Resistance to performance assessment and evaluation research is not uncommon among persons who work for human service agencies. The desire on their part to avoid participation can be for legitimate reasons. Increased paperwork that takes time away from serving clients is a frequent and stridently voiced complaint. Ethical issues are raised that call into question the wisdom of demanding control groups as part of the research design. Not serving some persons in order to justify the demands of methodology is, in the view of the dissenters, unfair. Hence, they resist on moral grounds. Sometimes an additional burden is placed on clients as a result of evaluation. They may be asked to respond to questions which are, in the judgment of staff members, unnecessarily time-consuming or an invasion of privacy.

Results of evaluative efforts are not always applied to programs or projects until too late to be helpful. Therefore, participation by staff members in those efforts is seen as wasteful. Sometimes, the data collected are meaningless to them and meet only the needs of evaluators or funding sources. Data which might be significant, as indicated above, can be useless to the extent that the collection procedures are invalid or not followed precisely.

Personal needs of staff members may also result in less than legitimate reasons for resisting participation in assessment efforts. Since performance assessment and evaluation are both judgments about merit measured against a standard, some staff persons, rightly or wrongly, take these results as judgments about themselves. They may feel insecure about the quality of their work or the integrity of their projects. Consequently, they sometimes prefer not to be involved or to cast doubt on the worth of the assessment efforts in order not to be judged in a negative light. A few persons will knowingly sabotage legitimate efforts to assess programs with which they are involved. Still other agency staff members will attempt to manipulate clients, records, or other sources of information in order to achieve a more positive set of findings. The resistance may take many forms, but the result is usually a decrease in the validity of the assessment findings.

Board members, directors of agencies, monitors, evaluators—indeed, everyone connected with services to people—must work to ensure that evaluation efforts are not resisted and that such efforts are supported and encouraged. Performance assessment and evaluation must be an integral part of human services so that clients and the agencies which serve them may benefit from new knowledge.

AGENCY SELF-ASSESSMENT CHECKLIST:
ASSESSING PERFORMANCE AND IMPACT

INDICATORS	STATUS			PERSON RESPONSIBLE
	Yes	No	Partial	
1. The agency has an overall scheme for determining accomplishments and problems in program effectiveness on a regular basis.	___	___	___	_____
2. The agency has an overall scheme for determining accomplishments and problems in program efficiency.	___	___	___	_____
3. The agency's data collection procedure enables staff members to collect data routinely and efficiently.	___	___	___	_____
4. The agency's data collection procedure provides the required information to outside sources, such as funding agencies.	___	___	___	_____
5. The agency's data collection procedure provides the required information to management, for program control purposes.	___	___	___	_____
6. Evaluation methods are in place and describe the impact of the service programs on the target population, program objectives, and costs.	___	___	___	_____
7. The agency has a procedure to provide follow-up, such as administrative action, technical assistance, or training, to correct problems identified by the assessment process.	___	___	___	_____
8. The agency periodically reviews all forms used for data collection to ensure their continued relevance and to improve their design.	___	___	___	_____
9. All staff members and volunteers are trained to complete the required forms.	___	___	___	_____

AGENCY SELF-ASSESSMENT CHECKLIST:
ASSESSING PERFORMANCE AND IMPACT
(continued)

10. Agency managers at all levels
     insist on prompt, thorough, and
     accurate record-keeping.   ____   ____   ____   _____

Coordination

11

Coordination advocates assume that human service agencies and their clients will benefit if agencies work together. Unfortunately, because of the finite nature of resources and the virtually unending needs in most communities, agencies generally compete with one another rather than coordinate their activities. The common funding mechanisms (grants and contracts) and the "political" nature of many funding processes do not necessarily result in the most effective and efficient agencies getting the most resources. Agencies may continue to receive funds despite the poor quality of their services or their coordination efforts because they are adept at grantsmanship or local politics.

Coordination has more proponents than detractors. The proponents argue that without coordination, services will continue to go to the most viable and easily served consumers, while those most in need will get short shrift. They suggest that coordination better satisfies the needs of unserved and underserved people by bringing a wider range of resources to bear. Coordination, they advise, increases cost-effectiveness because it lessens duplication of effort.

Coordination, like excellence, is an idea service providers say they prefer, but which is elusive in practice. Coordination is the conscious collaboration of service providers to maximize agency resources and benefits to clients. Coordination assumes that if agencies link together for relatively minor projects, such as the joint publicizing of a community health fair, or in a major way, such as combining their dollars to hire an outreach worker who will serve all of them, they will expand their individual resources. Many service providers expect that coordination will increase and improve services. Agency staff members, government bureaucrats, and elected officials all praise the value of coordination. Despite this theoretical support, however, extensive coordination is still uncommon among human service agencies in practice.

Several significant impediments to effective coordination exist. The major reasons why coordination efforts among agencies and service providers do not take place more often, and why these efforts, when made, usually do not meet the expectations for them are well known.

One significant barrier is the competition for finite funding to meet unlimited needs for services. In an era of increasing costs and decreasing funds for services, agencies tend to regard one another as adversaries. When one agency receives funds, the dollars available to others decrease. Not surprisingly, agencies competing for program funds resist coordinating with their competitors in implementing their programs later. This is as often the case for agencies funded with federal money as for agencies funded by private organizations, such as United Way/United Fund.

The corollary theory that if an agency is financially secure its readiness to cooperate with others will increase, unfortunately is not always the case. Community mental health centers (CMHC) operations are illustrative. There are nearly 800 CMHCs nationwide in urban and rural communities. They were initially funded with eight-year declining grants. Those serving poverty communities received 90 percent federal funding the first year. Other received 80 percent. All grants were reduced by ten percent each subsequent year. Policy-makers believed that the basic grant program operations would be increasingly underwritten by consumer fees, other grant support, and third-party reimbursement, such as Medicaid and insurance. Because of the eight-year nature of their support, these agencies should have felt financially stable and therefore willing to coordinate actively with others. Theoretically, CMHCs should have coordinated less with other agencies as the amount of their basic grants declined and they began to compete with other agencies for supplemental support. In practice, however, little difference appeared in most communities in the degree of coordination practiced by a CMHC early or late in its eight-year cycle. In other words, having a secure source of funding did not guarantee coordination.

The behavior of agency staff members and their constituencies are a second impediment to coordination. Community-based organizations operated by local interest groups, such as a neighborhood association Headstart day care project, are especially vulnerable. Sometimes service providers in such agencies, regardless of their job title, responsibilities, prior academic training or work experience, are insecure. They seem to fear others and are suspicious of "outsiders," occasionally refusing to work with them. They see coordination as an activity of little value.

Individuals who would, in theory, like to coordinate their activities with persons from other agencies may not do so for reasons other than fear. Professional territoriality may become a deterrent, with persons refusing to cooperate with other service providers. The justification is often made that the other service provider is not "professional" enough or is too professional and cannot relate to clients as "plain folks." Privacy may be given as a rationale, with some service providers unwilling to share what they know about clients. Differences in goals and values can also play a role. Some agency workers feel that their way is best and see no purpose to coordinating with others. Still others may lack commitment to their clients and be too apathetic to expend energy on coordination efforts.

Some agencies are so opposed to coordination that they actively work against it. They may intentionally misrepresent their views on issues, give faulty or inadequate information, or even urge their clients to lobby against other agencies. This behavior is not uncommon. Partisan action of this nature is frequently observed in situations where many agencies are vying with each other for the same clients, dollars, or recognition.

A third major barrier is the lack of incentive for coordination. While the federal government may occasionally require coordination in planning, compliance is difficult to achieve. It attempts to reduce duplication by making providers conscious of local needs and resources. The federal requirement for coordination in Part I of the Office of Management and Budget (OMB) Circular A-95 is illustrative. At least 60 days prior to submission to a federal funding source, proposals must be sent for review and comment by state and/or area clearinghouses. Clearinghouse comments about possible duplication and degrees of need are forwarded by the applicant along with the proposal to the funding source. The intent is to foster information sharing and improve service. The penalties for noncompliance, however, are obscure and infrequently enforced. In practice, agencies often receive federal requests for proposals less than 60 days prior to the due date, and clearinghouses frequently respond after funding decisions have already been made.

Once funded, agencies find little support for efforts at coordination. Without such a requirement by the funding source little coordination takes place. The federal government, recognizing this, has started requiring agencies in service categories such as transportation, manpower, and health to collaborate in priority setting and planning. A health systems agency (HSA), for instance, requires that applicants for federal categorical health funds not only prepare and adhere to plans, but also share resources. In order to get federal funds, hospitals in a community presumably must agree to refer certain types of patients to one another (e.g., open heart surgery) or close a particular type of facility (e.g., pediatric ward) in favor of a more cost-effective unit elsewhere. When such requirements can be enforced, agencies often agree to cooperate, complete the required forms, send representatives to the requisite interagency meetings, but still do not coordinate in fact or spirit. There can be a real difference between activity and action.

A council of governments (COG) unit in one community, which was interested in planning an accessible, coordinated, efficient transportation system for physically disabled and elderly residents, found the following situation. The public transit system, partly funded with General Revenue Sharing money, had buses that were not accessible to physically disabled persons. Accessible vans, bought with Older Americans Act money for transporting senior citizens to meals programs, sat idle except at lunchtime and were prohibited from taking persons under sixty as passengers. Some accessible vehicles available to persons of any age could only be used for transportation to medical appointments because of a regulation of the state funding agency. The school district had buses used only before and after school, but the additional insurance cost did not permit them to carry the elderly. The COG, which might have worked out the technical problems, found little interest in coordination on the part of these agencies for the purpose of providing a rational system of transportation. In fact, no agency seemed to care about another agency's consumers.

Still other impediments exist. Coordination requires time and energy. Some agencies, especially smaller ones, may not find the effort of attending numerous planning meetings worth the results. Legal or regulatory constraints may exist which, for example, might prohibit an agency from working with certain clients or sharing particular kinds of information. The complexity of a situation may militate against coordination, as in the example of the transportation planning difficulties cited above. History may also prevent coordination as in the case of agencies which had tried to work together previously and were unsuccessful.

Service delivery networks exist which can play a coordinative role for human agencies. One network is typified by planning council approaches to coordination. The second is nuclear in nature, with selected agencies clustered around a funding source. The third is represented by municipal-level integrated services departments.

Welfare planning councils, COGs, HSAs, mental health associations, and criminal justice planning boards are examples of established coordination mechanisms which exist in nearly every mid-sized to large community. These established coordination networks tend to pursue three rather limited purposes:

1. Information sharing (members tell one another what they are doing).
2. Data gathering and sharing.
3. Planning.

The planning role is generally only as effective as the sanctions for enforcement. Usually, the plans developed are not binding on any agency. Planning is sometimes used by funding sources, however, to allocate service dollars, as needs identified in a plan document supposedly pinpoint parameters for spending.

These established coordination efforts are popular with traditional human service agencies. Hospitals, for instance, expect to participate in local hospital council activities. However, the quality of that participation often leaves much to be desired. Too often participation means much talking and little agreement about joint action. Coordination frequently results in voluminous reports and plans, but few changes. The disadvantage to this coordination mechanism is that it can lull agencies, providers, consumers, and elected officials into complacency. Calls for genuine coordination, which might give one agency or group of agencies a competitive advantage over another or require an agency to do what it chooses not to do, are easily resisted or ignored. Usually no sanctions of consequence exist.

In most urban and in some rural communities another coordination system is composed of human service agencies clustered around funding sources. The nuclear pattern depicted in Figure 11-1 suggests that multiple funding sources make

Figure 11-1

A TYPICAL URBAN COMMUNITY SERVICE SYSTEM

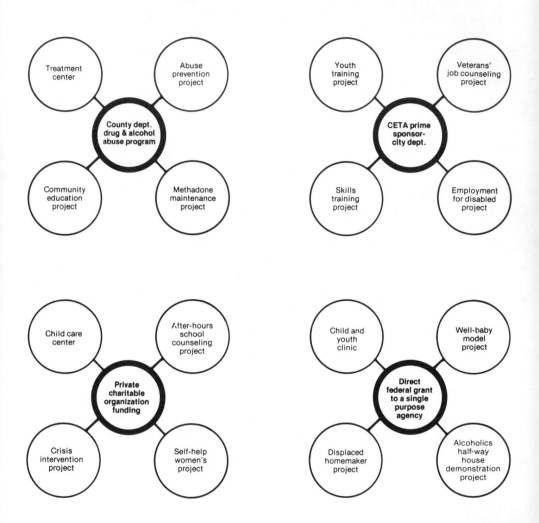

it difficult for anyone to coordinate all or even the majority of services. Even if a primary funding source, such as the county government in this illustration, mandates coordination among its grantees, this requirement has little effect on agencies funded from other sources. Many communities have dozens of nuclear service clusters.

State and local governments have been developing new agencies and reorganizing existing departments to bring together various human resources pro-

grams under a unified administrative framework. The purpose of these coordinative units is to develop a consistency in philosophy and goals, administrative control, and comprehensive integrated services to clients. The history of such efforts
shows some philosophic and administrative successes, but litle progress is evident at
the level of services to clients.

The reasons why such coordinated services are difficult to create administra-
tively are fairly clear. In Comprehensive Employment and Training Act (CETA)
programs, the older worker is a significant segment, or special service category, but
the definition of "older workers" is persons 45 years old and above. More persons
in the 45 to 55 age group are served by the programs generally than those over 55.
Under the Older Americans Act, a person must be 60 to be eligible for services.
Social Security defines its retiree population as those 65 and older, although some
people choose to receive reduced benefits at age 62. To be eligible for Medicare a
person must be older than to be served by CETA or an Older Americans Act program. In an integrated human services agency that may contain housing, employment, social services, antipoverty, criminal justice, youth, and aging programs, as
well as others, the variations in the regulations, eligibility requirements, and service strategies can be overwhelming.

Despite the complexity involved, considerable coordination could still take
place if the various divisions within the superagency worked together. Most often,
however, the personnel from various program components do not even have
regular contact with one another, though they may be housed in the same building.
They do not develop coordinated plans on which to base their allocations of funds
and, to avoid "interference," often do not share their plans until after the funds are
disbursed. Still more incomprehensible from the view of coordinated efforts, the
divisions frequently fund some of the same agencies to provide services to the same
clients without the least effort to ensure coordination of the projects.

A community's coordination of the delivery of human services can be gauged
by several criteria:

1. the level of jointly initiated projects, such as neighborhood centers or proposals for
   funding,
2. the level of referrals made by service providers to one another,
3. the degree of integrated activities between providers, such as joint outreach to
   clients, case conferences, or cooperative purchasing,
4. the service response rate at which selected needs are met (e.g., emergency service
   agencies collaborate to lessen time for ambulance arrivals).

These criteria can be used to chronicle the degree of existing coordination.
This approach is quite different from the way in which coordination is usually
assessed. Typically, the degree of integration of service-related activities is not
measured, but rather the number of agencies which belong to an association or the
number of people who attend a meeting.

Coordination has many forms, each of which can help to improve the effectiveness and efficiency of services to clients. The list which follows is suggestive of the range of possibilities for joint activities:

1. Co-location of staff members.
2. Joint outreach and/or intake.
3. Consolidation of records on common clients.
4. Outstationing of personnel in cooperating agencies' sites.
5. Integrated client support (e.g., transportation).
6. Case consultation or conferencing.
7. Sharing of volunteers.
8. Information exchange.
9. Joint training.
10. Centralized accounting or data storage.
11. Joint proposal development.
12. Consultation.
13. Shared equipment purchases and operation.
14. Alliances for advocacy and legislation.
15. Technology transfers.
16. Shared evaluations.
17. Shared personnel activities (e.g., transferable benefit packages).

The suitability of one coordination activity rather than another depends on the commitments and circumstances of each agency. Benefits to clients should determine the importance of any coordination activity undertaken by an agency. Benefits to the agency, such as good public relations, while not without merit, should remain secondary.

Making coordination work on behalf of clients, we believe, is the responsibility of local human services agencies and individual service providers, since the larger systems seem generally incapable of making coordination work. If there is a commitment to optimize the resources available to each client, a number of practical steps can be taken. Barriers notwithstanding, agencies can achieve a coordination of effort which will result in increased and improved services.

Agencies need a record of teamwork with other agencies. Trust is a crucial ingredient where agency, professional, and personal territoriality result in such large impediments to working together. Without trust little coordination is possible. Coordination requires deeds as well as words, jointly conceived and implemented activities, as well as letters of agreement. To coordinate, agencies must exhibit a sensitivity to the needs, values, and abilities of other agencies and individuals.

Agencies or individuals coerced into coordinative actitivies by threats, regulations, and controls react negatively and cooperate grudgingly at best. Inducements of a positive kind, such as sharing information and decision-making, participating in joint activities like training, and receiving public credit for real accomplishments, work much better.

To see that coordination operates fully and effectively, agencies need to establish the right climate at all levels within their organizations. The directors must take the responsibility to provide leadership, giving legitimacy to the enterprise through their own behavior. They can use the reward of public commendation and the sanction of private reprimand to reinforce positive staff attitudes toward coordination. Staff members must take the responsibility to cooperate with each other in the best interests of their clients, seeking ways to improve and extend their joint endeavors. Supervisors also play a significant role. They should follow up to ensure that the process is working and that the coordinating staff members receive adequate feedback.

Mechanisms or agencies do not coordinate—only people coordinate. Therefore, agencies need to communicate the agreements they have reached to the staff people who will work together. The workers' understanding should include the degree of coordination anticipated. At the lowest end of the continuum is the acquaintance of workers from different agencies with each other and with their roles in their respective agencies. The next higher level is information sharing which includes the active participation of staff members. Higher still is a consulting relationship in which suggestions are made back and forth regarding clients, procedures, and resources. At the top end of the continuum are joint planning and, finally, joint operations, which require the most coordination effort by staff members.

Making coordination work requires anticipating problems and issues among agencies which can become detriments to the successful implementation of joint efforts. The chart in Figure 11-2 shows the program, organizational, and resource areas which are most often identified as sources of coordination problems. Use of

Figure 11-2

POTENTIAL COORDINATION PROBLEM AREAS

Programmatic	Organizational	Resources
• Assessment of needs • Setting of objectives and priorities • Finding of funds • Planning for services • Delivering of services • Assessment of performance and evaluation of impact	• Type of agency • Location of project in agency or agency in system • Degree of responsibility and authority • Eligibility criteria	• Identification of resources • Creation of needed resources • Development of agreements to (or not to) provide services • Advocacy for services

the chart can help agencies anticipate issues that may arise before they become problems that are likely to make coordination impossible.

Examples of programmatic and resources issues are readily apparent. Less obvious are those problems which result from organizational issues. Suppose the youth development division of a city's human service agency has decided to join forces with a criminal justice program coordination task force sponsored by the state attorney general's office. Suppose, further, that the city's police department has refused to join the task force because of philosophic disagreements over the proposed treatment of youthful offenders and asks the head of the superagency to prevent its youth development division from participating as well. Another example might be an agency with a responsibility for providing legal aid services to low-income persons which is asked to join in a coordination agreement with an area agency on aging that has been criticizing it for not providing a sufficient portion of its legal services to the elderly.

With legitimization by each agency's director, a plan for realistic joint efforts, commitment, adequate supervision of the process, and a development of trust, coordination can be made to work on behalf of consumers. However, the climate of coordination, once established, has to be nurtured through mechanisms which permit its continued growth and, where desirable, expansion.

Two such mechanisms are (a) federations of human services agencies willing to coordinate at least some of their activities and (b) memoranda of agreement, which can define and delimit the coordinative efforts of as few as two agencies. The federation models are a compromise between the present *laissez-faire* approach predominant in the United States and a centrally planned service delivery system used in some other countries. The federation model takes some advantageous positions from each of the approaches. It retains individual agency integrity and program authority and can work equally well in stable and turbulent communities. Figure 11-3 depicts three alternatives along with action steps.

The intent of Alternative No. 1 is to bring agencies now operating in a *laissez-faire* environment closer to a federation mechanism.

Alternative No. 2 enables those operating in a somewhat centralized fashion and receiving service funds from the same source to jointly assess needs, plan target areas, manage cases, and share information. Alternative No. 2 gives agencies the responsibility to set priorities appropriate to their community's needs and resources. A funding source can return overall control to the involved agencies and assure that the above process results in genuine coordination by apportioning all grant service dollars on the basis of demonstrated coordination effectiveness and efficiency, and/or apportioning grant funds on the basis of service priorities established by the required joint planning.

Alternative No. 3 is a way of integrating coordination into agency policy-making. It recommends that agencies have board members—particularly consumers—who hold board membership in other human service agencies in a community. This practice is commonplace in business organizations where board members hold memberships on several different corporate boards simultaneously.

Figure 11-3

COORDINATION THROUGH FEDERATION MODELS

Alternative Federation Practices	*Possible Coordinative Action Steps*
1. Create a mechanism for administratively linking diverse local funding sources. Staff members meet to carry out steps a to e.	a. Conduct joint needs assessments. b. Review and comment on RFPs. c. Agree on common nomenclature. d. Agree on standards for services. e. Require review and approval (or comment) on proposals submitted by member agencies.
2. Create a mechanism for a single funding source to administratively link its grantees. Staff members join together for steps f to i.	f. Require joint needs assessments. g. Require target area service planning. h. Require case management, where appropriate. i. Require systematic information sharing.
3. Create a mechanism for policy-maker linkage throughout the system. Steps j and k are carried out.	j. Appoint community persons to policy board who are on at least one other board. k. Conduct periodic inter-agency education and problem-solving sessions.

Multiple board membership by consumers has several distinct advantages. First, board members can voice consumer needs that may cross service categories. Second, consumer members of boards can help other consumers learn what resources each agency has and how to get access to them. Third, sharing the linking function will make decisions about coordination more acceptable.

The interagency agreement can also be a useful mechanism to establish and maintain a coordination effort. Such agreements will generally include the following items:

1. Purpose.
2. Responsibilities.
3. Scope of joint activities.
4. Commitments of funds or staff time.
5. Duration of the agreements.
6. Reporting requirements.
7. Staff persons responsible for overseeing implementation.
8. Signatures of agency directors.

Once it has been determined that such an agreement is desirable, the extent that boards of directors or advisory committees should be involved must be decided. Then the impact of the agreement on staff members, fiscal systems and budgets, data collection systems and reporting, training, and, most of all, on services to clients should be analyzed. This analysis can provide a realistic assessment of the commitment required by the agreement and also the probable consequences.

Coordination has obvious benefits which range from economies of scale, such as joining together to purchase equipment, to improvements in the quality of services delivered. There are administrative, service, and personnel advantages in coordination. Figure 11-4 lists several coordination activities that agencies can pursue.

By coordinating their efforts, agencies can reduce the threat of competition, avoid duplication of effort, and improve their credibility with consumers of their services as well as the general public. They can increase the variety of professional disciplines brought to bear on behalf of their clients, and in the process improve the quality of their services. Agencies working together can provide the support, stimulation, and encouragement for each other that can help them all to provide more and better human services.

Sometimes it takes a catastrophe to stimulate agencies to coordinate their efforts. After a fire or flood, agencies seem more eager to collaborate than at other times. The problem is in sustaining the cooperation once immediate needs have been satisfied.

Figure 11-4

COORDINATION ACTIVITIES AND ADVANTAGES

Advantages	Examples of Activities		
	Administration	Personnel	Service
Economies of Scale	• Shared leasing of equipment • Shared purchase of supplies • Shared rental space • Shared insurance and retirement plans	• Shared use of receptionist • Multiple agency recruitment • Multi-agency use of consultants • Standardized compensation	• Shared outreach and referral • Joint information and referral • Shared transportation • Joint screening and assessment
Service quality	• Joint finding of experts • Joint proposal preparation	• Job enrichment (transfers) • Joint training • Minimum performance standards	• Multi-disciplinary approaches • Inter-agency case coordination • Shared client data
System	• Community-wide planning • Community-wide advocacy	• Technology transfers	• Standardized units of service • Standardized nomenclature

In one Pacific Northwest community the gradual shutdown of the forest industry meant widespread layoffs and underemployment. The crisis was slow in coming, taking place over several years. People were slow to sense that the misfortune of a few individuals was really a misfortune for the entire area. Not uncharacteristically, the human service agencies did little to take the lead. Indeed they reacted to the increase in unemployment by seeking more federal dollars for subsidized jobs. The competition among agencies for these scarce dollars resulted in antagonism and little concern for cooperation.

One organization, however, which felt that the region's needs required coordinated efforts was a grassroots community group started under the aegis of VISTA volunteers. The organization had been formed to improve services to off-reservation Indians. It had been in existence for three years when the unemployment problem became visible and when agencies began scrambling for dollars. The first clients the agencies dropped were Indians. The agencies rationalized that the Indians could always count on the Bureau of Indian Affairs and the Public Health Service for aid. The Indians began to suffer more than other groups, however.

To deal with the situation the grassroots community organization decided to sponsor a series of meetings for groups, such as local businesses and the chamber of commerce, unions, human service agencies, and local government. The meetings aimed at the problems of structural unemployment in the community. The service agencies, with the advice of the other groups, then established cooperative agreements and developed a plan for governmental funding sources to use in allocating manpower and economic development dollars to the community.

Coordination is not a natural state of affairs among human service agencies. Numerous program, personal, and political issues tend to keep agencies apart. However, with a commitment to make coordination work and appropriate joint efforts and mechanisms, agencies can reap the benefits of coordination for themselves and their clients. Coordination assumes that agencies and service providers with similar human service interests can and will work together. There are planning councils and networks of agencies in nearly every community, but proximity, administrative mechanisms, and agreements do not guarantee meaningful coordination. Economies of scale, maximizing limited resources, and improvements in services delivered are obvious benefits of coordination activities, yet agencies resist working together. Effective coordination requires commitment throughout the participating agencies, trust, and careful planning of joint activities.

CRITERIA AND POLICIES FOR COOPERATIVE RELATIONSHIPS

I.   BASIC PRINCIPLES FOR FORMULATING
AN AGENCY COOPERATIVE RELATIONSHIP POLICY

A.   A standardized policy should be developed which states the nature of the relationships to be maintained.

B.   Criteria should be established for the selection and evaluation of the relationships.

C.   All relationships should be reviewed periodically.

D.   Responsibility for maintaining each relationship should be assigned to a specific staff member.

II.   CRITERIA FOR SELECTION OF INTERAGENCY RELATIONSHIPS

A.   The relationship should:
   —provide the agency with increased information about clients, services, and/or problems,
   —stimulate staff development in terms of the agency's goals, objectives, and work,
   —enhance, strengthen, and promote the goals and programs of the agency,
   —improve and expand the availability and/or quality of services or programs,
   —increase the public visibility of the agency and its programs,
   —strengthen the total services of the community.

III.   FACTORS TO BE CONSIDERED IN DEVELOPING COOPERATIVE AGREEMENTS

A.   Is such an agreement consistent with the agency's purpose, goals, objectives, and priorities?

B.   Is a cooperative agreement the most effective and appropriate mechanism for organization and operation of the proposed program?

C.   What type of agreement is the most appropriate for the proposed program, i.e., consultation, planning, or operating responsibilities?

D.   How much staff time and/or agency resources will be required to support the cooperative agreement? Can this level of support be maintained?

E.   What are the potential problems inherent in the agreement? Can they be expeditiously resolved?

IV.   GENERAL PRINCIPLES FOR OPERATION OF COOPERATIVE AGREEMENTS

A.   Each relationship should be carefully selected. Before the agency enters an agreement it should be analyzed in terms of the above criteria and in terms of existing staff commitment.

B.   Responsibility for maintaining relationships should be assigned to staff members and board members in terms of their responsibilities, skills, and interests.

C.   Agency flexibility should be built into each relationship.

D.   Each relationship should be evaluated periodically and maintained only when it has a demonstrated value and effectiveness and reflects the agency's existing priorities.

   (Prepared by the Urban Elderly Coalition and reprinted with permission.)

AGENCY SELF-EVALUATION CHECKLIST: COORDINATION

INDICATORS	STATUS			PERSON RESPONSIBLE
	Yes	No	Partial	
1. The agency has identified all the public and private agencies in the target service area.	____	____	____	_____
2. Satisfactory linkages exist with those other agencies to which referrals are made.	____	____	____	_____
3. The agency routinely participates in area-wide services planning efforts.	____	____	____	_____
4. Periodic reports of agency activities are provided to other agencies and to community groups.	____	____	____	_____
5. The agency has a policy supporting appropriate joint efforts with other agencies and has executed memoranda of understanding.	____	____	____	_____
6. The agency has a procedure for assessing the effectiveness of interagency agreements.	____	____	____	_____
7. All staff members and volunteers are trained to understand the resources provided by other agencies and their limits.	____	____	____	_____
8. Agency managers at all levels insist that staff members and volunteers behave in a cooperative manner toward other agencies' personnel and clients.	____	____	____	_____

Publicizing Human Service Programs

12

Human service agencies with good projects sometimes hesitate to advertise their services and accomplishments for fear they will be seen as bragging. To the contrary, agencies have an obligation to keep the public informed about their activities. There are many reasons why human service agencies should use publicity to reach the general public or specific groups of people.

The purposes of publicity depend on the intended audiences.* One purpose is outreach, making potential clients aware of the services available and when, where, and how to obtain them. People want to know what types of services they can expect and what the costs will be. Once people become participants in a program, their information needs change. Then their education and that of their families and others in their informal support networks assumes considerable importance.

Public information is also a large part of the publicity which agencies communicate in order to educate, create good will, and obtain community support. Publicity provides the basis for recognition and helps establish the credibility which agencies need to survive. Publicity serves also to inform the community about opportunities for voluntary and paid work.

Targeted to specific groups, publicity can make service providers aware of possible referral sources, especially in large urban areas where many agencies do

---

*A variety of terms are currently used to describe the communication process. Modern theory, based in part on an engineering lexicon, uses terms such as "sender," "receiver," "message," "transmission," "feedback," and "medium." The older terms such as "speaker," "speech," and "audience" are still viable, however. We will be drawing on both throughout the chapter.

not know about other agencies in the field. Publicity can educate elected officials and government staff people as well as potential funding sources about an agency's services and resource needs.

To be effective, publicity must be presented in the right way to reach the right people at the right time. Unfortunately, many agencies pay little attention to the ways in which publicity can enhance their programs. In small human service agencies, publicity is frequently the responsibility of an overburdened executive director, while larger agencies may assign publicity as a part-time duty of a staff member or volunteer. Publicity serves an agency's purposes best when pursued regularly and vigorously by a specific individual who is responsible for this activity.

Shaping publicity to fit the audience and occasion is vital, regardless of the medium used to convey the information. A number of groups, or audiences, may want information about a program. The information should vary depending on their interests, abilities, and attitudes. Consider the following factors for each target group.

When deciding what should be communicated, a responsible person should start with how much knowledge the audience already has about a particular agency program and/or similar programs. Account should be taken of their feelings, beliefs, and attitudes as well. The members of the audience live, work, and play in cities, suburbs, rural areas; they use a variety of commercial and social institutions; they worship in different ways, and are bombarded by hundreds of divergent messages daily. Finding out what they have in common provides a basis for publicity. Information about the desired audience should be obtained, including age, sex, ethnicity, income level, and education.

People ordinarily read, listen to, or watch subject matter in which they already have an interest and that presents a point of view with which they are sympathetic. Although some groups, such as elected officials, may be concerned with information about a particular program's regulations and costs, the families of clients of the program may care little about such matters. Instead, they may feel the need for such information as hours, site locations, and fees. To get their attention, information should be selected to fit each audience's interests.

Adapting an agency's publicity to these factors increases the probability of successful communication. For example, a drug rehabilitation center which intends to distribute an information flyer to residents in its local area must first deal with the residents' attitudes. The center first has to explain that the recovering addicts in its program will not be robbing houses nearby or selling drugs to teenagers, as many of the residents fear. A brochure from this same center, developed specifically for the purpose of soliciting funds from local clubs and businesses, should contain information about the purposes of drug rehabilitation programs and their successes with addicts. The brochure might indicate how recovering addicts have gone from being welfare collectors to being taxpayers. The center may wish to place a feature story with the newspapers that follows the career of a former client from addiction to success in college. In addition, the center might distribute an information pamphlet to students at a nearby junior high school describing the dangers of taking PCP or glue sniffing. In each case the center will have to adapt the material to the information, interests, attitudes, and level of understanding of its particular audiences.

It is well known that persons who are joined together geographically, socially, politically, or professionally have some demographic characteristics, interests, and attitudes in common. Considering these commonalities in shaping the publicity for particular audiences increases communication effectiveness.

Agencies can use the answers to the following questions to adapt their publicity efforts to particular audiences or the general public.

> What information do the intended audience members already have about the agency and the program?
>
> What positive and/or negative beliefs do they hold about the agency and the program that need to be reinforced and/or changed?
>
> What common interests and concerns do they have?
>
> What demographic, economic, and social characteristics do they have in common?
>
> Who are the prospective audience's leaders and opinion makers?

The answers to these questions will provide a basis for developing an effective publicity effort.

Seeking male volunteers through public service announcements on daytime television programs probably will not be effective, since most men are at work during the day. Flyers advertising child care services distributed near stores where young adult women shop can be effective. However, if the child care program regulations require the families' incomes to be below the poverty level and the stores sell only high-priced merchandise, the approach will not work well. Knowing about the target group is important so that specific subject matter can be adapted to achieve specific results.

Regularly recurring events make good occasions to obtain publicity. An effective ongoing publicity effort will take advantage of these occasions to tell its story. For example, May of each year is proclaimed Older Americans Month throughout the United States. There are times when other groups—mothers, the blind, disabled children, veterans, to name just a few—are called to the attention of the public. Some agencies serving such clients use the opportunity to publicize their services on behalf of these groups. Mass media presentations about the group abound at such times, so the chance for getting an agency item on radio or TV or into the newspapers is good.

Special occasions also lend themselves to effective publicity efforts. One agency has a public party for each participant who reaches the age of 90. The story is covered by the local newspaper along with a reminder to the public of the services available from the agency. An agency serving young people puts the names of its enrollees having birthdays each month into its newsletter. Another agency has an annual dinner to honor its volunteers who have given 500 hours of service during that year, an event covered by the local television station. High-ranking public officials visiting programs often make good newspaper copy, while action projects, such as basketball games for persons in wheelchairs, make good television events. Creating such opportunities helps to obtain favorable publicity.

Credibility

Credibility is one of the most important ingredients of publicity. An agency which is credible is more likely to receive funding and more likely to be believed by the public. Publicity releases, speeches, and newsletters should always be designed to show an agency as credible.

Since credibility is gained only with difficulty and is easily lost, an agency should not try to substitute public appearance for program substance. The perception of credibility depends in large part on the quality of services. Another important factor is competence in accomplishing the quantitative goals as they are understood by the community. Some major corporations are seen as both effective and competent, yet are viewed with suspicion. Their statements on a variety of issues are not believed or, if believed, not accepted. Obviously other characteristics of credibility are involved. Foremost among these is good will. Agencies which are perceived as caring about their clients and their community gain good will and, hence, credibility. However, credibility is based not only on competency, effectiveness, and good will, but also on the communication of those attributes to clients, to their families, to specific groups with an interest in a project or program, and to the general public.

Deciding what publicity to seek

Deciding what publicity to seek is not a task an agency should undertake casually. Among several important decisions, the audiences and purposes for any publicity effort should first be determined. Next, the information, ideas, and examples that best lend themselves to the interests and needs of each audience should be chosen. Finally, language should be selected with the abilities and sensibilities of the audience in mind.

As noted above, agencies publicize their activities for a variety of reasons. These purposes, the intended audience, and the medium should determine the subject matter. As each factor depicted in Figure 12-1 is accounted for, the message becomes more focused and therefore more likely to reach its target effectively.

In a publicity effort to inform service providers about new services, for example, the services, eligibility requirements, and costs to clients should be included. If the new services compete with those of another agency and the service providers will have to be persuaded to refer clients, including such additional content as ways in which the programs differ may be necessary. Perhaps the new program will serve its clients in a more widely dispersed geographic area or accept especially hard-to-serve clients. The persuasive purpose and special audience characteristics should determine the content.

The medium of transmission will also influence the content of any message. The information that Mrs. Frances Ready has been selected by the board of directors to replace Mr. James R. Perry as its secretary may be appropriate for an agency newsletter but is hardly likely to make the *New York Times* or *St. Louis Post Dispatch*. On the other hand, unusual events or special human interest stories are always grist for the newspaper mill. If Mrs. Ready was a displaced homemaker who through the help of the agency's employment program got a job with a local bank and rose through the ranks to become its senior vice-president the information item takes on added human interest.

Figure 12-1

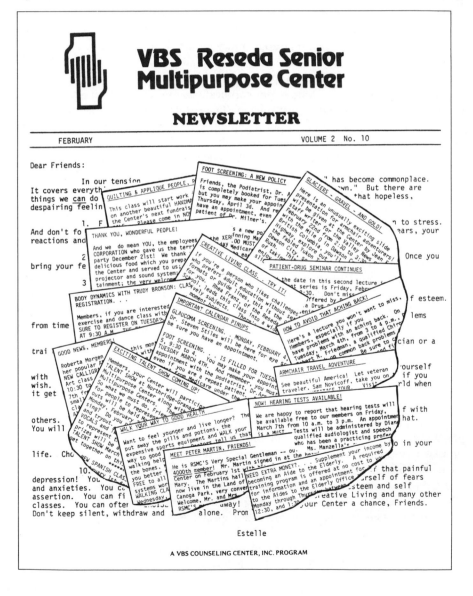

For general news items the following traditional formula still works well: *who, what, when, where, why,* and *how*. The *who* and *what* come first because they are usually the items that attract initial interest. An editor may wish to headline the information that Mrs. Ready has always lived in the county. Her position as the highest ranking woman in the banking business in the state also has news value.

Suppose an agency is going to hold an awards banquet for its volunteers and wishes to publicize the event so that the volunteers will receive recognition for their services. It also hopes that more volunteers can be recruited and the agency's achievements made known. The *who* in this case might highlight a youngster, a blind person, or the person with the most hours of volunteer time. The *what* is the banquet, followed by the *when* and *where*. The *why* might run to several paragraphs, detailing the diverse accomplishments of the volunteers and quoting their comments on why they have served. The *how* might state that pins given to those with 500 or more hours of service during the year were presented by the executive director of the agency.

The language requirements for publicity are simple to state, but not always easy to accomplish. The language that is used should be clear, adapted to the understanding of the intended audience, and, last but not least, concise. Brevity is a prime requirement today for messages which have to compete for attention in a marketplace filled with slick, professional communication.

In order to communicate with people who are not expert in human services, jargon should be avoided. It should never be assumed that ideas and concepts familiar to service providers are familiar to everyone else. Human service providers are specialists in many ways just like chemists, doctors, or carpenters. They have a language that is specialized and not at all familiar to the general public. (The list of terms in the Appendix of this book will testify to the truth of this statement.) Even such common terms as "need," "grant," "outreach" and "budget" may have different meanings for different persons.

Words should be used which convey ideas succinctly to a specific audience. In an earlier chapter we referred to the symbolic use of "Problem Pregnancy?" Most women who are in need of counseling, adoption, or abortion services because of social or psychological problems with their pregnancy will recognize that the message is not intended to convey a concern about the medical aspects of childbirth. So an agency helping runaway youth might post this notice: "Need a place to crash? Call Teentown at 555-5555." Their potential clients would have no trouble identifying the service involved.

The printed word, the spoken word, and the electronic media are all channels of communication. Publicity can be gained through newspapers, throwaways, pamphlets, posters, flyers, newsletters, and mail enclosures, through speeches to organizations, businesses, and clubs, and through radio and television news, feature broadcasts, and public service announcements.

All editors share the same responsibility to print *news*, regardless of the size of their paper or the population of the community. Newspapers want the facts and selected details, including the full names and addresses of local persons involved, and any important titles they may have. They want accurate facts. Mistakes reflect badly on papers and can make them reluctant to publish future material from an agency which has misled them in its news releases.

When possible, a newspaper wants the news when it happens. It publishes current events, not history. News stories can be submitted to a paper 48 hours before the event is to take place. This will enable the editor either to send a reporter to cover the event or to expect an account of what actually took place. In case of a cancellation, the paper expects immediate notification so it can "kill" the story.

The following rules for news releases are really quite simple and are basic to all newspapers.

1. Typing double-spaced on one side of 8½ " x 11 " paper.
2. At least 1½ " margins on both sides and the bottom.
3. The agency's name, address, and phone number in the upper left-hand corner of each page. Directly underneath "CONTACT PERSON:" with the name of the person who can best answer any questions the editor may have.
4. "RELEASE:" and either "IMMEDIATE" or the date the story can be printed should be in the upper right-hand corner.
5. The actual story should begin about one-third of the way down the first page. The second page, if needed, should carry the same headings as the first page and the fact that it is a continuation page should be indicated clearly.
6. Tributes, excessive adjectives, and folksy items should be shunned.

Pictures are quite often submitted along with the news story. If a picture is submitted, it should be:

1. A glossy print of the size used by the particular newspaper (usually 5 " x 7 " or 8 " x 10 ").
2. The principals in the photo should be grouped close together and, when possible, engaged in an activity.
3. An accompanying sheet should identify everyone in the picture.
4. The picture should not be clipped or written on.

Spoken word communication involves meetings, speeches, and person-to-person contacts. Staff members of an agency tend to forget that the best publicity is often what they routinely do and say in public. While a good program does not necessarily speak for itself, competent and caring staff members can be effective advertisers of an agency's services. Through speeches to such groups as the Tiger Club, Saint Anselm Boosters, or Highlands Historical Society, at meetings of service providers from other agencies, during personal contacts with elected officials, and in a host of other circumstances, staff members can concretely advance their agency's publicity efforts.

Radio and television are businesses just like a newspaper. However, since the cost for reporters, camera and sound technicians, and engineers is so high, many stations operate their local newscasting at a financial loss. This means that electronic media coverage may not be easy to get in substantial quantities. On the other hand, radio stations have a wider variety of news formats than does TV. Some have a disk jockey who will often read one or two minutes of news from the wire service teletype. Some radio stations in large metropolitan areas broadcast only news 24 hours a day.

The broadcast counterpart to the news editor on a paper is the news director, who may have the help of an assignment editor. These persons determine what news stories will be covered and get on the air. An agency should take its requests for news coverage to them. In larger radio and television stations, a specialist handles public service announcements. For talk show or feature show appearances, the best person to contact is usually the producer of the show.

When calling a news conference an agency should let stations know at least 24 hours in advance—48 hours' notice is better. It should be obvious that the agency must be sure the event is newsworthy. Another procedure is for an agency to send a news release about an upcoming event and request coverage. Remember, the governor visiting a basketball game played by blind youths may well be news, whereas the report of a regular board meeting probably is not.

To appear on talk shows or feature shows requires some creativity. If an important visitor is meeting with an agency, the visitor and the agency director may be asked to participate on one segment of a feature show. Usually the host or hostess of the program will appreciate a few minutes before air time to find out what questions should be asked so that the most newsworthy and interesting items can be elicited. This is an effective opportunity to tell the agency's story provided that the comments are not made to sound like a commercial.

Another way to reach the general public, and sometimes more targeted audiences, is through public service announcements. "Spots" or "PSAs," as they are commonly called, can be announced by a station employee, an agency staff member, or by a personality such as a mayor or a movie star. In all cases, the text must be prepared in advance. A spot announcement usually is 10, 30, or 60 seconds long and must be timed exactly. Radio stations which do not use a studio announcer will accept a tape. TV stations might prefer a live action videotape, but will usually settle for a well-prepared slide showing some activity, such as a client receiving service. An agency phone number may be superimposed over the picture and an audio tape played to give the impression of action.

In larger cities, broadcasters' associations exist which screen agencies wishing to do PSAs to ensure their legitimacy and allocate free air time (usually one month) so that all applicants get a fair share of the time available. Once a station agrees to accept an agency's PSA, they will advise the agency on what to prepare. Spot announcements on behalf of service do not bring in revenue to the stations. Therefore, stations will ordinarily broadcast them only when no commercial advertising is available. They do serve a publicity purpose, nonetheless, and are usually worth the effort.

AGENCY SELF-ASSESSMENT CHECKLIST: OBTAINING PUBLICITY

INDICATORS	STATUS			PERSON RESPONSIBLE
	Yes	No	Partial	
1. The agency has administrative procedures which specify how to relate to the news media, such as designation of contact persons and reviewing of news releases.	___	___	___	_____
2. The board of directors are experienced in handling publicity and their role is clearly stated and understood.	___	___	___	_____
3. The agency has a system for identifying all the print and electronic news media in its area.	___	___	___	_____
4. The agency has written materials suitable for use by the public.	___	___	___	_____
5. Publications are routinely disseminated to such organizations as other agencies, professional societies, and community groups.	___	___	___	_____
6. The agency has a speakers bureau of persons available for public appearances.	___	___	___	_____
7. All materials prepared or disseminated by the agency are bilingual when necessary.	___	___	___	_____
8. All staff members and volunteers are trained to discuss the agency programs with clients, their families, and general public.	___	___	___	_____
9. One person has the responsibility for coordinating all publicity efforts by the agency.	___	___	___	_____

Advocating for Human Services

13

Advocacy assumes either that something is wrong and that action is needed to right the wrong or that the *status quo* is desirable and should be maintained. Advocacy is an assertive stance suggesting that individuals can influence the social and physical world in which they live. Advocacy is rooted in the ethic with which Americans justify their right to control their lives.

However, many individuals find it difficult to put this philosophy into practice in today's impersonal, fragmented, and technologically oriented society. While the calls for self-help and independence are frequent, to believe that people with overwhelming problems can successfully advocate on their own behalf may be unrealistic. Impoverished, impaired, and isolated persons who require assistance may be unable to even make their needs known.

Human service agencies responsible for assisting these people often commit themselves to the task of stating the concerns of persons whose voices would otherwise not be heard. Advocacy by human service agencies means using their influence to make changes or to maintain conditions which will benefit prospective or current consumers of their services.

Advocates for human services are found in agencies and the community. They are employees, volunteers, and clients of agencies, and members of the general public with special concerns for persons in need of assistance. Advocates focus on their activities in several areas:

1. *changing internal agency or institution practices*, such as initiating an outreach effort to recruit additional staff persons who are members of a minority group,
2. *influencing public policy*, such as changing eligibility requirements for a state program so that more persons can receive services,

3. *influencing community attitudes and practices*, such as obtaining hospitalization rather than jail terms for alcoholics who frequent skid row or getting commercial enterprises to abolish their mandatory age retirement practices.

Agency-based advocates exercise important influence on behalf of clients. How much and what kind of results they achieve depends in part on their roles within their agencies.

Executive and project directors of agencies can and should be advocates for clients served by their agencies. This statement sounds right, since directors supposedly determine the rules and provide the leadership by which staff members are guided. However, directors are often partisans for their staffs and their organizations first and advocates for their clients second. For example, the hours of service are frequently set to suit agency personnel and not clients or their families. In disputes between clients and employees, the staff members' views usually prevail. Directors make the choice in the name of morale or to "support" their staff people. The most insidious lack of support for clients occurs, however, when directors allow incompetent or indifferent staff persons to continue serving clients. Regard for employees' needs too often takes precedence over advocacy for clients.

Directors should advocate for clients in their agencies by insisting on high standards of performance; by making rules that favor clients and bending, as needed, those that do not; by modeling behavior that demonstrates caring and responsibility toward clients, and by rewarding the client advocacy efforts of their staff members. Especially in public agencies, which rarely regard risk-taking positively, directors need to encourage the advocacy efforts of staff members.

Agency directors have a role on behalf of their clients in the larger community as well. They should argue for the necessary resources to aid their client population, not just their own clients, on every occasion. Special pleading for an agency's clients only is seen as self-serving and has undesirable effects. Directors should seek to testify before Congressional and state legislative committees, to lobby elected and bureaucratic officials, and to educate the general community. The guidelines for each of these presentations are similar. They include the following simple and easy-to-follow rules:

1. Be concrete, use examples as well as statistics.
2. Use plain language, avoid jargon.
3. Make specific, practical suggestions.
4. Always be polite, avoid self-righteousness and threats.
5. When giving testimony formally, have copies of the statement to distribute.

Staff members advocate for their clients in many ways within their agencies also. They may bend the rules to the advantage of their clients. For instance, an intake worker may *suggest* to a prospective client how to answer a question so that he or she will meet the eligibility requirements for service. They serve as communication links between board members and the executive director on the one hand and advocacy groups on the other. Agency personnel sometimes lobby elected officials or board members for changes, although this may put them in conflict with their directors, many of whom reserve this activity for themselves.

One specially assigned role played by staff persons in some settings is that of ombudsman. Most often in the United States the ombudsman position is found in health care institutions, where it is often called "patient advocate." The patient advocate acts as spokesperson for people who are unable to make their sentiments known or to get actions taken which they believe are necessary for their well-being. For instance, a person unhappy with a decision about the room assignment made by a hospital admissions clerk might complain to the patient advocate and, as a result, be placed in a more satisfactory location. The patient advocate also interprets the institution or health care setting to patients, explaining regulations and procedures. Suppose the person cited in the previous example could not be reassigned because of a shortage of available beds. The patient advocate would have the task of offering an explanation to that person as to why he or she could not be moved.

While the implementation of this role benefits individual clients considerably, it is relatively benign with respect to organizational changes. Unlike the Adjutant General's investigative role in the armed forces, patient advocates and other ombudsmen do not ordinarily have the authority to order changes. Patient advocates in hospitals, for instance, frequently report to a director of nursing, whose sympathies or obligations may be directed toward support of staff convenience.

Internal advocacy has risks which impede action for many staff people. Dismissal or loss of advancement must be considered as a realistic threat. Personal attachments to co-workers may be severed if advocacy efforts are seen as disloyal or threatening to other employees. Always present, also, is the possibility of co-optation. Service providers who "complain a lot" on behalf of clients may find themselves in the position of justifying some conditions of which they do not approve, such as their agency's not providing services on weekends. This reduces their credibility in advocating changes in other areas.

Instead, to reduce the risks of advocating for change within an agency, they should seek results, not attention. Service providers should let people from the outside, whose jobs are not threatened, take the lead. They should supply them with data and ideas without spying or "finking" on the agency. Also, they should seek institutional and personal support. The insistence of an entire staff usually accomplishes more than an individual effort. If accused or threatened, they should show how the accusations are irrelevant. Finally, all agency employees must be sure the improvements which will result from the advocacy effort are worth the price of dismissal and be willing to pay that price.

Staff members can provide substantial advocacy for human services in the community, too. In addition to aiding the efforts of others, they can serve as communicators of needs, problems, and values. Agency personnel should be the conscience of the public, reminding everyone of the necessity for supporting their client population.

Board and advisory committee members also can influence what happens to clients in their agencies. They determine what services will be delivered as a matter of policy, often help to set standards of performance, and can use their position to raise issues relating to services. They have an obligation to take advantage of their unique position to advocate for human services in the community. Few people accuse them of self-serving motives, since they are not paid and can speak out freely. They can speak in the community with the status afforded representatives of agencies providing human services and can receive reimbursement for travel to testify at their state capitals or in Washington, D.C. Often, they also are members of the client group on whose behalf they are advocating, which gives added impact to their messages. Active board members often serve with more than one agency, which will provide still other advocacy opportunities.

Advocacy, especially when the concern is for an individual client, may easily become meddling in administrative affairs, however. For example, a father may complain to a board member of poor treatment given his child by an agency employee. The board member should not go to the staff person directly, but rather report the incident to the executive director. If the father complains later that the staff member is retaliating against the child, the board member should once again report the complaint to the director. Board members overstep their appropriate boundaries when they interfere between staff persons and clients.

Board and advisory committee members who exhibit only apathy toward clients' needs and services support the *status quo* by their inaction. When clients' needs receive less attention and support than do those of agency personnel, board members must share the blame.

Volunteers, like board and advisory committee members, have the advantage of advocating in the community on behalf of a client population without having their motives challenged. Some directors of agencies, who have advocacy experience, prefer to use volunteers rather than salaried personnel as agency advocates in the community for this reason. However, volunteers are not as accountable to the agency as staff members, which is the reason still other agency directors hesitate to make them "official" representatives in advocacy efforts.

As internal advocates, volunteers find themselves in a difficult role. Often, volunteers clearly see changes needed to improve services, yet their suggestions for improvements in practices and procedures, however justified, may go unheeded or even result in resentment from staff members. Volunteers, like others, probably find their advocacy most successful when they find allies and speak with one voice.

The principles for advocacy within one's own agency which follow provide a basis for determining short-range tactics and long-range strategies.

1. Establish a need for the proposed changes.
2. Determine that the end, if achieved, will be worth the cost in any disruption, ill will, or dollars which may result.

3. Plan, do not leave events to chance.

4. Find influential allies first and large numbers of allies second; do not go it alone, if possible.

5. Prepare long- and short-range alternatives so that some success can be obtained even if the desired end is not completely achieved.

6. Include implementation steps in desired objectives so that specific actions and not just casual assurances are won.

7. Always heed the timing of any effort.

8. Let the best suited individuals spearhead the effort, not those who want attention or glory or who have a kamikaze pilot's attitude.

9. Document everything necessary to support facts and assertions.

10. Prepare a "battle book" with arguments, rebuttals, and data so others can be knowledgeable when they join forces.

11. Be persistent but not abrasive.

12. Allow those in opposition to save face; never attack them personally as these people may be allies on another issue.

Community-based advocates frequently mobilize to effect changes because of the tendency of so many agencies to place their survival above services to clients. For example, in one large metropolitan area in which public employees ordinarily provided many of the human services, a public referendum resulted in a decision to permit contracts to be let to private agencies for the services. Although the voters believed that contracted services would be less expensive, as a matter of fact little contracting of services resulted. Many of the public employees, not wishing to jeopardize their positions, even resisted discussing the merits of contracted services. Resistance to change is often as strong in agencies as it is in individuals.

Community-based advocates may be members of voluntary associations, such as neighborhood improvement groups, professional societies, and local chapters of national membership organizations. Paid community organizers can be advocates on human service issues as can unpaid individuals whose motive is to make things better for themselves or others.

Advocates are sometimes consumers, such as members of a welfare rights organization, sometimes concerned outsiders, such as members of a church group, and sometimes both. Finding situations or systems with which they are not satisfied, these advocates, both as individuals and in groups, serve as change agents. While individuals have often been effective, many advocacy efforts are group affairs.

Advocacy by groups is a six-step process. These steps are as follows:

1. Identify specific, reasonable objectives.

2. Identify assets which can help to attain the objectives.

3. Identify barriers which can hinder attaining the objectives.

4. Develop strategies and tactics.

5. Assign roles and follow-up responsibilities.
6. Implement an advocacy plan.

Identifying specific, reasonable objectives is a more important first step than many action-oriented advocates believe. Thinking they know "what's wrong," some do not see any point in setting out their hoped-for accomplishments. Consequently, what they finally decide is needed may not become clear until they have taken so many inappropriate actions that they have harmed their cause. Others, from inexperience or in the name of strategy, leave their objectives vague and beyond any hope of reasonable accomplishment. A senior citizens committee which sets as its primary objective the improvement of housing for all older persons in the community, or a substance abuse council which states that its objective is the eradication of drug abuse are examples. Perhaps the senior citizens committee should focus on a campaign to get an increase in the number of Section 8 housing subsidies available, or get the city council to pass an ordinance requiring housing developers to rent 10 percent of all their new apartment units at prices elderly persons can afford, or get property taxes for elderly homeowners lowered.

A specific objective serves to focus the advocacy effort on an accomplishable end and sets the result against which actions can be judged to determine their effectiveness. Specific objectives reduce the friction which results from individuals interpreting in their own way the "cause" on behalf of which a group is working. This is a hazard which can be detrimental to a group's advocacy efforts.

To obtain specificity in advocacy objectives, one must begin by identifying complaints. This will help to determine what needs to be changed or, at least, what is currently not working well. The more data gathered the better, up to the point where data gathering becomes a substitute for advocacy. Once determined, the general areas of discontent should point to common concerns about policies or practices that require action to correct. This also applies to situations in which advocacy may be directed toward maintaining the *status quo*, as when a group feels that its constituents will lose some service currently provided unless steps are taken to prevent that loss.

Next, the objectives should be stated in terms of ends that can be accomplished. An objective stated as "make the agency understand the minority community better" is too vague, does not indicate the actions needed, and does not lend itself to measurement of its success. This objective is better stated in this way: "Increase the percentage of minority employees in the Community Development Department who hold managerial positions to equal the percentage of minority persons in the community." Note that objectives for advocacy groups do not ordinarily have specific degrees, or levels of accomplishment, and timetables, although they may have. Since such groups have less direct control, the degree of accomplishment and time factors often are hard to determine.

Identifying assets which can help to attain the objectives is the second step. Let us suppose that the Community Development Department in the example above is part of the bureaucracy of a city with a city manager and council form of government. One minority group organization decides, after considerable internal discussion, that underrepresentation is their community's biggest problem, as persons like themselves are not being fairly represented at the management level of any city department. Since their group represents the majority of consumers of Community Development Department services, they decided to make this department the focus of their initial efforts.

They can begin by asking the following questions:
Will we need money to conduct our advocacy campaign?
Who in the department can help us and what kind of help can they provide?
What resource people in other departments will help us?
What resource people in our community will help us?
Which elected or appointed officials will help us?
What state or federal agencies operating under what laws or regulations can help us?
What resources beside funds and people do we need?

From an employee of the Personnel Bureau who is friendly to their cause they get data on the number of minority group employees at all levels of the department. They decide a stronger case can be made if women's organizations and other minority groups are involved, so they invite representatives from these groups to join them. One member of their group plays golf frequently with the city editor of the newspaper. Another works in the city manager's office. Research turns up information about nondiscrimination clauses in several of the department's federal contracts. Looking both in and beyond the larger community, a community-based advocacy group can find many sources of assistance.

The above illustration points to a process for identifying assets. Community-based advocacy works best by bringing like-minded people together and involving them in finding resources. Every community has human and material assets that can be tapped for advocacy. Few communities, however, are cohesive or motivated enough, or have residents who are experienced enough, to work together to identify and use those assets. Indeed, one outcome of community-based advocacy is that people learn to recognize the resources close at hand.

Identifying barriers which can hinder attaining the objectives requires attention as well. There are as many barriers to advocacy as there are assets. In communities and neighborhoods where people have little in common except their feeling of powerlessness, the barriers can easily be overwhelming. A group can as easily be turned off as on. Therefore, barriers should be identified realistically, but against a backdrop of ends to be achieved.

Sometimes the probable sources of resistance are obvious, but many times they are not. The director of the Community Development Department, in the example above, denied any prejudice against employees who are members of minority groups and claimed that she must follow the civil service rules of the Personnel Bureau in promoting. The person in charge of personnel practices denied that the civil service rules discriminate and suggested that everyone has an equal chance on the tests for promotion. Department supervisors, whose recommendations are part of the promotion procedure, also denied any responsibility.

Generally, it cannot be assumed that all persons who are indifferent or opposed to the views of the advocacy group are barriers. Many times people who are indifferent are really unaware of the facts. Some who are opposed base their opposition as much on their feelings of personal threat as on a commitment to an opposing point of view. These persons can often be made allies by convincing them that their fears are groundless and that cooperation will benefit them.

Developing strategies and tactics is a stage in the advocacy process in which the experiences of others can be useful. Much has been written in professional journals and books as well as in popular magazines and newspapers about change strategies. This material is beyond the scope of this chapter. However, there are several basic rules of thumb which can be stated here.

First, never underestimate the strength of those with an opposing position, especially if they are defending the *status quo*. Those seeking change must take action, while those resisting change often do best by doing nothing. Second, never underestimate the time, the energy, and the disappointments that will inevitably be part of an advocacy effort—even a successful one. Those who forget this rule will find it difficult not to become discouraged. Third, select alternative approaches that build on the group's strengths. Allies are vital assets, but the basic resource is the group which has the primary commitment.

Tactics are a means for carrying out strategies, not an end in themselves. In the Community Development Department example above, the group decided that the best strategy was to obtain promotions of minority personnel without embarrassing either the city bureaucrats or the elected officials. They decided to do this so that when the desired changes were made, the newly promoted persons would be able to work cooperatively with the other employees in an effort to make the agency more aware of, and sensitive to, the needs of minority group member clients. Therefore, the advocacy group resolved not to involve the newspaper editor with whom they had contact nor the federal agencies but instead to keep the issue unpublicized. The group decided, further, to use these possible assets and the unfavorable publicity they could generate as a potential threat. A threat which is perceived as real can be as powerful a motivating force as the reality itself.

Assigning roles and follow-up responsibilities, the next step in the advocacy process, is crucial. Lip service is easy to give. Unless people are willing to contribute their time and effort, however, an advocacy effort will fail. To assure that the work is done, every meeting should end with a review of the tasks that will have to be accomplished before the next meeting and who will do them. Also, for each assignment there should be a second person who will follow up if needed. Checklists with "dos" and "don'ts" can be helpful.

Generally, it is desirable to call for volunteers, but if those leading the advocacy process have the authority to make assignments, they should not hesitate to call on the most competent people. To achieve the objectives of advocacy the people who care most have to be involved. Their involvement reinforces the "rightness" of the cause. However, people who can get the job done, regardless of the degree of their commitment, are necessary also.

Implementing an advocacy plan is the final step in the advocacy process. Numbers, timing, and contingency planning are three of the important considerations here. In one state, a bill was introduced in the legislature which would have seriously curtailed funds previously available for educational services to persons with physical and mental disabilities. The organizations for the disabled, both professional and consumer groups, recognizing that they might lose these funds, decided to put aside their past differences and develop an advocacy effort. They created a telephone tree so that a letter-writing campaign could be started on short notice. That is, the members of a leadership committee composed of representatives of each of the major organizations, agreed to call five persons in their organization and ask them each to call five other persons. This procedure would be repeated until everyone was contacted.

As the bill proceeded through both houses of the legislature, considerable lobbying was undertaken. The experienced lobbyists on the commitee knew that elected officials who would support their request for continued funding would do so for one of three reasons: (a) they had already decided the continued services were a good idea, (b) they owed favors to, or wanted favors from, members of the participating organizations, or (c) they did not want to incur the enmity of the state's disabled population. The legislators in this last category were targeted for the letter-writing campaign.

The committee requested a friendly legislator to introduce an amendment at the last possible moment which would have the effect of killing the bill for that session of the legislature. They felt the timing was important as they did not want to give the sponsors of the bill time to mobilize their forces. While all of these tactics were going on around the legislature, a small delegation from the leadership committee began to lobby the governor's staff and to direct letters from disabled persons to the governor. This was done as a contingency so the governor could be persuaded to veto the bill in case it should pass.

A reminder is needed here about the federal Hatch Act. This legislation precludes federal employees and persons funded with federal funds from engaging in political campaigning during their working hours. Unpaid persons, such as board members, must also exercise discretion if the agency has a tax exempt status.

There is far more to community-based advocacy than we were able to present here. Perhaps, the most important idea is not how to do it, but that those working with and for human service agencies and those based in the community should find ways to advocate together on behalf of those who are in need of assistance.

AGENCY SELF-ASSESSMENT CHECKLIST:
ADVOCACY

INDICATORS	STATUS			PERSON RESPONSIBLE
	Yes	No	Partial	
1. The agency has a policy that clearly states advocacy is integral to the agency's mission.	___	___	___	_____
2. Agency staff members are encouraged to help clients make their needs known to the agency.	___	___	___	_____
3. The agency has a policy regarding staff members' efforts to organize groups of clients to make their needs known to other agencies and to local government.	___	___	___	_____
4. The agency has a procedure and assigns personnel to review regulations and legislation on behalf of its constituents.	___	___	___	_____
5. The agency has a procedure for handling consumer complaints regarding all aspects of agency operations.	___	___	___	_____
6. The agency has employees with responsibility to advocate for individual clients within the agency.	___	___	___	_____
7. The agency has a policy regarding affirmative action and nondiscrimination in its own activities and in the activities of its subcontractors and vendors.	___	___	___	_____
8. The agency has a policy regarding staff involvement in advocacy linked to political action.	___	___	___	_____

Using Volunteer Services

Without the voluntary systems now operating in the United States the quality of human services would be drastically decreased. The primary voluntary system is informal. It consists of assistance provided by families, friends, neighbors, and even strangers, and is, no doubt, of greater quantity and more individualized quality than the services provided by agencies funded by government and private sources. The neighbor who "looks in" each day on the blind woman living next door, the nephew who mows the lawn and changes burned-out light bulbs for his elderly aunt, the letter carrier who coaches a Little League baseball team, the mother with five children of her own who takes a pregnant, single teenager into her home are all part of a vast system of voluntary activities.

A component of this system, often overlooked, operates within the agencies that provide human services. A teacher who stays beyond regular hours to counsel a troubled youngster, a community worker who shows up on Sunday at the park to prevent members of rival gangs from fighting, a drug abuse counselor who stands by day after day to help an addict through drug withdrawal each provides volunteer services.

A second system of voluntary action is supported through more formal agency or organization sponsorship. The auxiliaries and candy-stripers who function in medical settings, the people knocking on doors collecting for the March of Dimes, the VISTA volunteers serving in poverty communities throughout the nation are examples of organized voluntary action. The smallest town or village has many such organized groups.

Four reasons for actively seeking and employing volunteers are primary. First, volunteers are an excellent source of extra help with the myriad administrative program tasks of an agency. Second, volunteers bring a broad range of technical skills and experience to an agency. Third, because they are not salaried, volunteers have a different perspective of an agency and its mission. Their ideals and ideas can be quite valuable in modifying agency policy and practice. The fourth reason for employing volunteers is for legitimation. To the extent they are representative of an agency's clients, the volunteers give the agency more credibility in the eyes of the consumer. For example, a community mental health center serving a Puerto Rican community can enhance its ability to relate to its present and potential clients by augmenting salaried personnel with local volunteers who speak Spanish and know the neighborhood customs.

Volunteers provide services, technical assistance, and advice. Those volunteers giving direct services to people form the majority of the volunteer effort. They are indispensable to the programs of many agencies. Also of value are the many skilled people who provide professional-level information, training, and technical assistance at no cost and through whose efforts program quality is often substantially increased. Volunteers who serve on boards of directors, advisory councils, and in other advisory capacities make a much needed and highly useful contribution, too.

Why do people volunteer? Motives vary considerably. The rewards for voluntary help differ with the volunteers' sense of what is important to them and with the values of the community or organization. Some people are quite satisfied to offer their services, expecting only to receive an opportunity to serve. Others wish something more in return. A simple thank you, the chance to be involved in a community service, the recognition that a candy-striper's uniform brings are all rewards. Other people are motivated by more tangible things. A recognition pin, an awards banquet, or a newspaper article which includes their names can motivate some people to action. The range of possible motivations needs to be given careful attention. Relating to volunteers, as in relating to salaried personnel, no one motivation or reward may satisfy completely. Further, no one reward will satisfy all volunteers in all activities.

The assumption that volunteers always seek rewards and recognition may be misleading. People are motivated for complex reasons. Probably the best form of motivation is the self-motivation that comes from belief in a cause or action. Some volunteers get deeply involved, contribute extraordinary effort, and persevere when they believe their efforts will help achieve something important. The religious missionary is a case in point. While some missionaries may work for the reward of a place in heaven, others do so because they believe in the tenets of their religion and want people to value those same tenets.

This belief in a group's goals or activities is basic to collective action. That is, beliefs held in common—the justness of a cause, the rightness of an action—bind people together. Recognition pins, newspaper articles, and laudatory remarks at recognition dinners, while useful, are not as effective in motivating people to work together.

Human service agencies are in a particularly good position to develop issues in which people feel they have a common stake because their goal is service to people in need. People get involved when they recognize how an issue affects them. A sense of the personal impact of their actions on their lives increases their willingness to volunteer.

The recognition that others hold similar sentiments regarding particular activities eventually leads to the formation of organizations. These organizations are composed of people who voluntarily band together to do something that all of them believe in. This, of course, is in marked contrast to other types of organizations where people work together because they are paid to do so or because they are forced to comply with an organization's rules.

Voluntary associations are particularly American. In the early 19th century, Alexis de Tocqueville, the French traveler and journalist, described the United States as a place where people of every calling and cause got together to advocate their special interests. Voluntary associations continue today as a significant social institution. Their importance lies in the numbers of people involved. Every community has them. The Lung Association, homeowners' associations, the National Retired Teachers Association, and the Sierra Club are examples. Voluntary associations are active in pursuing the special interests of their membership.

Many people join more than one voluntary organization, depending on their feeling that an association represents their interests. Not everyone in an organization is active or influential in its decisions. However, some people who are officers in one may hold similar roles in other organizations. They can and do influence the actions of several associations and therefore have the potential for influencing decisions affecting the entire community.

The voluntary associations can help human service agencies with political, financial, and personnel support. By one definition, the voluntary associations in a community are one element of its power structure. Their influence and agreements help determine resource allocation in the community. Further, because voluntary associations represent special interests, they tend to be quite vocal in advocating for service agencies that complement their own interest. Hence, human service agencies should give important consideration to voluntary associations when planning and implementing projects.

Getting maximum use and avoiding abuse of volunteers' services requires planning. Before undertaking to seek out and use voluntary helpers, agencies need to answer "Yes" to the following questions.

Does the agency have the resources necessary to provide support for each volunteer? At a minimum, volunteers require training, supervision, space, equipment, and considerable emotional support. An agency needs staff or other volunteers who can supervise and train the nonsalaried workers. Most importantly, staff members of an agency must commit themselves to supporting volunteers as an integrated and valued part of that agency's projects. Agency personnel must see the volunteers as important contributors. If travel is extensive or other out-of-pocket ex-

penses are required of the volunteers in order to participate, an agency will need funds to reimburse such costs. Similarly, an agency may find it necessary to increase its liability insurance or assume legal costs in using volunteers. Financial and resource outlays for the support of volunteers invariably are larger than initially anticipated.

Among the costs which are real but often unplanned are salaries for staff who are used to provide support for volunteers' activities. If rapid and frequent volunteer turnover negates the benefits of training efforts, an agency has to question whether the voluntary activity is worth the cost in staff time. If a paid supervisor is needed, but few volunteers are recruited, the cost is too high. If benefits do not exceed costs by an agreed-upon margin, an agency is wise not to initiate or to continue, in the instance of an on-going program, a volunteer component. Volunteers are never free; there are always costs.

However, the benefits are considerable for agencies with effective volunteer components. An agency has less control over a nonsalaried volunteer, but with careful selection and assignment the productivity of volunteers can match or exceed that of salaried persons.

Are the volunteers' services seen as relevant, competent, and dependable by clients, staff members, and the volunteers themselves? Washing the office coffee pot may be a necessary task, and some volunteers will willingly undertake it, but its relevance to an agency's program objectives is negligible. There is little question about the relevance of a volunteer who translates newsletters into Tagalog for Filipino/American senior citizens. Judgments about the relevance of a particular activity are often made by the volunteers themselves. When they see their tasks as irrelevant, they just stop coming. Few volunteers relish the idea of being "free help." They prefer to think of themselves as an important adjunct to staff effort aimed at achieving an agency's objectives.

Are volunteer efforts at a level of competence sufficiently high to warrant their use? Just as some persons have not yet accepted the services of nurse practitioners when they expect to be treated by physicians, so some clients feel that volunteer help may not be as good as the service provided by salaried personnel. In many cases, an individual volunteer may be as skilled as a staff member doing the same job. However, being competent and being perceived by consumers as competent are not the same. Therefore, great care must be taken to ensure that volunteers are competent, that their roles are limited to what they can do, or learn to do, well and that their services are presented so clients see them as capable. Staff members also must view volunteers as able to perform at the required level of skill. This calls for adequate screening, training, and supervising, as well as weeding out those volunteers who cannot perform consistently at an acceptable level.

Volunteers should be available to do the jobs to which they are assigned. Few things are more demoralizing to clients and staff members than expecting some service which can no longer be delivered. Agencies which build service levels by depending on the constant output of volunteers should recognize the risk. Volunteer activities are worthwhile only so long as they can be depended upon.

If voluntary activities are seen as relevant, competent, and dependable by the volunteers themselves and those whom they serve and with whom they work, the effort that volunteers make will be worthwhile.

Do the activities performed by the volunteers avoid putting them in competitive or demeaning positions in relation to staff members and clients?

Sometimes the only difference between a staff person and a volunteer is that the staff member receives a salary. While there is merit to treating the volunteer as a nonsalaried staff person; but when this happens, it may threaten the volunteer and salaried staff member alike. Some salaried personnel contend that volunteers are unreliable, require too much training and supervision, and too easily violate the confidentiality of clients. These charges are sometimes true. At other times, they result from concerns about competition.

The relationship between salaried staff and nonsalaried volunteers can produce conflict. Addressing this problem is important because of its potential for adversely affecting services. No benefit comes from creating a situation in the work environment that harms services. Integrating volunteers into the agency work force with minimum disruption best serves the primary purpose for involving volunteers, to broaden the base of resources available to serve clients.

Involving salaried staff in the identification of roles, selection, and assignment of volunteers will reduce conflicts associated with assimilating volunteers into an agency. First, the staff members should identify roles and develop job descriptions for the volunteers. Next, staff persons should participate in establishing criteria for the selection of volunteers. Finally, some staff members should sit on interview panels to help select volunteers.

This approach assumes that if salaried personnel are asked to determine how volunteers can be used, develop criteria for selecting volunteers, and participate in the selection of volunteers, there can be a significant reduction in the potential for conflict. A careful analysis of the tasks and activities the agency must perform made with the input of both salaried personnel and volunteers can also help to resolve differences and create a climate of mutual trust and respect.

If some volunteers are unreliable, take too much in agency resources, or violate clients' confidentiality, they should be dropped. If all volunteers are seen by the staff members in this way, it may be that the volunteers' job duties are not appropriate and/or that the volunteers and staff members need to discuss together what roles it would be most desirable for each to play.

Consumers' perceptions of volunteers, while usually personal in relation to each volunteer, can be moved in a general positive direction by providing adequate support for the volunteers. If salaried staff members "bad mouth" volunteers in front of clients or show their disdain when working with volunteers, those served will notice this behavior. Mutual support and respect between staff members and volunteers pays off in the positive regard given volunteers by the clients. Consumers will also tend to view volunteers favorably if the volunteers are trained to do their tasks well and are placed appropriately, enabling them to provide good services. In addition, when volunteers are well selected and trained, their positive attitude toward clients is likely to result in good feelings from the clients with whom they have contact.

Legitimation of volunteers by an agency's board of directors and executive director is also necessary. An annual rewards day banquet or testimonial can mean much to volunteers whose work is often unheralded. However done, an agency must show its staff, the community, its clients, and the volunteers themselves that the voluntary effort is needed, wanted and appreciated.

One of the best ways to provide support for volunteers is through the establishment of a volunteer component within an agency. It need not be elaborate. If there are enough active volunteers, an agency can make a staff member or a volunteer responsible for coordinating volunteer affairs. This role might consist of activities such as recruitment, selection, training and supervision. To effectively integrate volunteers into an agency, the volunteer component should be in active liaison with the agency management at all levels.

In large organizations with traditional volunteer involvement, such as hospitals, the volunteer component is usually well established. Some hospitals have a department of voluntary services, sometimes with one or more paid directors. The traditional volunteer departments are frequently external to the basic hospital administration and often become quite political. We do not believe the establishment of such units outside agency control is necessarily the best approach for non-institutional settings.

Developing jobs and planning work assignments for volunteers is similar

to those tasks for salaried personnel. Assignments generally fall into three categories: (1) new activities which need to be done; (2) current activities which are required, but which are not being fully accomplished; and (3) current activities which it would be desirable to increase if sufficient personnel were available. Volunteers may, in addition, find innovative ways to carry out activities that the agency has not recognized.

Generally, those agencies which have reasonable, flexible, and worthwhile assignments are the ones best able to recruit and hold volunteers. What is a reasonable assignment? The criteria here are necessarily negotiable between an agency and a volunteer. An agency that needs volunteer drivers to transport children from low-income families to summer camp can consider this a reasonable assignment only for persons who have a car, have adequate liability insurance, can afford the gasoline, and are available during the hours each day when the transport is needed. An agency which draws its volunteers from a group of people who cannot meet these conditions because of the costs involved or the necessity to be at work when the services are needed would be wise to use staff members for this activity and find volunteers to perform the duties the staff persons might otherwise be doing.

Reasonable also means that volunteers find their proposed activities possible in terms of the skills they have or can develop, satisfactory in terms of hours and working conditions, and acceptable in terms of out-of-pocket expenses they may have for such items as transportation, meals, and uniforms.

An agency that can adapt its assignments to the individual conditions which volunteers present is flexible. When hours can be arranged or rearranged to meet their schedules, when job duties can be pared down, shared, or otherwise altered to match their skills and interests, and when work sites can be moved to suit their convenience, without harm to clients, increased numbers of volunteers can be recruited and maintained.

Some assignments, of course, can only be done in a certain way at a certain time. When these requirements must be met, the needs of volunteers should not be allowed to disrupt or diminish services to clients. However, many activities can be handled by trained volunteers provided the assignments are scheduled appropriately and the agency has a system for regulating work. One method is to assign jobs requiring constant and prescribed activities to volunteers who can assist regularly. For those volunteers who cannot participate regularly, a daily or weekly listing of short-duration assignments can be posted. As the volunteers arrive, they can choose tasks that can be completed in the time available, receive instruction when necessary, and sign the assignment sheet to indicate their accomplished tasks.

Short-term assignments might include such activities as replacing books on the shelves in the agency library, making folders and filing intake forms in the correct storage areas of a free clinic, repairing separated puzzles or broken toys in the child care center playroom, or making follow-up phone calls to ensure that referral agencies have given the necessary services.

What is a worthwhile assignment? Any assignment that volunteers agree to do which matches their needs and interests and agency needs is worthwhile. The motivation of volunteers when matched by their assignment creates a feeling of satisfaction. Among the commonly expressed reasons volunteers give for donating their time are a desire to be of service to others, to engage in interesting and growth-promoting activities, to "get out of the house" for a change of pace, to be with people, and to participate in status-building or ego-enhancing activities. To the extent that their motivations are recognized and rewarded, volunteers are likely to find the work worthwhile and will continue donating their time.

To provide a variety of worthwhile experiences for a group of volunteers takes imagination. An agency in a rural area met an expressed need of its board members by opening a thrift shop next to the highway. The shop, operated by the board members, raised funds for activities not covered by the agency's grant funds. One agency created a loan-a-volunteer program so that its volunteers could have an opportunity to work at new assignments and meet new people, yet remain part of the agency. Still another agency developed a rotation system like that used by industry to train executives. After six months of service in the agency, a volunteer could elect to be assigned as an assistant to a key staff member. This enabled the volunteers to get a better picture of the daily operation of the agency and to make a contribution at higher levels in the agency than would usually be the case.

The variety of significant activities a volunteer can perform is extensive. The following is a list of some common assignments which can be done by voluntary workers:

1. Facilitating contact with clients, family, and the public by answering phones, handling appointments; escorting or transporting clients; telephoning shut-ins or follow-up cases.

2. Raising funds by collecting clothes, newspapers, metals; running thrift or gift shops; holding exhibits or events.

3. Serving clients by leading group discussions; providing entertainment; making home visits; delivering meals, materials, or messages; assisting professional workers with client activities; teaching crafts or languages; supervising play, health, recreational, or educational activities; giving information, counseling, or tutoring.

4. Assisting staff members by collating printed materials; filing, typing; translating materials into other languages; repairing toys, fixing plumbing or furniture; assembling and processing records.

5. Facilitating agency-community relations by bringing voluntary associations into the agency's decision process; calling upon community groups for assistance and advocacy.

Recruit volunteers by giving the task constant effort. No single recruitment method works for all organizations in all communities. Make the best attraction for gaining new volunteers a reputation as a successful provider of services, a place where volunteers are treated well and given significant work opportunities. Volunteers should not be recruited unless there is a specific need for their services.

Whether an agency recruits by using a volunteer committee, an unpaid volunteer director, or a paid volunteer coordinator, probably the best volunteer recruitment is through word-of-mouth. People who are pleased with an agency, whether as volunteers or clients, are the best recruiters.

Recruitment efforts should be based on the realities of the community and the motivations, interests, abilities, and needs of the volunteers. The community should be analyzed to identify sources from which volunteers can be drawn. If an agency has historically served blacks the probability of recruiting volunteers who are black will be much higher than for an agency which has never served them. If an agency is located in a small town in which nearly everyone is employed during the day, the recruitment of volunteers for service during working hours will be difficult. Thus, knowing the community can save an agency effort and expense by focusing the recruitment activities on persons who are likely to serve.

In communities with volunteer bureaus, their services should be used to recruit their members. Other groups which might be approached are:

1. civic associations, fraternal societies, social organizations and clubs,

2. religious groups,

3. parent-teacher school organizations and neighborhood improvement groups,

4. service organizations such as De Molay or the Junior Chamber of Commerce,
5. labor unions,
6. professional associations,
7. youth groups and senior citizen groups.

For a number of reasons, persons recruited from the organizations cited above will tend to be white and middle-income. They are the people who most frequently volunteer and are the easiest people to recruit. Further, they are familiar with and comfortable with the norm of volunteerism. Women form the largest pool of volunteers, although this condition is changing rapidly as more women abandon voluntary activities for paying jobs.

Persons from low-income and minority groups provide many volunteer services, but they do so infrequently in agencies oriented to middle-class populations. Low-income people tend to view volunteerism as a luxury and as an activity engaged in by someone who has education, status, and leisure. In essence, they see volunteers as people who are quite different from themselves.

Volunteers can be recruited from low-income and minority groups by tapping organizations and people respected by them. Blacks in the United States have an historic affinity for their churches. Their church leaders, therefore, can be quite helpful in any effort to recruit volunteers. Many Mexican/American and other national groups also invest considerable time in church-related activities as well as in fraternal organizations. The prominent members of these local minority communities will know persons who are potential volunteers and may be willing to recommend them if an agency can offer its volunteers a valuable experience, money to cover out-of-pocket expenses, and give reasonable assurance that needy people from *their* local areas will benefit from the agency's services.

Once it has been determined what tasks volunteers should do and where volunteers are most likely to be found, the next step will be to contact them and sell them on the project. Present volunteers can be excellent recruiters. Staff members can also be good recruiters as they meet people in their work, at meetings, at community events, and at social functions. Person-to-person contact is effective.

Selected volunteer workers and staff members can meet with organizations and individuals who are potential sources of volunteers. Also, a publicity campaign can be developed to attract attention to an agency's volunteer component. Prospective volunteers can be contacted by writing letters to the members of organizations or by placing notices in their newsletters. The letters and notices indicate what help is needed, why the project is worthy, and how they can participate.

Volunteers have the same needs as the people who are paid to do a job. In order to satisfy their needs, it is necessary to know what they will do and what skills they have. Underusing or misusing volunteers is wasteful and can harm an agency's efforts. To assign a retired accountant to stuffing envelopes underuses the volunteer, and possibly will cause the person to go elsewhere.

In recruiting and keeping volunteers, an important consideration is to match work assignments with their interests and skills. One way to do this is to establish a skills inventory. Prepare job descriptions for each volunteer position, ask volunteer applicants to complete regular personnel application forms, and interview volunteers as any other employee.

Screening potential volunteers is important. Some volunteers can cause

more trouble than their services are worth. A person should be volunteering first to meet the needs of an agency and its clients, and only secondarily to meet his or her own needs. Volunteers will not start or continue to provide services if their own interests and needs are not met to some extent, but those volunteers who are primarily interested in socializing or in telling their troubles to clients are a detriment rather than an aid to an agency.

For recruiting and placing large numbers of applicants, a panel interview is useful as an initial screening device, reserving final judgment until the volunteers have been on the job for a short while. The best time to weed out those who are not likely to perform well is before they start. This is probably best done by an interview coupled with an application form, which identifies the volunteer's previous paid and voluntary work and current availability. The panel or individual interview can be used to explore attitudes toward the consumer group, interests and motivations, and possible work assignments. Investigate previous work habits and personality characteristics in the interview, too. The more data available, the more correct are the decisions for accepting or rejecting candidates.

A potential volunteer who does not like to work in a noisy environment or who is easily irritated by constant change may not be suitable for an agency that provides child care services. Similarly, a person who refers to consumers by offensive ethnic labels would be a risk as a volunteer. On the other hand, a person who needs to have everything neat and tidy might not make a good counselor for drug users, but might be very helpful in the office doing clerical tasks. The final criterion in each case should be that the volunteer can provide worthwhile assistance without causing harm to the clients.

Volunteers who have received training and supervision, but are not performing satisfactorily should be moved or terminated quickly. Nobody gains from delaying the decision.

Effective orientation and training of volunteers is vital to a successful volun-

teer effort. Once volunteers have been accepted by the agency, their abilities should be measured against the job they will be asked to do. The differences, if any, are the training requirements. Volunteer and staff member training are similar in many respects, but one difference is readily apparent. Salaried persons can be required to attend and participate in training sessions, while volunteers generally are donating their time for training.

To the extent that volunteers and staff members have the same training needs and are at approximately the same level of accomplishment, they can be put in training sessions together. This approach saves time and funds. By training together, the relationship between staff members and volunteers can be strengthened since they will share the same information and experiences.

Sometimes, however, this approach may not be desirable. If the two groups are not at the same level of accomplishment, resentment may develop if one group is held back for the other. Or if there is considerable sensitivity among the staff members about appearing "ignorant," "foolish," or "incompetent" in front of volunteers, the joint training effort may have undesirable effects.

Careful consideration should be given to the scheduling of training. Some volunteers prefer to be trained on the job while others may prefer to make additional time available. Making regular attendance at training sessions a precondition of acceptance into, and continuation in, a project is possible, of course. An agency with this policy should advise volunteers of this requirement when they apply.

How long volunteer workers will continue to donate their services and how committed and responsible they will remain can be influenced by their preservice orientation. Orienting volunteers to an agency or organization and its activities generally consists of making sure they know:

—the purpose of the agency,
—the staff, other volunteers, and clients with whom they will work,
—the community and site in which they will work,
—the tasks that they and others will be required to perform.

To illustrate how one of these areas for orientation might be handled, consider an agency in a city of 350,000 persons. It has a grant to identify blind, disabled, or elderly persons who are eligible but have not received Supplemental Security Income payments under the Social Security Act. To accomplish its purpose of finding these eligible persons, the agency recruits eight older persons, each of whom is willing to donate twenty hours a week of volunteer time. The first week is devoted to orientation training.

The volunteers, as part of the orientation, tour that part of the community in which they will work. The volunteers get a list of items of information to acquire, such as where older persons shop for food, go for medical care or to cash their Social Security checks. The volunteers then go to a local beauty parlor, a doctor's office, a service agency site, park, bus stop, and public health clinic among other places where elderly people congregate and chat with them in order to identify still other places and services that senior citizens use frequently. The information collected is used by the volunteers to identify new sites where potential clients gather and referral sources for services that their clients might need. This training is educational, practical, and fun.

Supervision and support of volunteer workers requires time. The investment is worthwhile only if it results in satisfactory volunteer performance. Supervision can be provided through one staff person who only looks after volunteers or through a number of staff persons, each of whom is responsible for both salaried and nonsalaried people. A volunteer director (paid or unpaid) may handle orientation, griev-ances, and administrative details, such as keeping track of schedules and informing volunteers of agency policy. Staff members may provide specific job training, over-see day-to-day assignments, and evaluate performance. However it is done, some person or persons in the agency should be responsible for the volunteers' safety, their knowledge of and participation in agency projects and events, and the quality of their performance.

Volunteers must feel rewarded for their efforts. Reward systems vary con-siderably in agencies which utilize volunteer assistance. In one small child-care agency, the only full-time employee handles the volunteer program and provides daily reinforcement of the volunteers' efforts on a personal and individual basis. An agency which provides a range of services to the elderly in a multipurpose center publishes a monthly newsletter in which it features an article on one volunteer in each issue. A drug abuse project has a birthday party each month for all the staff, clients, and volunteers whose birthdays fall in that month. A hospital has an annual awards banquet at which the administrator speaks and gives out pins representing hours of donated service. The method is probably less important than the principle: if properly trained, supervised, assigned, and recognized, volunteers can provide excellent services in support of the goals of a human services agency.

AGENCY SELF-ASSESSMENT CHECKLIST:
USING VOLUNTEER SERVICES

INDICATORS	STATUS			PERSON RESPONSIBLE
	Yes	No	Partial	
1. The agency uses objective criteria, available for public review, in recruiting and selecting volunteers.	——	——	——	————
2. The agency has a procedure for providing all volunteers with orientation and skills training as needed prior to placement.	——	——	——	————
3. The agency provides in-service training for all volunteers assigned to a work site or task.	——	——	——	————
4. Persons from the target community are recruited for volunteer assignments.	——	——	——	————
5. At least one agency employee or volunteer has overall responsibility for assistance to volunteers.	——	——	——	————
6. The agency uses the same procedures in developing specifications, such as job descriptions, for volunteers as for salaried personnel.	——	——	——	————

Glossary

A-95—a process established by the Office of Management and Budget (OMB) which created clearinghouses designed to coordinate the spending of federal funds.

Act—legislation voted by both houses of the Congress and signed by the President.

Accounting—maintenance of financial records to provide ongoing, up-to-date knowledge of an agency's financial position.

***Ad hoc* committee**—a specific purpose committee established for a limited time. *See also* Standing committee.

Administrative overhead—agency expenses not directly charged to a project.

Advisory committee—serves an agency or project by providing ideas and feedback on needs and services.

Advocacy—actions which are intended to create institutional and/or personal change, institutionalize change, and influence public policy at all levels of government.

Agency—an incorporated organization engaged in the provision, coordination, or administration of human services.

Allocation—assignment of money or other resources for a given purpose.

Applicant agency—an agency which applies for grant funds.

Appropriation—money made available for a particular activity. *See also* Authorization.

Assets—property (including money) which belongs to a person or agency.

Audit—formal examination of financial accounts to ensure records are in order and that money has not been used improperly.

Audit trail—financial and program records that clearly indicate how funds were spent.

Authorization—legal or administrative approval of an action; legislative approval for spending levels contained in acts requiring funding for implementation. *See also* Appropriation.

Block grant—funds made available by the federal government to states, counties, and cities for a wide range of purposes under local control. *See also* Categorical grant.

Board of directors—persons who are legally empowered to make decisions for a corporation and to authorize all contracts and expenditures.

Boiler plate—standard material, such as a statement about the demographic make-up of a community, which is used by an agency in all its proposals.

Bond—a certificate from an insurance company stating that it will repay any financial loss which results from the actions of the individual who is bonded.

Budget—an agency's plan for expending expected income over a specific time period.

Bureaucracy—hierarchal organizations which value objectivity, routine procedures, impersonality, and predictability.

Bylaws—the rules that govern the way a board of directors or advisory committee operates.

Carryover—grant funded monies unspent in one project year that are approved by the funding source for spending in the next funding year.

Catchment area—the service territory of an agency.

Categorical grant—funding that restricts expenditures for a specific purpose for a specific category of people. *See also* Block grant.

Code of Federal Regulations (CFR)—a publication of the federal government which lists all current regulations.

Charitable organization—a nonprofit agency engaged in philanthropy or community service which receives its funds from donations.

Client—a person receiving services.

Council of Governments (COG)—regional, voluntary, intergovernmental planning and coordination agencies.

Community-based organization (CBO)—a private, nonprofit agency at the local, or community, level.

Compliance—following the rules or requirements.

Component—one part of a program or system.

Comprehensive—a full range of services to meet the needs of a target population.

Confidentiality—protecting a client's rights to have personal information kept from the public.

Consultant—a specialist employed on a *per diem* basis for a temporary assignment, such as to develop a program, prepare documents, evaluate an activity, or conduct training.

Consumable supplies—inexpensive items which are used up regularly, such as pencils, paper, or clips.

Consumer—*See* Client.

Continuation grant—funding for subsequent years after the first year in a multiyear program.

Contract—an agreement to perform a particular task within a fixed period of time.

Contract compliance—assessment of agency performance, usually by the funding source(s), to ensure that contractual obligations, legal requirements, etc., have been met.

Coordination—planning or working together to achieve a desired common end.

Cost-plus contract—specifies a fixed profit over actual costs for carrying out a project.

Cost sharing—predetermined cost of project(s) that agencies are required to meet with their own resources; same as matching share, q.v.

Data processing—collection, classification, and complilation of quantitative information.

Demographic—descriptions of a population including such items as number, age, sex, ethnicity, income, education, and health status.

Demonstration project—a project intended to evaluate what a particular service intervention can accomplish. *See also* Model project.

Designation—selection of an agency by a political subdivision, to serve in an official role, such as an area agency on aging or a health systems agency,

Didactic training—demonstration and instruction; the traditional classroom lecture method.

Disallowance—refusal to reimburse for an expenditure considered improper.

Discretionary funds—money that is set aside in a public department or agency to be spent by decision of the director.

Dissemination—distribution of project reports and findings to others for information and/or replication.

Direct costs—identifiable expenditures for carrying out a project, such as salaries, equipment purchases, and rent.

Earmarked funds—money set aside for a specific purpose.

Effectiveness—clients' gains as measured against anticipated gains; impact.

Efficiency—agency's actual output as measured against anticipated output.

Eligibility—legal qualifications for receiving program benefits.

Evaluation—analysis of program outcomes.

Executive committee—usually made up of the officers of the board of directors and acts for the board between meetings.

Expenditures—money which is spent to meet financial obligations.

Federal—referring to the government of the United States.

FICA—Federal Insurance Contributions Act, which determines Social Security contributions.

Financial—pertaining to money. *See also* Fiscal.

Financial management—the allocation and control of financial resources to assure maximum efficiency and effectiveness in achieving an agency's objectives.

Fiscal—pertaining to the management of money.

Fiscal year (FY)—the budget calendar; the federal fiscal year is October 1 to September 30.

Fixed fee contract—specifies the maximum charge an agency may levy to accomplish an agreed-upon work program.

Formula—factors such as population size, health status, or number of persons over age 65, used to determine the allocation of funds among governmental jurisdictions or agencies.

Foundation—a nonprofit corporation established for the purpose of supporting charitable, educational, health, etc., endeavors.

Fringe benefits—compensation in addition to salary, ordinarily including such items as health insurance, Social Security contributions, unemployment insurance, and worker's compensation.

Full-time equivalent (FTE)—describes the amount of personnel time involved in a particular activity; e.g., two half-time employees equal one FTE.

Funding source—governmental agency or foundation that provides grant funds or contracts for services.

General services—assistance to service components, such as pickup and delivery, building maintenance and repair, printing and duplicating, and telephone.

Goal—broad, general statement of anticipated accomplishment.

Governance—the system that organizations create to govern themselves.

Governing board—the main decision and policy-making unit of a public or private nonprofit agency. *See also* Board of directors.

Grant—an award of funds that can be spent only for the specific purpose stated in the notice of grant award from the funding source.

Grantee agency—the recipient of a grant award.

Guidelines—directions, rules, and information memoranda which should be followed, but are not mandated. *See also* Regulations.

Hard match—a term used for matching share when the agency's share must be in money. *See also* Soft match.

Hard money—program dollars committed for an indefinite period. *See also* Soft money.

Indirect costs—expenses for operating an agency or institution not directly chargeable to a particular project, such as payroll preparation, building maintenance, and accounting.

In-kind contributions—contributions such as supplies, space, and volunteer services made by private groups or individuals; soft match.

Inquiry letter—a brief description of a proposed project sent to a potential funding source in advance of submitting a proposal.

Interventions—planned activities, such as counseling or job placements which are designed to ameliorate needs.

Jargon—specialized words and phrases usually unintelligible to the public which are used by people in the same work or profession.

Line item—a specific line, or reference, for each expenditure in a budget such as telephone costs, a secretary's salary, rent, or purchase of a desk.

Matching share—that part of a grant award which must be provided by an agency in order to obtain the funds. *See also* Hard match; Soft match.

Management information systems (MIS)—collection, analysis, and dissemination of data to determine an agency's current status and trends.

Model—a representation of basic activities and relationships which apply to all parts of a system.

Model project—implementation of a unique or exemplary program that can be emulated by others; ordinarily less rigorous evaluation is required than with a demonstration project. *See also* Demonstration project.

Monitor—funding source representative who has administrative responsibility for ensuring grantee complies with the fiscal and program requirements of its grant or contract.

Need—a standard that expresses community concern arising from the perception of a problem that an individual or group has.

Needs assessment—activities such as interviews, surveys, examinations of the literature, and evaluations of demographic data which produce information that identifies areas of need.

Nonprofit agency—an organization that seeks to provide a service rather than make a profit.

Notice of grant award (NGA)—official notification by a funding source that a grant or contract has been approved and funded.

Objective—a statement of desired outcome, or result, which is specific, measurable, and time limited; stated usually as product or process outcome.

Obligated funds—money set aside for uses which have been previously specified.

Ordinance—a law.

Peer review—assessment of the worth of proposals for funding or performance of a project by persons who have similar backgrounds or training or do similar work.

Per diem—daily rate of payment or expense reimbursement.

Performance assessment—determination of program efficiency and effectiveness through monitoring, contract compliance, and evaluation.

Planning—formal or informal process of analyzing needs, determining objectives and criteria of accomplishment, and developing related program activities and budgets.

Policies—statements which are guides to action, set boundaries, and are designed to secure a consistency of purpose.

Priorities—placement of items in order of importance.

Process—the manner in which a particular result is achieved.

Program—a comprhehensive set of general services, such as educational or employment program. *See also* Project.

Program budget—indicates the gross costs for projects or component activities and not line item costs.

Project—a specific, limited service or set of services designed for a specific, limited client group by a particular agency. *See also* Program.

Project officer—a person assigned by a funding source to serve as liaison between the funding agency and the grantee agency.

Proposal—a request for funding which states a need and describes a methodology to ameliorate that need.

Provider—*See* Service provider.

Public law—legislation passed by Congress and signed by the President; identified by P.L.-(session of Congress)-(number of the law), e.g., P.L. 93–112, the Rehabilitation Act of 1973.

Quorum—the number of members that have to be present in order to make decisions at a meeting.

Referral—procedure for sending an individual to another agency to receive service.

Regulations—clarifications of legislative intent which have the force of law and with which agencies must comply. *See also* Guidelines.

Reprogramming—approved use of leftover unobligated funds in ways that were not anticipated in the original budget.

Request for Proposals (RFP)—a document distributed by a funding source which details the procedures, timetable, and requirements to apply for grant or contract funds.

Resources—sources of support which include money, people, equipment, etc.

Review panels—*See* Peer review.

Scope of work—*See* Work program.

Service provider—individuals who provide services to clients, such as drug abuse counselors, nurses, job developers, and outreach workers.

Services—activities that assist clients to meet their needs.

Soft match—non-cash items, such as volunteer time and donated equipment, used for matching share. *See also* Hard match.

Soft money—program dollars committed for a specific time and limited purpose. *See also* Hard money.

Solicited proposal—prepared in response to a Request for Proposal. *See also* Unsolicited proposal.

Special conditions—special requirements attached by the funding source to an agency's grant or contract.

Staff member—employee of an agency.

Staffing pattern—organization of the people employed by an agency, including reporting relationships.

Standing committee—a permanent committee of a board of directors or advisory council. *See also Ad hoc* committee.

Steering committee—a managing or directing committee.

Strategy—an overall plan or method for accomplishing a desired end. *See also* Tactic.

Supplemental grant—funds awarded in addition to those originally awarded for the initial project.

Tactic—a short-range plan or method for accomplishing a desired end. *See also* Strategy.

Target area—a geographic location in which a large number of potential clients are living.

Target population—a group of persons who are potentially eligible for a particular program or project.

TBA—*To Be A*ppointed, a term used in proposals to indicate that no employee presently fills the position indicated.

Technical assistance—aid provided by someone or something (a manual) outside an agency which helps it solve a specific problem.

Titles—the major subdivisions of legislative acts; usually designated by roman numerals.

Trustee—an alternative title sometimes used to designate a member of the board of directors.

Unobligated funds—money which has not been set aside for any specific purpose.

Unsolicited proposal—preparation and submission of a proposal not in response to a Request for Proposal. *See also* Solicited proposal.

Wiring—the preselection of an agency for funding.

Work program—statement of activities and tasks which define what a project will do to accomplish its objectives.

Appendix

LIST OF IMPORTANT ADDRESSES

1. Any Representative
   The House of Representatives
   The Capitol
   Washington, DC 20515
   (202) 225-7000

2. Any Senator
   The Senate
   The Capitol
   Washington, DC 20510
   (202) 225-2115

3. House Document Room
   (for copies of bills and committee reports)
   Capitol Building
   Washington, DC 20515

4. Senate Document Room
   (for copies of bills and committee reports)
   Capitol Building
   Washington, DC 20510

5. Superintendent of Documents
   Government Printing Office
   Washington, DC 20402
   (202) 783-3238

6. Data User Service Division
   Bureau of the Census
   Department of Commerce
   Washington, DC 20233
   (303) 763-5512

7. Library of Congress
   Reader Services Department
   Washington, DC 20540
   (202) 426-5530

One source of information which contains numerous addresses of U.S. Government agencies and statistical data bases in an easy-to-read format is *Washington Information Workbook*. It can be found in library reference departments or ordered from Washington Researchers, 918 Sixteenth Street, N.W., Suite 102, Washington, DC 20006   (202) 833-2230

FEDERAL INFORMATION CENTERS FOR U.S. GOVERNMENT REGIONS

Region

1. JFK Federal Building
   Cambridge Street, Rm. E-130
   Boston, MA 02103
   617-223-7121

2. Federal Building
   26 Federal Plaza, Rm. 1-114
   New York, NY 10007
   212-264-4464

3. Federal Building
   600 Arch St.
   Philadelphia, PA 19106
   215-597-7042

4. Federal Building
   275 Peachtree St., NE
   Atlanta, GA 30303
   401-221-6891

5. Edward McKinney Dirksen Building
   219 So. Dearborn St.
   Chicago, IL 60604
   312-353-4242

6. Fritz Garland Lanham Federal Building
   819 Taylor St.
   Ft. Worth, TX 76102
   817-334-3624

7. Federal Building
   601 E. 12th Street
   Kansas City, KA 66106
   816-374-2466

8. Federal Building
   1961 Stout St.
   Denver, CO 80294
   303-837-3602

9. Federal Building and U.S. Court House
   450 Golden Gate
   San Francisco, CA 94102
   415-556-6600

10. Federal Building
    915 2nd Avenue
    Seattle, WA 98174
    206-442-0570

Since federal departments have offices throughout each region, these regional information centers provide a convenient mechanism for locating specific offices.

ERIC CLEARINGHOUSES

There are currently 16 ERIC Clearinghouses, each responsible for a major area in the field of education. Clearinghouses abstract, index, and prepare annotated bibliographies of materials in education.

ADULT, CAREER, AND VOCATIONAL EDUCATION (CE)
Ohio State University
1960 Kenny Rd.
Columbus, OH 43210   (614) 486-3655

COUNSELING AND PERSONNEL SERVICES (CG)
University of Michigan
School of Education Building, Room 2108
East University & South University Sts.
Ann Arbor, MI 48109   (313) 764-9492

EDUCATIONAL MANAGEMENT (EA)
University of Oregon
Eugene, OR 97403   (503) 686-5043

ELEMENTARY AND EARLY CHILDHOOD EDUCATION (PS)
University of Illinois
College of Education
Urbana, IL 61801   (217) 333-1386

HANDICAPPED AND GIFTED CHILDREN (EC)
Council for Exceptional Children
1920 Association Drive
Reston, VA 22091   (703) 620-3660

HIGHER EDUCATION (HE)
George Washington University
One Dupont Circle, N.W., Suite 630
Washington, DC 20036   (202) 296-2597

INFORMATION RESOURCES (IR)
Syracuse University
School of Education
Syracuse, NY 13210   (315) 423-3640

JUNIOR COLLEGES (JC)
University of California at Los Angeles
Powell Library, Room 96
405 Hugard Avenue
Los Angeles, CA 90024   (213) 825-3931

LANGUAGES AND LINGUISTICS (FL)
Center for Applied Linguistics
1611 North Kent Street
Arlington, VA 22209   (703) 528-4312

READING AND COMMUNICATION SKILLS (CS)
National Council of Teachers of English
1111 Kenyon Road
Urbana, IL 61801   (217) 328-3870

RURAL EDUCATION AND SMALL SCHOOLS (RC)
New Mexico State University
Box 3 AP
Las Cruces, NM 88003   (505) 646-2623

SCIENCE, MATHEMATICS, AND ENVIRONMENTAL EDUCATION (SE)
Ohio State University
1200 Chambers Road, Third Floor
Columbus, OH 43212   (614) 422-6717

SOCIAL STUDIES/SOCIAL SCIENCE EDUCATION (SO)
Social Science Education Consortium, Inc.
855 Broadway
Boulder, CO 80302   (303) 492-8434

TEACHER EDUCATION (SP)
American Association of Colleges for Teacher Education
One Dupont Circle, N.W., Suite 616
Washington, DC 20036   (202) 293-7280

TESTS, MEASUREMENT, AND EVALUATION (TM)
Educational Testing Service
Princeton, NJ 08541   (609) 921-9000

URBAN EDUCATION (UD)
Teachers College
Columbia University
Box 40
New York, NY 10027   (212) 678-3437

SAMPLE PERSONNEL POLICIES

A. Discrimination Prohibited
There will be no discrimination in hiring or personnel practices because of race, creed, color, sex, disability, age, or national origin.

B. Recruitment
All vacant positions are open to all qualified applicants. Public announcements of job openings may be made in order to attract the best qualified applicants for each position. If an employee is equally qualified to fill a vacant position, he or she will have preference over applicants who are not employees.

C. Selection
Screening and selection procedures will be used to determine the qualifications and ability of candidates to perform the duties of a position. Work and life experience on a year for year basis may apply toward some formal education requirements, as appropriate.

D. Employment Status
The first three months will be a probationary period.

E. Conditions of Work
The normal full-time work week will be a forty-hour week.

All employees will be paid bimonthly. Work performed from the 1st to the 15th is paid on the 20th; work performed from the 15th through the end of the month is paid on the 5th.

F. Personnel Performance Review
The probationary period may be extended by an employee's supervisor. Termination during the probationary period will not be subject to the grievance procedure, except on grounds of discrimination because of race, creed, color, national origin, sex, disability, or age.

There will be a written evaluation of all employees before the completion of their probationary periods, one month prior to each anniversary date of the employees, and at such times as the employees or their supervisors leave the agency.

G. Discharge
For serious and willful disregard of rules and instructions, an employee may be discharged by the Executive Director.

H. Grievance Procedure
The employee will discuss the grievance with the Executive Director who will respond within five working days. If the grievance remains unadjusted, it may be presented to the Personnel Committee.

This will be the final step for appealing grievances.

I. Conflict of Interest
Two or more members of the same immediate family, husband, wife, offspring, parents, brothers and sisters, or brothers- and sisters-in-law, may not be regularly employed in a situation where one has a supervisory relationship with the other.

J. Honoraria and Fees
Employees may not receive separate fees for services or independently contact agency clients. The norms, ethics, and rules will be set by the Personnel Committee and enforced by the Executive Director.

K. Purchasing Policy

No employee is allowed to charge for goods and services without prior approval from the Executive Director or a fiscal officer. Any employee charging without prior approval automatically assumes the full liability for such action.

L. Position Classification

The responsibilities required of applicants for each position are indicated in job descriptions approved by the Personnel Committee.

Salary level will be based on wage surveys to determine prevailing rates of pay.

Performance will be reviewed annually and may result in increases of up to 5 percent of the base salary. Salary increases to compensate for raises in the cost of living may also be given periodically.

It is recommended that starting salaries be at the base rate. Salaries will not be above the second step without approval of the Personnel Committee.

M. Holidays

The eight approved holidays are as follows:

Labor Day	Washington's Birthday or President's Day
Thanksgiving	Memorial Day
Christmas Day	Independence Day
New Year's Day	Day to be agreed upon annually

If a holiday is observed on an employee's scheduled day off or a vacation, he or she will receive an extra day off or an extra day of vacation credit.

N. Vacations

Vacation leave will accrue at the rate of one day for each completed month of employment. A maximum of twenty-four days of vacation time may be accumulated.

If a holiday falls during an employee's vacation, that day will not be charged against his or her vacation balance.

Vacation time shall accrue, but may not be taken by employees during their probationary period.

O. Sick Leave

An employee may receive sick leave with pay. Sick leave will accrue at the rate of one-half day per month from the date of hire, and will be cumulative up to a maximum of 12 days.

Employees will not be compensated in cash or time off for any accumulated unused sick leave when they are separated from employment.

An employee may receive up to two working days off with pay annually for purposes of religious observances or death in the immediate family.

P. Unpaid Leaves of Absence

Employees will be eligible for leaves of absence after completion of their probationary periods. All leaves of absence will be granted at the discretion of the Executive Director.

Q. Fringe Benefits

The Board of Directors will, from time to time, adopt fringe benefit packages in accordance with the best interests of personnel and the financial status of the corporation. Employees, both full and part time, will be eligible for these benefits.

SAMPLE ARTICLES OF INCORPORATION

We, the undersigned, hereby form a nonprofit corporation under the provisions of the General Nonprofit Corporation Law of the State of _____ , and hereby state:

  I. The name of this corporation is (name of organization).

 II. This is a nonprofit corporation which does not contemplate pecuniary gain or profit to the members thereof and is organized solely for public benefit purposes. The corporation shall not have any capital stock.

III. The purposes for which the corporation is formed are:

    A. The specific and primary purposes are:

        1. Through research, demonstration, and service to _____. (State specific intents of the corporation. For instance, "service to all unemployed and underemployed persons who live in. . ." or "service to all persons in need of primary health care and who are eligible because of. . .")

        2. To receive and administer funds for study, demonstration and research, and service all for the public good.

    B. The general purposes and powers are to do any and all acts and things which may be done by any nonprofit educational and charitable (name state) corporation, as provided by the General Nonprofit Corporation Law of the State.

IV. Notwithstanding any of the above statements of purposes and powers, this corporation shall not, except to an insubstantial degree, engage in any activities or exercise any powers that are not in furtherance of the primary purposes of this corporation.

 V. The principal office for transaction of the business of this corporation is located in the County of _____, State of _____.

VI. The names and addresses of the persons who are to act in the capacity of directors until their successors are chosen are as follows:

NAME	ADDRESS
Arthur Jones	Vice President Bank of Anytown 300 Spaulding Road Anytown, FL 30000
Roberta Smith	1214 Hope St. Anytown, FL 30000
T. R. Johnson	Northside Senior Citizens Project 521 No. Maple St. Anytown, FL 30000

VII. This corporation is not organized, nor shall it be operated, for pecuniary gain or profit, and it does not contemplate the distribution of gains, profits, or dividends to the members thereof and is organized solely for nonprofit purposes. The property, assets, profits, and net income of this corporation are irrevocably dedicated to educational and charitable purposes and no part of the profits or net income of this corporation shall ever inure to the benefit of any director, officer, or member thereof or to the benefit of any private shareholder or individual. Upon the dissolution or winding up of this corporation its assets remaining after payment of, or provision for payment of, all debts and liabilities of this corporation, shall be distributed to a nonprofit fund, foundation, or corporation, which is organized and operated exclusively for educational and charitable purposes and which has established its tax exempt status under Section 501 (c)(3) of the Internal Revenue Code and Section _____ of the Revenue and Taxation Code. If this corporation holds any assets in trust, such assets shall be disposed of in such a manner as may be directed by decree of the superior court of the county in which this corporation's principal office is located, upon petition therefor by the Attorney General or by any person concerned in the liquidation.

IN WITNESS WHEREOF, the undersigned, being the persons hereinabove named as the first directors, have executed these Articles of Incorporation this _____

of _____, _____.   day
        month   year

(Signed)

_____

Arthur Jones

_____

Roberta Smith

_____

T. R. Johnson

SAMPLE BYLAWS

ARTICLE I. NAME

The name of the Corporation is (name of organization).

ARTICLE II. PRINCIPAL OFFICE

The Corporation will maintain its principal office in the County of _____, State of _____ , but may have offices and transact business at such other places as the Board of Directors may from time to time direct.

ARTICLE III. MEMBERSHIP

1. The voting membership of this Corporation will consist of all members of the Corporation in good standing, including the directors of the Corporation.
2. Election to regular membership will be by the Board of Directors, but may also be made by a two-thirds (⅔) vote of the total membership of the corporation at any annual meeting or at a special meeting of the members duly called for the purpose.
3. The Board of Directors will have a summary power, by vote of a majority of its members, to suspend or terminate the membership of any member for conduct which disturbs the order, impairs the good name, or endangers the welfare, interest, or character of the Corporation.

ARTICLE IV. BOARD OF DIRECTORS

1. The management of this corporation will be vested in a Board of Directors made up of _____ persons.
2. The members of the Board of Directors will be elected by the membership at the annual meeting of the members of the Corporation and serve for terms of _____ years.
3. At the first meeting of the Board of Directors after the annual meeting of the members, the Board of Directors will elect a slate of officers as specified in Article V of these Bylaws. Vacancies on the Board may be filled for the unexpired terms by the remaining Directors.
4. A majority of the Board of Directors will constitute a quorum for the transaction of business. At any meeting of the Board, a majority vote of those present will be necessary to the adoption of any resolution or the taking of any action.
5. No member of the Board of Directors shall receive remuneration for services rendered or derive, directly or indirectly, any pecuniary profit or any material advantage from his or her appointment. Members of the Board of Directors may be reimbursed for their audited out-of-pocket expenses.
6. When the Corporation is planning or conducting a community services project, an appropriate advisory committee selected from the population to be served by such project will be appointed by the Board of Directors. The Chairperson of the advisory committee will be entitled to attend the meetings of the Board of Directors and to participate in the deliberations of the Board concerning the community service project, but will not have the right to vote.

ARTICLE V. OFFICERS OF THE CORPORATION

1. The officers of the Corporation will be the Chairperson, Vice-Chairperson, Secretary, and Treasurer.

2. The Chairperson will preside at all meetings of the Corporation and of the Board of Directors. He or she will be an *ex-officio* member of all committees of the Board. The Vice-Chairperson will assume the authority and duties of the Chairperson in his or her absence. The Secretary will keep a record of all the proceedings and conduct the correspondence of the Corporation and of the Board of Directors. The Treasurer will keep a record of all receipts, disbursements, and other financial transactions of the Corporation, and shall have custody of all the funds. He or she will make all deposits and issue all warrants of the Corporation.

ARTICLE VI. MEETINGS OF THE CORPORATION

1. Unless otherwise specified by the Board of Directors, the Corporation will hold its Annual Meeting on the _____ _____ of _____, at _____.
                   (week)   (day of week)   (month)   (time)

2. Special meetings of the members and the Board of Directors may be called at any time by the Chairperson.

3. A quorum for the transaction of business at any Corporation meeting will consist of not less than one-third of the members of the Corporation, present in person.

ARTICLE VII. DISSOLUTION OF THE CORPORATION

Upon dissolution of the Corporation, after all debts of the Corporation have been paid, the remaining assets and property of the Corporation, if any, will be conveyed to any charitable, nonprofit or governmental entity, but all in keeping with any contractual agreements with Federal, State, and local governments and any laws, ordinances, or regulations of such governments.

ARTICLE VIII. AMENDMENTS

These Bylaws may be amended by the Board of Directors at any regular meeting of the Board, except that the Board of Directors may not adopt any amendment to these Bylaws changing the authorized number of directors. These Bylaws may also be amended by a vote of a majority of a quorum of Corporation members.

Adopted by the Board of Directors on ._____ (date) _____.

Amended on _____ (date) _____

_____ (date) _____

_____ (date) _____

Index

DATE DUE			

Azarnoff   185356